Library of
Davidson College

*STUDIES IN ANCIENT ORIENTAL CIVILIZATION • No. 46*
THE ORIENTAL INSTITUTE OF THE UNIVERSITY OF CHICAGO

*Thomas A. Holland • Editor*
with the assistance of Thomas G. Urban

# THE ORGANIZATION OF POWER
## ASPECTS OF BUREAUCRACY IN THE ANCIENT NEAR EAST

*Edited by*
McGuire Gibson
and
Robert D. Biggs

Second Edition with Corrections

The Oriental Institute of the University of Chicago
*Studies in Ancient Oriental Civilization* • No. 46
Chicago • Illinois

Library of Congress Catalog Card Number: 91–60541

ISBN: 0–918986–72–9
ISSN: 0081–7554

*The Oriental Institute, Chicago*

© 1987, 1991 by The University of Chicago. All rights reserved.
Published 1991. Printed in the United States of America.

Second Edition with Corrections

# TABLE OF CONTENTS

Symposium Program .................................................................................................................. vii

Editors' Preface to the Second Edition ...................................................................................... ix

Editors' Preface to the First Edition .......................................................................................... x

List of Abbreviations ................................................................................................................. xi

Introduction. *McGuire Gibson* ................................................................................................. 1

1. "In a City Without Watchdogs the Fox is the Overseer": Issues and Problems in the Study of Bureaucracy. *Michael G. Morony* .................................................................. 5

2. The Administrative and Economic Organization of the Ur III State: The Core and the Periphery. *Piotr Steinkeller* .......................................................................................... 15

3. Ur III Bureaucracy: Quantitative Aspects. *Miguel Civil* ................................................. 35

4. Charisma and Control: On Continuity and Change in Early Mesopotamian Bureaucratic Systems. *Piotr Michalowski* ....................................................................... 45

5. Legitimation of Authority Through Image and Legend: Seals Belonging to Officials in the Administrative Bureaucracy of the Ur III State. *Irene J. Winter* ............................. 59

6. Administration of the Temple of Inanna at Nippur under the Third Dynasty of Ur: Archaeological and Documentary Evidence. *Richard L. Zettler* .................................... 101

7. The Organization and Functioning of the Royal Mortuary Cults of the Old Kingdom in Egypt. *Ann Macy Roth* .................................................................................................. 115

8. Ptolemaic Bureaucracy from an Egyptian Point of View. *Janet H. Johnson* .................. 123

9. Some Perspectives on Byzantine Bureaucracy. *Walter Emil Kaegi, Jr.* .......................... 133

10. The Role of Bureaucracy in the Provisioning of Cities: A Framework for Analysis of the Ancient Near East. *Robert C. Hunt* ......................................................................... 141

# SYMPOSIUM PROGRAM*

### THE ORGANIZATION OF POWER: ASPECTS OF BUREAUCRACY IN THE ANCIENT, MEDIEVAL, AND OTTOMAN NEAR EAST

Sponsored by The Oriental Institute and the Department of Near Eastern Languages and Civilizations, University of Chicago, April 16–17, 1983

### PROGRAM

Saturday, April 16

McGuire Gibson, University of Chicago
*Opening Statement*

Michael G. Morony, University of California, Los Angeles
*\*Issues and Problems in the Interpretation of Bureaucracy*

Piotr Michalowski, University of Michigan
*\*Discontinuity and Change in Early Mesopotamian Bureaucratic Systems*

Miguel Civil, University of Chicago
*\*Toward an Economic History of Ur III*

Piotr Steinkeller, Harvard University
*\*The Administrative Organization of the Ur III State: The Core and the Periphery*

Marc Cooper, Southwest Missouri University
*Ur III Royal Administration Centered on Puzrish-Dagan*

Irene Winter, University of Pennsylvania
*\*The Relationship of the King to his Officials in Ur III*

Richard L. Zettler, University of Chicago
*\*The Structure of the Inanna Temple in Ur III*

Ann Roth, University of Chicago
*\*The Administration and Functioning of Old Kingdom Royal Mortuary Temples*

---

\*Papers preceded by an asterisk are included in this volume, though not necessarily with the same title. Among the papers not included here are several which were committed elsewhere.

Sunday, April 17

Janet Johnson, University of Chicago
*Ptolemaic Administration from the Egyptian Point of View

Walter E. Kaegi, University of Chicago
*Some Perspectives on Byzantine Bureaucracy

Lawrence Stager, University of Chicago
Ancestral Estates and State Formation in Ancient Israel

Fred M. Donner, University of Chicago
Administrative Bureaucracy in the Umayyad State

Roy P. Mottahedeh, Princeton University
Administration in Western Iran and Southern Iraq, 900–1050 A.D.

John Woods, University of Chicago
The Life Cycle of Nomadic-Sedentary Empires: Anatolia to Central Asia in the Middle Islamic Periods

Carter Findley, Ohio State University
Personal Policy in Transition from Patrimonialism to Rational-Legalism: Aşçı Dede Ibrahim Halil (ca. 1828–1910)

Albertine Jwaideh, University of Toronto
The Land Commission of Baghdad Province and the Administration of the Ottoman Land Code, 1869–1914

Robert McC. Adams, University of Chicago
General Summation

Robert Hunt, Brandeis University
Commentary

# EDITORS' PREFACE TO THE SECOND EDITION

The original edition of this volume sold out rather quickly. Because orders continued to come in for it, it was decided to reprint the volume.

We have taken advantage of this opportunity to correct a few typographical errors that had been found. At the same time, we gave authors an opportunity to make corrections of their own and to update references in their footnotes (especially in the case of articles that were not yet published at the time of the original edition). Several corrected readings have been made in Appendix 1 in the article of Irene Winter.

The font of the original edition was Bookman. The font now used in Oriental Institute publications is CuneiformOriental. The entire volume has been reformatted, resulting in different pagination from the original edition. Consequently, when *The Organization of Power* is cited in the future, it will be necessary to specify when the second edition is the one being used.

Once again we wish to thank Thomas G. Urban for his help in preparing this revised edition.

McGuire Gibson

Robert D. Biggs

# EDITORS' PREFACE TO THE FIRST EDITION

In editing the papers in this volume, we have not tried to impose a rigid consistency in the spelling of personal names or place names, preferring to leave such matters to the preference of the individual authors. Thus, for example, one will find Amar-Sin, Amar-Suʾen, Ur-Nammu and Ur-Namma. Nor have we insisted on capitalization of the first letter of personal and geographical names in transliteration.

For the sake of typographical simplicity, ḫ is given throughout as h in Sumerian and Akkadian. As is customary in cuneiform studies, Akkadian words are given in italics and Sumerian words in roman. We have not italicized Akkadian elements in personal names, however.

In general, the abbreviations are those of the *Chicago Assyrian Dictionary*, especially for citing cuneiform texts. In several articles additional abbreviations are used and these are listed separately in the individual articles. Some other frequently-used abbreviations which are not given in *CAD* or which differ from those in *CAD* are given on pp. xi–xii.

We are grateful to Janet H. Johnson, Director of The Oriental Institute, for agreeing to have this volume appear in this series. We are indebted to Thomas A. Holland, Oriental Institute Publications Coordinator, and John Palmer, Publications Assistant, for the work they have done to produce this volume. David Baird was responsible for the computer composition. We are very grateful to him. Thomas Urban, coming to the articles with fresh eyes, gave us very valuable help with the final proof-reading.

McGuire Gibson

Robert D. Biggs

# LIST OF ABBREVIATIONS

List of abbreviations not found in the *Chicago Assyrian Dictionary*

| | |
|---|---|
| *ASJ* | *Acta Sumerologica* (Hiroshima, Japan, 1979–) |
| AUAM | Unpublished tablets in the Andrews University Archaeological Museum |
| Boehmer, *Glyptik* | R. M. Boehmer, *Die Entwicklung der Glyptik während der Akkad-Zeit* (Berlin, 1969) |
| Buchanan, *Early Seals* | B. Buchanan, *Early Near Eastern Seals in the Yale Babylonian Collection* (New Haven and London, 1981) |
| Collon, *British Museum* 2 | D. Collon, *Catalogue of the Western Asiatic Seals in the British Museum, Cylinder Seals*, vol. 2, *Akkadian-Post Akkadian Ur III Periods* (London, 1982) |
| Frankfort, *Cylinder Seals* | H. Frankfort, *Cylinder Seals* (London, 1939) |
| Frankfort, *Stratified Cylinder Seals* | H. Frankfort, *Stratified Cylinder Seals from the Diyala Region*, OIP 72 (Chicago, 1955) |
| Garelli, *Le Palais et la royauté* | P. Garelli, *Le Palais et la royauté*, RAI 19 (Paris, 1974) |
| Moortgat, *Rollsiegel* | A. Moortgat, *Vorderasiatische Rollsiegel* (Berlin, 1940) |
| Oppenheim, *Eames* | A. L. Oppenheim, *Catalogue of the Cuneiform Tablets of the Wilberforce Eames Babylonian Collection of the New York Public Library*, AOS 32 (New Haven, 1948) |
| von der Osten, *Newell* | H. H. von der Osten, *Ancient Oriental Seals in the Collection of Mrs. Edward T. Newell*, OIP 22 (Chicago, 1934) |
| Owen, *NATN* | D. I. Owen, *Neo-Sumerian Archival Texts Primarily from Nippur in The University Museum, The Oriental Institute and the Iraq Museum* (Winona Lake, Indiana, 1982) |
| Parrot, MAM | A. Parrot, *Documents et monuments*, Mission Archéologique de Mari, vol. 2/3 (Paris, 1959) |
| Porada, *Corpus* | E. Porada, *Corpus of Ancient Near Eastern Seals in North American Collections*, vol. 1, *The Pierpont Morgan Library Collection* (Washington, D.C., 1948) |

| | |
|---|---|
| *PRAK* | H. de Genouillac, *Premières recherches archéologiques à Kich*, 2 vols. (Paris, 1924 and 1925) |
| Sauren, *NY Public Library* | H. Sauren, *Les Tablettes cunéiformes de l'époque d'Ur des collections de la New York Public Library* (Louvain-la-Neuve, 1978) |
| *Seals and Sealing* | M. Gibson and R. D. Biggs, eds. *Seals and Sealing in the Ancient Near East*, Bibliotheca Mesopotamica, vol. 6 (Malibu, 1977) |
| Sigrist, *NSAT* | M. Sigrist, *Neo-Sumerian Account Texts in the Horn Archaeological Museum*, Andrews University Cuneiform Texts, vol. 1 (Berrien Springs, 1984) |
| Wiseman, *Seals* | D. J. Wiseman, *Cylinder Seals of Western Asia* (London, n.d.) |

Other frequently-used symbols:

| | |
|---|---|
| DN | divine name |
| GN | geographical name |
| PN | personal name |
| RN | royal name |

# INTRODUCTION

### MCGUIRE GIBSON
*University of Chicago*

Over the past fifteen years, I have organized four symposia dealing with various aspects of social organization as evidenced in the ancient written and archaeological record.[1] Except for the first one, these symposia were organized very informally, were not publicized, were not funded, and yet attracted a group of scholars from great distances at the expense of their universities or themselves. The informality of the arrangements and the lack of publicity were thought to engender an atmosphere of easy exchange in which the usual restraint of a meeting would be relaxed and the result would be lively and innovative discussions.

In the previous symposia, we have touched on a variety of social organizations, including bureaucracies, as evidenced in documents and archaeology. In the symposium that was the basis for this volume, we were addressing institutional structures directly.

In this symposium, Mesopotamia/Iraq was the major focus, with other areas included for illustrative or comparative purposes. Scholars with a known interest in the subject of bureaucracy, or at least administration, were asked to join a group of Chicago colleagues for a weekend of discussions. The timing of the symposium, April 16 and 17, 1983, was determined in part by the fact that some of the participants would be in Chicago then on MacArthur Foundation business.

There was no definite commitment prior to the symposium to publish the papers, a fact that made it easier to draw in participants at short notice. We knew in advance that some of the contributions were already promised elsewhere, but we wished to have the participation of particular scholars because we thought their contributions would be especially relevant to other papers.

The governing idea behind the symposium was the free interchange of ideas and the crossing of disciplinary, geographic, and temporal borders in search of common ground for discussion of social organization. It has been thought that merely bringing together scholars who might not otherwise know of one another's work and letting them discuss problems of approach to different bodies of material would afford valuable intellectual stimulation. It is my personal conviction that there has been much continuity in social and economic organization from the ancient Near East to the present and that the pre-

---

1. April 1, 1972: Symposium on irrigation, Long Beach, California; published (T. E. Downing and M. Gibson, eds., *Irrigation's Impact on Society*. Tucson, Arizona: The University of Arizona Press, 1974).
    March 21–23, 1975: Symposium on the function of seals, Oriental Institute, Chicago; published (M. Gibson and R. D. Biggs, eds., *Seals and Sealing in the Ancient Near East*. Malibu: Undena, 1977).
    June 2, 1978: Symposium on "The Achaemenids as Overlords"; not published except in specific articles by participants, e.g., R. L. Zettler, "On the Chronological Range of Neo-Babylonian and Achaemenid Seals," *JNES* 38 (1979) 257–70.

Islamic/Islamic scholarly dichotomy is an unfortunate barrier to understanding of that continuity. There have been instances of major organizational innovation and change during that span of time. But only in a study of the continuities can innovations be recognized. Scholars of Islamic and Ottoman society may not be aware that there are in Mesopotamian, Egyptian, and other ancient sources aspects of administration that are remarkably similar to, if not the same as, those they describe in their own fields. Likewise, the scholar of the ancient periods may not know of or may dismiss as irrelevant a bureaucratic mechanism, a routine, or an institution in Islamic context that may have had its origins in ancient society. Certain organizational features may be independent inventions, may be features that appear in a number of civilizations and may therefore be merely the most sensible ways of organizing work, rather than evidence of a tradition. But if scholars in different areas and periods remain unacquainted with similar structures elsewhere, a more verifiable synthesis of their own fields will remain elusive. If a symposium (and its publication) does nothing other than spark an idea and cause an individual to see his own material in a new light, or even evoke a reasoned rebuttal, it has served a very useful purpose.

Over the past thirty years, there have been numerous studies of institutions, associations, economic structures, and bureaucracies in Medieval European, Japanese, Chinese, Islamic, and other branches of history. Now, the field of ancient Near Eastern languages, having reached the end of its decipherment stage, is increasingly addressing itself to those institutions that regulated ancient society as well as questions related to demography, economy, and other socioeconomic areas. Near Eastern archaeology, influenced by the "New Archaeology," the "New Geography," and the "New History," has also been seeking answers to socioeconomic problems such as site function, societal interrelations, and subsistence patterns, usually employing an ecological model. We in the field of ancient studies can learn a great deal from those who have already dealt with the same issues, especially from social and economic historians of the Islamic periods, since they have examined cultural responses of later ages to environmental and societal conditions in the same geographical areas.

The reason for choosing bureaucracy as a focus for discussion is that it is more easily recognizable and more abundantly recorded than other social structures. Documents of all periods reflect governmental action and must, necessarily, give an insight into administrative units, routines, and personnel, even when not explicitly stated. Temple administration, likewise, has left a wealth of documents. Official titles give clues to functions, or at least allow the discrimination of specific individuals as functionaries in administrative activities. What records do not usually do is make explicit informal relationships between officials such as kin-relations, patron-client arrangements, ties by village of origin, religious favoritism, and similar links. In Chicago, the city that made "clout" a household word, we are not surprised to find that in other times and places, individuals, families, and combinations of interests made use of and prospered from the organizations they served, and probably served well. Such personal elements operating within a bureaucracy may be misinterpreted as integral to the institution, rather than as a sub-system operating within the structure. For instance, the domination and manipulation of a bureaucratic structure by a family, a larger group of kin, or an interest group might not be recognized if the researcher were not aware of the potential existence of such a group and be prepared to recognize it through clues in the archive or in parallel documents. If possible, one must isolate the institution (as ideally conceived) from the intricate interplay within that structure of such informal, personal relationships. When the structure is understood, one can then analyze the workings of the personnel within it, seeing in what ways the structure is "bent" for individual purposes and changed in temporary or permanent ways.

Basic to our understanding of the relationship of bureaucracy to those informal, personal interests in any period in the Near East is a comprehension of the nature of the informal groups, the waxing and waning of the strength of kinship organizations; the existence, even in the most urbanized setting, of

# INTRODUCTION

lineage and other ties; the role of custom in the regulation of very large parts of ancient, medieval and modern life, even in situations where civil law is supposed to carry out the same function. The continuing existence of tribal modes of organization alongside of, but usually subordinated to, state institutions, even though not often made explicit in written records, must be assumed in any period, at least for Iraq if not for other areas. This duality in organization, tied to the unstable environment of southern Iraq, has for millennia furnished a variety of responses to particular situations;[2] it has also made it much more difficult to lay out neat organizational charts, hierarchical tables, and majestically proceeding stages of social and organizational development. The variety of roles any one individual might have—as a member of one or more bureaucratic organizations, as a member of one or more informal associations, as a member of a family, an extended family, a lineage, a tribe, or as a member of a particular group identified in religious or linguistic terms—may or may not be recorded, depending on circumstances.

In many of the presentations here, the role of "big families" as the key element in administrative structures, both palace and temple, is paramount. The continuity of those "big families" within an administrative unit, despite the changes in politics and government, was for the ancient Near East the chief mechanism by which cultural tradition was made possible. It is not surprising to find that "big families" were also an essential feature in medieval and Ottoman times, that a *waqf* for the sustained welfare of a mosque is remarkably like the system whereby a Sumerian family was itself maintained while it administered a temple at Nippur for generations. It should also not be surprising that the social history of most other areas of the world shows a similar interweaving of informal social organizations within "rational" bureaucratic entities.

The symposium entitled "The Organization of Power: Aspects of Bureaucracy in the Ancient, Medieval, and Ottoman Near East," did, in fact, cover the chronological range indicated. The medieval Islamic and the Ottoman contributions, however, were almost all unavailable for publication. Some had been promised elsewhere or were already in press. The substance of Fred Donner's paper on administrative bureaucracy in the Umayyad state, addressing the transition from pre-Islamic to Islamic administration from early Arabic sources, appeared in the *Journal of the American Oriental Society*.[3] Hoping to see the transition to Islamic practice from another viewpoint, we asked Michael Morony to address the question of continuity from the Sasanian dynasty in Iraq. Having covered this question in his *Iraq after the Muslim Conquest*,[4] Marony volunteered the more general essay on Weber's notions on bureaucracy in relation to the Middle East which is included here. Roy Mottahedeh's paper on administration in Iran and Iraq during the Middle Islamic period, which supplied a temporal link between Early Islamic and Ottoman bureaucratic practice, was a variation on a published article.[5] John Woods presented a thought-provoking, elegant interpretation of administration in the context of nomadic-sedentary Turkic empires, but he is reworking it for a larger synthesis. Two contributions on Ottoman administration, by Carter Findley and Albertine Jwaideh, were also committed elsewhere.[6] Findley's,

---

2. For discussions of aspects of various kinship organizations in Mesopotamian society, see M. Gibson, "Violation of Fallow and Engineered Disaster in Mesopotamian Civilization," in Downing and Gibson, *Irrigation's Impact*, pp. 7–20; "Current Research at Nippur, Ecological, Anthropological, and Documentary Interplay," in M.-T. Barrelet, ed., *L'Archéologie de l'Iraq* ... (Paris, 1980) 193–205; and especially R. McC. Adams, "The Mesopotamian Social Landscape: A View from the Frontier," in C. B. Moore, ed., *Reconstructing Complex Societies*, BASOR Supplement 20 (1975) 1–20; "Strategies of Maximization, Stability, and Resilience in Mesopotamian Society, Settlement, and Agriculture," *Proceedings of the American Philosophical Society* 122 (1978) 329–35.
3. "The Formation of the Islamic State," *JAOS* 106 (1986) 283–98.
4. *Iraq after the Muslim Conquest* (Princeton, 1984).
5. "Bureaucracy and the Patrimonial State in Early Islamic Iran and Iraq," *Al-Abhath* 29 (1981) 25–36.
6. Publication details not specified.

dealing with the career of one official, gave a unique picture of a bureaucrat's career, rich with petty but extremely high-level personal intrigue, maneuvers for advancement, and ultimate frustration of ambition. Jwaideh's paper dealt with provincial administration in a particularly critical period of change in Iraq, laying out a background upon which to view local aspirations and reactions to administered change.

The volume presented here is, then, a more compressed, but more unitary one than originally envisioned. We have retained almost all the papers on ancient administration and these are in large part new, important, ground-breaking statements on particular institutions. We have lost Lawrence Stager's important contribution on the relationship of kinship groups to state formation in ancient Israel, but that was already in press under the title "The Archaeology of the Family in Ancient Israel."[7] Five of the papers devoted to the Ur III period comprise a major reassessment of that most bureaucratized of Mesopotamian eras.

We could have expanded the Egyptian side of the symposium and the volume a great deal, but my own Iraq-centered interest intervened. Our program was already growing too long to keep its "informal" character; since my planning had been centered upon the question of continuity from ancient to modern bureaucracy in Iraq, I thought it more appropriate to limit the Egyptian section to two case-studies that might be comparable to Mesopotamian practice. The Egyptian contributions, widely separated in time, deal with religious administration in relation to central government (directly comparable to Zettler's paper) and the complexities of government when territory has come under new rule (comparable to Steinkeller's and Winter's contributions).

Walter Kaegi's paper on Byzantine bureaucracy was elicited to allow some discussion on the role of that bureaucratic tradition, as against ancient Near Eastern, in the evolution of Islamic and Ottoman practice. His contribution is essentially an outline for future research, laying out areas that may reward effort in the Byzantine field, but also helping others to formulate questions for use on their own data.

Invited discussants for the symposium included Robert McC. Adams (then provost, Chicago), who gave a general summation; Robert Hunt (Anthropologist, Brandeis), who has broadened his comments into a long essay for this volume; Henry Wright (Anthropologist, Michigan); Halil Inalcik (Historian, Chicago), and John Padgett (Political Scientist, Chicago).

The Oriental Institute and the Department of Near Eastern Languages and Civilizations of The University of Chicago gave official sponsorship to the symposium and the Institute helped defray some minor local costs. Professor and Mrs. Adams hosted a dinner for the participants.

Once again I wish to thank Robert Biggs for joining me in editing the papers in this volume.

---

7. *BASOR* No. 260 (1985) 1–36.

# CHAPTER 1

## "IN A CITY WITHOUT WATCHDOGS THE FOX IS THE OVERSEER":[1] ISSUES AND PROBLEMS IN THE STUDY OF BUREAUCRACY

MICHAEL G. MORONY
*University of California,
Los Angeles*

How should bureaucracy be studied? How applicable is the modern model of bureaucracy outside of Europe? In the circular and inductive fashion common in the social sciences bureaucracy tends to be defined in the abstract in terms of those institutions which are called bureaucratic. The etymology of bureaucracy from the French "bureau" only emphasizes the feature of functional specialization in an administrative system organized by departments.[2] However, from eighteenth-century France to the modern United States, bureaucracy has been used for a form of administration or management that combines the use of written records, centralization, hierarchic chain of command, and professionalism with specialization.[3] Size is sometimes included in this definition because it increases the need for organization to improve efficiency.[4] The modern analysis of bureaucracy by sociologists tends to be idealized and functionalist but includes attention to the social bases of bureaucracy.

When bureaucracy is understood in terms of purpose rather than structure, it is seen as a form of administrative organization that is expected to maximize efficiency.[5] In contrast to the organizational structure, the inner workings of bureaucracy are analyzed in terms of informal and unofficial patterns of behavior.[6]

1. Sumerian proverb; S. N. Kramer, *The Sumerians: Their History, Culture, and Character* (Chicago and London, 1963) 226.
2. "Bureau" comes, in turn, from the Old French *burel*, a coarse woolen cloth covering a desk or table. For a history of the term see C. A. Emge, "Bürokratisierung unter philosophischer und soziologischer Sicht," *Akademie der Wissenschaften und der Literatur: Abhandlungen der Geistes- und Sozialwissenschaftlichen Klasse* 18 (Mainz, 1950) 1205–23.
3. The classic definition was by Max Weber, "Essay on Bureaucracy," in *From Max Weber: Essays in Sociology*, tr. H. H. Gerth and C. Wright Mills (New York, 1946) 196–244; also in F. E. Rourke, ed., *Bureaucratic Power in National Politics* (Boston, 1965) 3–14. Weber's definition of bureaucracy included a system of general rules or standards for operation and omitted centralization although that might be implied in hierarchy. See also P. M. Blau, *Bureaucracy in Modern Society* (New York, 1956) 19, 28–31, and H. Jacoby, *The Bureaucratization of the World* (Berkeley, 1973) 14–27.
4. Blau, *Bureaucracy*, p. 14; A. Downs, *Inside Bureaucracy* (Boston, 1967) 24–25.
5. Blau, *Bureaucracy*, pp. 60–61; Rourke, *Bureaucratic Power*, p. ix.
6. Blau, *Bureaucracy*, pp. 45–57. See also N. P. Mouzelis, *Organisation and Bureaucracy: An Analysis of Modern Theories* (Chicago, 1969).

Although other forms of administration have bureaucratic features, the fact that centralized bureaucracy developed in modern Europe as an alternative to feudal, participatory, and local forms of government, with which it competed, has been a source of value judgments, issues, and problems in the interpretation of bureaucracy. Bureaucratic centralization in particular was one means used by absolute monarchs during the seventeenth and eighteenth centuries, in alliance with the commercial bourgeoisie, to end feudal disorder, privilege, and local oppression.[7] The desirability and effectiveness of this means has naturally been judged according to the interests of those making the evaluation. To the extent that the expansion of the federal bureaucracy in the United States was for the wartime allocation of resources, social welfare, civil rights, or consumer protection, it conflicted with the freedom to exploit, oppress, or defraud.[8] Those who lost such privileges have tended to defend the advantages of wealth in terms of "liberty" and "free enterprise." As a result, whether or not a bureaucracy is "responsible" by preserving personal freedom has become an issue in the literature.[9]

Proponents tend to emphasize the rationality of bureaucracy in terms of its mechanistic efficiency[10] and impartiality. The former echoes eighteenth-century justifications of bureaucracy as a tool to increase royal power against feudal inefficiency in terms of Natural Law with a subsequent Utilitarian overlay. The latter justifies bureaucracy in terms of rationality and fairness in hiring and promoting officials on merit and in the treatment of clients as a reaction to privilege and unfair advantage.[11] Critics tend to regard the cure as worse than the ailment and represent bureaucracy as replacing one form of oppression by another more efficient, dehumanized, and mechanistic one.[12]

Because bureaucracy institutionalizes certain kinds of changes and makes them effective, the process is difficult to reverse. Whether or not a bureaucracy is desirable, then, depends also on whether one considers those changes to be desirable. Blau, for instance, considers bureaucracy to be necessary for the "deliberate introduction of a social innovation on a large scale,"[13] while Sullivan recognizes it as a vehicle for change, but compares the result to totalitarian dictatorship.[14] In any case, once established, bureaucracy tends to preserve the new *status quo*, including itself.[15]

For those who assume that bureaucracy works, order and efficiency are seen as potential or actual threats to personal freedom and as likely to create dependence.[16] One argument against this is that it does not work very well, and that internal conflicts and actual inefficiency undermine total control.[17]

7. S. N. Eisenstadt, *The Political Systems of Empires* (London and New York, 1963) 14–15; Jacoby, *Bureaucratization*, pp. 28–35, 37.
8. For a review of the problems in the spoils system that led to the professionalization of the Civil Service in 1883 see H. Kaufman, "The Growth of the Federal Personnel System," in Rourke, *Bureaucratic Power*, pp. 129–31.
9. See N. J. Powell, *Responsible Public Bureaucracy in the United States* (Boston, 1967).
10. Blau, *Bureaucracy*, pp. 31–32, 58; Downs, *Inside Bureaucracy*, pp. 2, 84–87; Weber, "Essay," pp. 6–8.
11. Downs, *Inside Bureaucracy*, pp. 68–69; Weber, "Essay," p. 7. Blau (*Bureaucracy*, p. 115) argues somewhat apologetically that impartiality can serve a democratic function.
12. Blau, *Bureaucracy*, p. 103; Powell, *Responsible Public Bureaucracy*, p. 35; L. Sullivan, *Bureaucracy Runs Amuck* (New York, 1944) 275.
13. Blau, *Bureaucracy*, pp. 91–92.
14. Sullivan, *Bureaucracy Runs Amuck*, p. 79.
15. F. E. Rourke, *Bureaucracy, Politics, and Public Policy* (Boston, 1969) 128–29.
16. Blau, "Bureaucracy and Democracy," in *Bureaucracy*, pp. 101–18; Downs, *Inside Bureaucracy*, pp. 132, 253, 259–60; Jacoby, *Bureaucratization*, p. 1; Powell, *Responsible Public Bureaucracy*, pp. 34–35, 45. Downs argues, for instance, that bureaucracy increases freedom by providing more options.
17. Powell, *Responsible Public Bureaucracy*, p. 163; Rourke, *Bureaucracy*, p. 147. H. Rogger (*Russia in the Age of Modernization and Revolution, 1881–1917* [London and New York, 1983] 47–48) suggests that the inefficiency of the czarist bureaucracy was a "saving grace."

Efficient or not, bureaucracy tends to be criticized most often when the interests of administrators differ from the interests of those who are administered.[18] According to Kharasch, "Much irritation is wasted on institutions which function quite well by their own internal standards, but poorly in terms of public service."[19] Kharasch himself is critical of "powerful, wasteful and dangerous" institutions that ought to be "useful, productive and humane."[20] It is generally from this point of view that bureaucrats are criticized for being inefficient, self-important, unimaginative, indecisive, and bound by routine,[21] sometimes with appeals to the stereotypes of bureaucrats in nineteenth-century literature such as Balzac's *The Civil Service* and Gogol's "Inspector General." [22]

Among bureaucrats themselves conflicts of interest can develop within a bureaucratic system. When they affect its efficiency they tend to be considered "dysfunctions." From the top looking down, the need to delegate authority in order to implement policy can result in the abuse of power, neglect of duties, and economic "corruption" when insubordinate subordinates use delegated power to pursue their own private interests.[23] From the bottom looking up, the interest of insecure subordinates in preserving their positions can lead them to emphasize conformity and loyalty at the expense of initiative, promotion by seniority instead of by merit, and personal competition over group interest that works to obstruct administrative efficiency.[24] Paradoxically, bureaucratic subordinates tend to be faulted whether they fail to give their superiors honest, constructive criticism or use their expertise to influence policy.[25]

How much of the above discussion is useful in studying pre-modern, non-western administrative systems? When the concept of bureaucracy is applied deductively outside of modern Europe, the value judgments noted above tend to be projected along with it. Because Weber defined bureaucracy in terms of executive, decision-making functions and excluded the scribal staff, he denied the existence of bureaucracy in the ancient Orient and regarded its administrative systems as patrimonial.[26] Wittfogel distinguished "serving" from "controlled" and "ruling" bureaucracies, but his work was based mainly on China and he tended to generalize on the basis of the modern Soviet system.[27] For Wittfogel, ancient ruling bureaucracies were despotic because military and religious institutions were integrated with agro-managerial systems of administration thus preventing comparable, competing forms of organization from developing. Bureaucracy is controlled in modern, Western democracies because bureaucratic forms of

---

18. Rogger, *Russia*, p. 48; Rourke, *Bureaucracy*, p. 148.
19. R. N. Kharasch, *The Institutional Imperative: How to Understand the United States Government and other Bulky Objects* (New York, 1973) 105.
20. Ibid., pp. 9, 245.
21. Blau, *Bureaucracy*, pp. 13, 86; Powell, *Responsible Public Bureaucracy*, pp. 2–3, 35; Rogger, *Russia*, pp. 47, 51; Rourke, *Bureaucracy*, pp. 129, 135–36; A. M. Schlesinger, Jr., "Roosevelt as Chief Administrator," in Rourke, *Bureaucratic Power*, pp. 89–91; Sullivan, *Bureaucracy Runs Amuck*, p. 196; K. A. Wittfogel, *Oriental Despotism* (New Haven, 1959) 52.
22. Blau, *Bureaucracy*, p. 86; Kharasch, *Institutional Imperative*, pp. 45–46; Rogger, *Russia*, p. 49; Sullivan, *Bureaucracy Runs Amuck*, pp. 59, 285.
23. J. S. Coleman, *Power and the Structure of Society* (New York, 1973) 97–98; Powell, *Responsible Public Bureaucracy*, p. 1; Rogger, *Russia*, pp. 50, 51, 54.
24. Blau, *Bureaucracy*, p. 33; Rogger, *Russia*, pp. 44–45.
25. H. Finer, "Administrative Responsibility in Democratic Government," in Rourke, *Bureaucratic Power*, p. 184; Rogger, *Russia*, pp. 44, 46; Weber, "Essay," p. 8. For an analysis of the literature on the domination of policy by bureaucrats, see D. Waldo, *The Administrative State* (New York, 1948) 89–103. Finer calls this "the new despotism," while Rogger (p. 47) compares the "politically conscious policy-making bureaucracy" of Prussia, France, and Austria favorably to that of Russia.
26. Weber, "Essay," p. 4.
27. Wittfogel, *Oriental Despotism*, pp. 105, 106, 337.

management (specifically in business) exist outside of and in competition with government.[28] This self-serving liberalism is clearly a projection of modern, Western values. It is questionable whether (1) monopoly over a form of organization explains despotism or (2) the administrative systems of ancient and Islamic Western Asia actually had such a monopoly. Eisenstadt's highly abstract study of pre-modern centralized bureaucratic empires provides a much better theoretical framework, especially for the interrelations between political systems and social structures.[29]

One strategy for an analysis would be to take the abstract model of bureaucracy and see how much of it is applicable to the pre-modern administrative systems of Western Asia. Whoever adopts this method should be prepared to find features that are not present in the modern, Western model. One should also realize that it is impossible to avoid entirely making value judgments, but that it is possible to minimize the damage if one is at least aware that one is doing it. At any rate, it is more productive to avoid judging an administrative system in terms of what one thinks it ought to do and rather to evaluate it (if one must) with regard to how well it works on its own terms and performs the functions for which it was created, whether one approves of those purposes or not. The best way to determine the effectiveness of a system is to measure what it actually does against what it is intended to do. With this in mind one should ask the following questions when considering particular systems.

The first question is what is the purpose of the system. Ostensibly the purpose of all such systems is the exercise of control, but there can be differences over what is controlled and why. Unlike modern, Western systems that were developed at first to curb feudal disorder[30] and to mobilize resources, the purpose of bureaucratic administration in the early Sumerian city-states was to organize economic activity on a relatively large scale; this organization developed because of the size, complexity, and duration of the undertaking.[31] In Old Kingdom Egypt it appears to have been a means of territorial unification and mobilization of resources on an even larger scale, while the bureaucratization of Assyria after 738 B.C. under Tiglath-Pileser III (744–27) was to enhance centralized power at the expense of local authority in the Assyrian homeland and at the expense of tributaries who were replaced by governors in an expanding imperial system.[32]

Whatever the purpose of a system may be, how is it carried out? Control may be exercised in several ways, but in a bureaucratic system this is done by keeping records, collecting income, and paying salaries. In the temple and palace organizations of ancient Western Asia scribal officials were employed for documentation and administrative communication. Economic records were born along with bureaucracy, and archives are evidence of its existence.[33] Written documents facilitate two forms of control. As a form of collective memory that can be checked against human memory or prevarication, records assist control across time, preserving an account of what is collected and what is supposed to happen to it.[34] Along with the verbal messages, written communications assist in control of subordinates who are physically out of reach. Written documents were an essential part of imperial administration before electronic communications.

---

28. Ibid., pp. 49–52, 100, 338, 365, 368.
29. S. K. Eisenstadt, *The Political Systems of Empires* (London and New York, 1963).
30. Sullivan, *Bureaucracy Runs Amuck*, p. 118.
31. G. Roux, *Ancient Iraq* (Harmondsworth, 1980) 128.
32. Ibid., pp. 282–83.
33. A. L. Oppenheim, *Ancient Mesopotamia: Portrait of a Dead Civilization* (Chicago, 1964) 23–24, 70, 230–31, 235; Roux, *Ancient Iraq*, pp. 128, 163.
34. Oppenheim (*Ancient Mesopotamia*, p. 230) points out the practical need for such records when officials serve for temporally limited terms.

How are such systems organized? How hierarchic, centralized, and specialized are they? In highly developed systems, what is the difference and relationship between central and provincial institutions? Specialization in the central administration may be measured in terms of the number of positions with different responsibilities as in Old Kingdom Egypt, or in terms of the relative elaboration of departments with their own staffs of officials as in Islamic states. For comparative purposes the development of administrative profiles, i.e., of the offices and their responsibilities, is useful, but such typologies by function should be weighed against the overlapping of personnel. Are the officials as specialized as the offices they hold, or do they switch from one to another? Does the same person hold several offices at the same time? Are positions monopolized by a relatively small group of officials? Do these features occur more at the upper than the lower levels of the system? Is such versatility the antithesis of professionalism? By the end of the third millennium B.C. there appear to have been thousands of highly specialized Sumerian scribes divided into two ranks.[35]

Hierarchy can be measured in terms of how many levels there are in the system, whether or not there is a chain of command, how much discretion officials are allowed, and who appoints, dismisses, or transfers subordinate officials. Early Sumerian temples already had highly developed hierarchies descending from the chief administrator to superintendents, inspectors, overseers, controllers, and scribes.[36] Clues to the degree of hierarchy in a system can also be found in the way geographical units of administration are grouped as in the three-tiered nome system of Old Kingdom Egypt.

The nature of hierarchy, the degree of specialization, and the size of administrative units in a geographically extended system indicate the extent of centralization. Is there a single administrative pyramid as in Old Kingdom Egypt or are there separate lines of authority from the center to each province or district? Are there parallel, functionally specialized, hierarchies of provincial officials, and, if so, how, if at all, do they intersect? The combination of powers at the provincial level granted to Old Kingdom nomarchs, Neo-Assyrian governors,[37] and early Islamic governors indicates greater provincial autonomy and relative administrative decentralization. Combining powers seems to be an early feature of developing or expanding systems, but it can also contribute to political fragmentation should the central administration break down. In particular systems the separation of powers and the introduction of specialization at the provincial level seems to be a subsequent development for greater central control. One of the earliest examples of this is under the Third Dynasty of Ur at the end of the third millennium B.C. where district governors held administrative, judicial, and fiscal powers but were appointed, dismissed, and transferred by the ruler who also appointed a separate military governor.[38] The recurring pattern in Western Asia appears to be the division of local authority among separate military, fiscal, and judicial officials as in the Achaemenid system of Darius (522–486) after 520 B.C.[39] There were similar divisions of responsibility in the Sasanian and early Byzantine systems, and in some Islamic states.

However they are organized, do political bureaucracies compete with alternative systems? Apart from tributary, confederative, or decentralized regimes such as those of the Kassites or Parthians where regions outside of bureaucratic control were also likely to be politically autonomous, state bureaucracies appear to have had two main rivals. One was the religious institution wherever temples, churches, or *masjid*s had their own property and administrative organization. In the late third millennium B.C., palace-centered organizations competed with temple-centered organizations of the same type in Sumerian cities,

---

35. Kramer, *The Sumerians*, p. 230. [See also I. Winter in this volume, eds.]
36. Roux, *Ancient Iraq*, pp. 128–29.
37. Ibid., p. 283.
38. Ibid., p. 162. [See also the discussion by P. Steinkeller in this volume, eds.]
39. Ibid., p. 377.

though they emerged later as the nucleus of territorial administrative systems. Perhaps because of their structural kinship, from ancient temples to Islamic *awqāf*, the administration of religious institutions was capable of being incorporated into "secular" administrative systems by powerful regimes. The earliest example is, again, the Third Dynasty of Ur where the temples survived with their own organization but paid taxes to the ruler who also collected and distributed their revenues for them.[40] Temples, churches, and *awqāf*, might also be controlled non-bureaucratically by putting relatives of the ruler in charge of them, but, depending on the personalities involved, this method creates a potential not only for loyal but administratively autonomous religious institutions, but also for the effective representation of their interests to the ruler. Under certain circumstances, powerful, autonomous religious institutions could challenge or undermine a "secular" regime as during the Neo-Babylonian (Chaldaean) or middle Sasanian periods.

The second rival of bureaucracy was the palace organization out of which it had grown, but which survived as an alternative to it. From antiquity to Safavid Iran expanded royal household systems for mobilizing resources which had their own bureaucratic features competed with "regular" fiscal bureaucratic systems. Sometimes the territory of a state was divided between them.

However powerful or circumscribed a system may be, how does the actual machinery of administration work? What do the officials do? What happens to documents? How are seals used on them, and what is the significance of such authentication?[41] Attention should also be paid to the mechanics of administering military and religious institutions.

Who runs the system? How are officials chosen and organized? What is their social origin? Do bureaucratic officials constitute a profession or a class? Is service hereditary and, if not, how do officials perpetuate themselves or transfer their expertise? How are officials trained? Are the scribal schools at Nippur and Ur during the Third Dynasty of Ur related to increasing professionalism and the expansion of the bureaucracy?[42] Is the apprentice type of in-service training in Islamic systems a feature of patronage? How long do officials hold their positions, how often are they rotated, and is advancement by merit or by patronage?

How are officials paid? How often are they paid? The frequent distribution of movable forms of wealth increases the dependence of officials on the regime they serve. Daily rations indicate the greatest degree of dependence as in Old Kingdom Egypt where local officials received daily rations of bread, meat, and jugs of beer. The same applies to the king's table at Mari and elsewhere. Alternatively, salaries in kind as paid to the employees of Sumerian temples,[43] or later salaries in cash served to keep officials dependent. By the same token, paying officials by giving them access to the sources of wealth makes them less dependent. Is land attached to a position, or are the rights to income assigned to officials such as the ensis of the Third Dynasty of Ur who paid themselves from the taxes collected in their own districts?[44] This alternative form of payment tends to confuse official with private activity, interests, and rights and can raise the question of the inheritance of such rights by the relatives of such officials. It is also something of an administrative short-circuit. By eliminating the intermediate tax-collecting, salary-paying part of the bureaucracy it may be less expensive and more efficient in the short run. But even when it is a reward for loyalty, it can lead to the alienation of resources, decentralization, and political fragmentation.

40. Ibid., p. 264. [See also R. Zettler in this volume, eds.]
41. M. Gibson and R. D. Biggs, eds., *Seals and Sealing in the Ancient Near East* (Malibu, 1977).
42. Concerning scribal schools see Kramer, "Education: The Sumerian School," in *The Sumerians*, pp. 229–48; Oppenheim, *Ancient Mesopotamia*, pp. 242–43; and Roux, *Ancient Iraq*, pp. 202, 331–32.
43. Roux, *Ancient Iraq*, p. 128.
44. Ibid., p. 164.

Since a bureaucratic system is a type of administrative institution, we may ask what features of an institution it has. Is there a set of standardized practices? Is the organization capable of replication, expansion or contraction as was the Neo-Assyrian empire of Tiglath-Pileser III in which conquered territory became provinces by organizing it like Assyrian districts?[45] What kind of buildings do bureaucrats inhabit? Can the plan of a building be related to the structural organization of administration? How do the tablets found in different rooms of the palace at Mari provide clues to the organization of records and correspondence?[46]

Why does bureaucratic administration work? Why do officials follow orders? What happens (if anything) when orders are not obeyed? The unique problem created by the need to delegate power in authoritarian, hierarchic systems is how to enforce central control over subordinate and distant officials and how to secure their conformity to the regime's policies. When such a system works, some form of sanction is operating. Why sanctions are effective or expected to be so reveals assumptions about human nature and about the values of a particular society. For instance, one persistent image in Western Asia describes officials as anatomical extensions of the ruler.[47] If the hand of a powerful ruler is said to be "long," it is because the officials make it so.

Religion can be an important sanction for authority. Of particular significance for bureaucracy are the ancient creation myths that represent creation as organization, as bringing order out of chaos, and as being accomplished by command.[48] Because the išakku of Lagash represented Ningirsu or Sumerian lugals exercised Enlil's responsibilities on earth, their officials participated in the cosmic order. The fact that the ancient Egyptian ruler was considered to be divine gave him ownership, authority, and responsibility over Egypt. The ability of the Egyptian ruler to create by command is implied in the Memphite theology according to which the commanding speech of Ptah brought thought to reality. Ptah thus continues to create wherever there is thought and command. Authoritative utterance or commanding speech (hu) was one of the qualities of Egyptian kingship, meaning that the ruler gave the kind of orders that were obeyed. In both doctrine and ritual the ruler, as a god, gave Egypt its seasons, abundant water, and crops. In fact, he actually did so through his officials who regulated irrigation, and who, by measuring the fields after the annual Nile flood, brought actual order out of real chaos. Doctrine thus sanctioned administration, while successful administration justified doctrine.[49] Among Muslims, reward or punishment in the hereafter was used as a sanction for officials. The Commander of the Faithful, ʿAlī ibn Abī Ṭālib (A.D. 656–60), is said to have told his tax collectors that eternal reward or punishment depended on their behavior.[50]

Another way of discouraging the arbitrary exercise of authority by subordinates is through control mechanisms designed to deprive officials of any more power than they need in order to perform their duties. It is assumed that officials will get away with as much as they can as expressed in the Sumerian proverb, "In a city without watchdogs the fox is the overseer." Internal administrative checks can take the form of institutionalized competition among parallel officials with overlapping responsibilities or

---

45. Ibid., p. 283.
46. Ibid., p. 202.
47. The secretary ʿAbd al-Ḥamī (d. A.D. 750) called officials the ears, eyes, tongues, and hands of the ruler; B. Lewis, *Islam—From the Prophet Muhammad to the Capture of Constantinople* (New York, 1974), vol. 1, p. 186.
48. It is worth noting that Weber saw chaos as the antithesis of bureaucracy ("Essay," p. 9). See also Sullivan, *Bureaucracy Runs Amuck*, p. 275.
49. J. A. Wilson, "Egypt," in H. and H. A. Frankfort, *Before Philosophy* (Harmondsworth, 1959) 88–91, 93, 95–96.
50. Abū Yūsuf, *Kitāb al-kharāj*, tr. E. Fagnan, *Livre de l'impôt foncier (Kitāb el-Kharādj)* (Paris, 1921) 182.

shared functions.[51] Such conflict among officials or departments can be either a device for control, a cause of administrative paralysis, or a source of creativity. Local officials can also be controlled, or the effects of their discretionary use of power can at least be restricted spatially and temporally by limiting their territorial jurisdiction[52] and by rotating them frequently. An additional check on local officials is to supervise them through royal inspectors such as the sukkals of the Third Dynasty of Ur, the *qurbatu* officials of the Neo-Assyrian empire, or the Achaemenid eyes and ears of the king.[53] In general, the need to balance such forms of control against the ability of officials to carry out their duties puts such a system into what Rourke calls an "unstable equilibrium."[54]

Mechanistic controls are largely based on the expectation that officials will act according to their own self-interest, that officials will obey if they fear the consequences of disobedience. Fear of punishment and dismissal are probably universal sanctions, but it is worth noting that the fear of public exposure was expected to restrain the behavior of an ancient Egyptian official,[55] while the Muslim *qāḍī*, Abū Yūsuf, expected the fear of judicial review to curb oppression by officials.[56] There is a different sort of appeal to self-interest in warnings to officials that oppression will destroy their own base of economic support, as when the Muslim governor, Ziyād ibn Abīhi, told his officials to treat the peasants well because "as long as they prosper, you prosper."[57] It is difficult to imagine a more specific appeal to bureaucratic self-interest than the maxim ascribed to the Sasanian monarch Khusraw II that "he who does not obey his superior is not obeyed by his subordinates."[58]

Dependence also serves as a means of control over salaried officials, freed slaves, or new men who owe their position to the ruler. But the fear of losing status and support is not the only sanction for such officials. They can also be motivated by a sense of obligation for favors, or gratitude for benefits that cements patron-protégé relationships and generates loyalty. One of the best examples is the Islamic ethic of *niʿmah* (gratitude) that created ties of *iṣṭināʿ* or *intisāb*, a foster parent relationship, between patron and protégé. The patron raised, educated, and trained his protégé in his own profession. The protégé's obligation to his patron resembled that toward a parent.[59] Self-interest, dependence, and obligation were combined in the practice of some Islamic regimes of co-opting local natural leaders at the point where the administrative regime intersected with its subjects. The rulers recognized the authority of such leaders over their followers while making them responsible for their followers' behavior.[60]

The mutual trust among officials based on such obligations and group solidarity based on common interests and professional identity are a major alternative to coercive controls. Trust and solidarity contribute to family rule because relatives are expected to be bound to the regime by kinship ties. Trust also contributes to the solidarity and loyalty among the members of administrative factions who consider

---

51. C. J. Friedrich, "Public Policy and the Nature of Administrative Responsibility," in Rourke, *Bureaucratic Power*, pp. 165–75; Downs, *Inside Bureaucracy*, pp. 119–20; Powell, *Responsible Public Bureaucracy*, p. 16; Rogger, *Russia*, p. 52; Schlesinger, "Roosevelt," p. 99; Sullivan, *Bureaucracy Runs Amuck*, p. 17; Wittfogel, *Oriental Despotism*, p. 345.
52. Roux, *Ancient Iraq*, p. 283. The reform of Tiglath-Pileser III included reducing the size of Assyrian districts by increasing their number.
53. Ibid., pp. 162, 283, 337. See also A. L. Oppenheim, "The Eyes of the Lord," *JAOS* 88 (1968) 173–80.
54. Rourke, *Bureaucratic Power*, p. xviii.
55. Wilson, "Egypt," p. 99.
56. Abū Yūsuf, *Kharāj*, p. 171.
57. Ibn Qutayba, *Kitāb ʿuyūn al-akhbār* (Cairo, 1964), vol. 1, p. 10.
58. Thaʿālibi, *Ghurar akhbār mulūk al-furs wa siyaruhum*, ed. and tr. H. Zotenberg, *Histoire des rois des Perses* (Paris, 1900) 690.
59. R. P. Mottahedeh, *Loyalty and Leadership in an Early Islamic Society* (Princeton, 1980) 72–79, 82–84.
60. S. El-Ali and C. Cahen, "'Arīf," *Encyclopaedia of Islam*[2], vol. 1, pp. 629–30.

each other to be reliable. The faction created by the Nizam al-Mulk kept the Saljuq empire running for a generation after his death.[61]

Explanations for why such systems work thus combine bureaucratic sociology with administrative ethics. A bureaucratic system depends ultimately on the personal loyalty, integrity, and reliability of persons the ruler can trust to carry out his orders, whether they be personal friends, members of his entourage, or royal confidantes. The delegation of responsibility to reliable subordinates tends to put the system at the mercy of the ruler's judgment in the choice of those in whom to place his trust because misplaced trust can result in betrayal. The need for an ethical dimension to administrative behavior led officials to rely on the ethics of equity. But justice as equity in administration could lead officials to take refuge in regulations. The ancient Egyptian official was expected to act impartially according to law and precedent but was told that "the officials' place of refuge lies in acting in conformance with the regulations" by fulfilling a promise made to a petitioner.[62] Sasanian royal informers were required to possess religious and ethical virtues that would ensure their reliability,[63] and there is a similar tradition of ethical requirements for Muslim tax collectors.[64] During late antiquity this tended to be institutionalized by involving religious leaders in state administration. Bishops and *mobad*s were employed as checks on secular officials, to administer law, and to seal documents. The Muslim Commander of the Faithful, Muʿāwiya (A.D. 660–680), is said to have put a *qāḍī* in charge of his department of the seal,[65] and Muslim *qāḍī*s were sometimes put in charge of taxation.[66] However, opposing ethical and mechanistic solutions to the delegation of power in this way tends to set up a structuralist dichotomy.

The "systems analysis" treatment of bureaucracy in general tends to be somewhat static, producing a synchronic picture of a particular system at a particular time. It is useful to consider bureaucracy in terms of the historical processes of development or change, although one should be wary of evolutionary schemes. Sullivan's states of development[67] are specific to the modern West and have no application to Western Asia. Eisenstadt's scheme is more appropriate but evolves from less developed to more developed.[68] The dynamic of an expanding bureaucracy is somewhat circular. Since highly developed systems are more expensive, an expanding bureaucracy requires increasing income to pay for it, greater control over resources, and still more officials to collect and disburse revenues. The increasing specialization and delegation of authority in an expanding administrative system either creates a new elite of officials or enlarges an existing one.[69] They also create new problems that generate new solutions.

What happens when a bureaucratic system breaks down? What constitute "abuses"? Who defines them? Whether defined by a misserved ruler or by oppressed subjects, administrative "corruption" is

---

61. C. E. Bosworth, "The Political and Dynastic History of the Iranian World (A.D. 1000–1217)," *Cambridge History of Iran* (London and New York, 1968), vol. 5, pp. 69–70.
62. Wilson, "Egypt," p. 99.
63. M. Boyce, *The Letter of Tansar* (Rome, 1968) 50.
64. Abū Yūsuf, *Kharāj,* p. 172; M. Khadduri, *Islamic Law of Nations: Shaybānī's Siyar* (Baltimore, 1966) 283–84.
65. Jahshiyārī *Kitāb al-wuzarāʾ wa-l-kuttāb* (Leipzig, 1926) 21.
66. Abū Yūsuf, *Kharāj,* p. 137; Ibn Khallikan, *Biographical Dictionary,* tr. M. de Slane (Paris and London, 1843–71), vol. 2, p. 2.
67. Sullivan, *Bureaucracy Runs Amuck,* p. 118.
68. Eisenstadt, *Empires,* pp. 4, 309–60.
69. Powell, *Responsible Public Bureaucracy,* pp. 175–76; Rogger, *Russia,* p. 50. For the displacement and succession of goals see Blau, *Bureaucracy,* pp. 93–95.

usually some form of inequity or a use of power for private ends.[70] In some recorded cases, it amounts to oppressive taxation and the misappropriation of property by officials.[71] What constitutes bureaucratic "reform"? Whose interests does it represent? Does it merely restore efficiency,[72] or does it extend the ruler's power further than before? The reforms of Urukagina (ca. 2400 B.C.)[73] and the so-called Code of Ur-Nammu (ca. 2050 B.C.) associated the abolition of abuses with new regulations.[74] The process of reform is one of the historic sources of law and is usually justified in terms of some ideal.

The issues regarding change within a particular system broaden into questions of long range change or continuity across subsequent systems and the possibility of the "influence" of different systems on one another. The main problem in reconstructing most systems is the discontinuous nature of the evidence. The temptation to use comparative analysis to make up the difference, to rely on the common features if not timeless sameness of Western Asian systems and to use one system to understand another, has been too great to resist. There has been some arguing back and forth, for instance, between Babylonian and Islamic systems in the way Ellis used Løkkegaard who used Clay.[75] But mere similarity is not enough. Similar features may belong to dissimilar systems and are not, in themselves, proof of "influence" or continuity. It is necessary to show how such features survived, to identify the means of continuity or transmission, to outline the social history of the administrators of one regime who were employed by its successor, or to demonstrate that the bureaucratic institutions of an imperial system survived in its successor states after it broke up. Survival needs to be weighed against revival because the inherent problems of delegation and their obvious solutions tend to reconstitute similar systems. One should be wary of etymologies. The fact that the Iranian word for scribe (*dabīr*) is derived from the Sumerian word for scribe (dub-sar) does not, in itself, prove that Iranian and Sumerian scribes were the same in any other respect. The meaning and use of such terms need to be understood in their context as do the actual responsibilities of officials, whatever their titles.

This is obviously a relativist and functionalist solution to some of the problems of the historical study of bureaucracy in Western Asia. The implications of fragmentary information and isolated details need to be weighed against all known possibilities. Which kind of system is it most likely to belong to? Where does it fit in that system? In general one should remember that the configurations of circumstances are more important than separate features. One should also balance the static description of the way systems work against how they change over time, and consider the value systems that motivate officials and the sanctions that restrain them. Those who study Western bureaucratic systems should also recognize that these systems are not unique but need to be put into a broader framework.

70. Wilson, "Egypt," pp. 96–97; Wittfogel, *Oriental Despotism*, p. 171.
71. E.g., in ancient Lagash, Kramer, *The Sumerians*, pp. 79–81.
72. Eisenstadt, *Empires*, pp. 169–71, 291–92; Wittfogel, *Oriental Despotism*, pp. 171–72.
73. Kramer, *The Sumerians*, pp. 82, 84, 317–22.
74. It is now generally recognized that the code formerly attributed to Ur-Nammu dates rather to the reign of Šulgi. See P. Steinkeller in this volume, p. 17, n. 10.
75. Rachel Clay, *The Tenure of Land in Babylonia and Assyria* (London, 1938); M. Ellis, *Agriculture and the State in Ancient Mesopotamia* (Philadelphia, 1976); F. Løkkegaard, *Islamic Taxation in the Classic Period* (Copenhagen, 1950).

# CHAPTER 2

# THE ADMINISTRATIVE AND ECONOMIC ORGANIZATION OF THE UR III STATE: THE CORE AND THE PERIPHERY

PIOTR STEINKELLER
*Harvard University*

The area and period considered in this paper is Mesopotamia at the time of the Ur III dynasty (2112–2004 B.C.). Beginning with not much more than a parochial city-state, the House of Ur succeeded within two generations in spreading its influence over the whole of Western Asia and in building what amounted to a multinational empire. The phenomenal rise of this empire was matched only by the suddenness and completeness of its demise; in less than a century after its creation, no trace of it remained.

The Ur III dynasty was founded by Ur-Nammu, who, by assuming the title "King of Sumer and Akkad," i.e., of southern and northern Babylonia, laid claim to hegemony over both lands. A recently published text, however, casts serious doubt on whether Ur-Nammu did in fact exercise effective control over northern Babylonia.[1] Yet even if we were to assume that the reputation of Ur-Nammu as a unifier

---

Abbreviations are those of the *Chicago Assyrian Dictionary* with the following changes and additions:

| | |
|---|---|
| Forde, *Nebraska* | Nels W. Forde, *Nebraska Cuneiform Texts of the Sumerian Ur III Dynasty* (Lawrence, Kansas, 1967) |
| Jean, *ŠA* | Ch. F. Jean, *Šumer et Akkad* (Paris, 1929) |
| Kang, *SACT* | S. Kang, *Sumerian and Akkadian Cuneiform Texts in the Collection of the World Heritage Museum of the University of Illinois* (Urbana, 1972–) |
| Langdon, *TAD* | S. Langdon, *Tablets from the Archives of Drehem* (Paris, 1911) |
| Limet, *TSDU* | H. Limet, *Textes sumériens de la III$^e$ dynastie d'Ur* (Brussels, 1976) |
| Nesbit, *SRD* | W. M. Nesbit, *Sumerian Records from Drehem* (New York, 1914) |
| Owen, *NATN* | D. I. Owen, *Neo-Sumerian Archival Texts Primarily from Nippur* (Winona Lake, Indiana, 1982) |
| *PDT* | M. Çığ, H. Kızılyay, and A. Salonen, *Die Puzriš-Dagan-Texte der Istanbuler Archäologischen Museen* (Helsinki, 1954) |

1.  This text is the Sippar fragment of the "Ur-Nammu Code" (F. Yildiz, "A Tablet of Codex Ur-Nammu from Sippar," *Or.* n.s. 50 [1981] 87–97), restoring a large section of the prologue and some of the laws. The question whether northern Babylonia was controlled by Ur during Ur-Nammu's reign is raised by the following passage in the prologue: ud-ba Akšak(!)$^{ki}$ Már-da$^{ki}$ X$^{ki}$ Ka-zal-lu$^{ki}$ ù maš-gán-bi Ú-za-ru-um$^{ki}$ níg An-ša$_4$-an$^{ki}$-a nam-árad hé-íb-ak-e á $^d$Nanna lugal-gá-ta ama-ar-gi$_4$-bi hu-mu-gar, "at that time, Akšak(!), Mar(a)da, X, Kazallu, and their settlements, (and) Uṣarum, (and) whatsoever had been enslaved by Anšan, through the strength of Nanna, my lord, I established their freedom" (Sippar fragment lines 125–34; for the

of Babylonia is historically valid, there is little doubt that it is Šulgi, Ur-Nammu's son and successor, who should be considered the true builder of the Ur III state.

In the second half of Šulgi's reign, which lasted forty-eight years, the Ur III state entered into a period of rapid territorial expansion, mainly to the east of the Tigris and in southwestern Iran. The process of subjugating those territories and of incorporating them into the Ur III state, which began in Šulgi's twenty-fourth regnal year,[2] seems to have been completed shortly before his death.

This phase of foreign conquest coincided at home with a series of remarkable political, administrative, and economic reforms, as a result of which Babylonia emerged as a highly centralized bureaucratic state, with virtually every aspect of its economic life subordinated to the overriding objective of the maximization of gains.

A study of the reign of Šulgi specifically, and of the Ur III period in general, cannot but leave one with the impression that the reforms were carried out according to a grand master plan, whose author, we have every reason to believe, was Šulgi himself. The existence of such a blueprint is suggested, on the one hand, by the brevity of the period during which these transformations came about (less than twenty years, with ten years being the most likely figure), and, on the other, by the striking degree of systemic cohesion that characterized the institutions of the Ur III state.

Among the most important of Šulgi's reforms[3] we can list the following:

1. The deification of Šulgi (no later than the year Šulgi 20).[4]

2. The creation of a standing army Šulgi 20).[5]

3. The reorganization of the system of temple households Šulgi 21).[6]

---

reading Akšak(!)$^{ki}$ in line 125, see S. N. Kramer, "The Ur-Nammu Law Code: Who was Its Author?" *Or.* n.s. 52 [1983] 455, n. 15; given the context, the reading X$^{ki}$ as Šubur$^{ki}$ in line 127, given by Yildiz, p. 87, seems doubtful; one would expect here another northern Babylonian city; P. Michalowski suggests to me, based on a collation of the tablet, the reading Gír-kal$^{ki}$). If, as taken by Yildiz, p. 93, and myself, but against Kramer, p. 455, the verb in line 134 is to be translated in the first person singular (as indicated by -gá-, "my," in line 133), then the event described in this passage would have to be assigned to Šulgi's reign, for in all likelihood it is Šulgi who was the author of the code (see n. 10 below). The picture presented by other evidence bearing on the status of northern Babylonia during the reign of Ur-Nammu is inconclusive. On the one hand, the "Cadaster of Ur-Nammu," an Old Babylonian text purporting to describe the territories under Ur-Nammu's control, includes the northern Babylonian provinces of Girtab, Apiak, Urum, and Mar(a)da (F. R. Kraus, *ZA* 51 [1955] 45–74; Steinkeller, "On the Reading and Location of the Toponyms ÚR×Ú.KI and A.HA.KI," *JCS* 32 [1980] 25–27); on the other hand, no exemplars of Ur-Nammu's royal inscriptions have been discovered at any of the northern Babylonian sites (the text Ur-Nammu 14, which W. W. Hallo, "The Royal Inscriptions of Ur: A Typology," *HUCA* 33 [1962] 26, classified as coming from northern Babylonia, stems, in fact, from the southern Babylonian Keš; see *Rép. géogr.* 2, p. 96). [A recently excavated Isin tablet, to be published by C. Wilcke, seems to provide conclusive evidence that the war with Anšan described in lines 124–34 of the "Ur-Nammu Code" took place during the reign of Ur-Nammu. This tablet, which is an Old Babylonian copy of Ur-Nammu's historical inscription, contains an account of the military conflict between Ur-Nammu and Puzur-Inšušinak of Elam (courtesy C. Wilcke). In all probability, the same event is meant in each case.]

2. As evidenced in that year's name-formula, recording Šulgi's first foreign conquest: mu Kár-har$^{ki}$ ba-hul, "the year Karhar was destroyed" (*BE* 1 125:22).

3. A comprehensive study of Šulgi's reforms is still to be written. See, provisionally, E. Sollberger, "Sur la chronologie des rois d'Ur," *AfO* 17 (1954–56) 17–18; J. Klein, *Three Šulgi Hymns: Sumerian Royal Hymns Glorifying King Šulgi of Ur* (Ramat-Gan, 1981), p. 36; see the review by D. R. Frayne in *BiOr* 40 (1983) 94–95.

4. See, most recently, Steinkeller, "More on the Ur III Royal Wives," *ASJ* 3 (1981) 81.

5. Year-formula of Šulgi 20: mu dumu Úrim$^{ki}$-ma lú-giš-gíd-šè ka ba-ab-kéš, "the year the citizens of Ur were conscripted as spearmen" (*BE* 1 125:16).

6. I assume that this is the event that the year-formula of Šulgi 21 refers to: mu $^d$Nin-urta énsi-gal $^d$En-líl-lá-ke$_4$ é $^d$En-líl $^d$Nin-líl-lá-ke$_4$ eš-bar-kin ba-an-dug$_4$-ga $^d$Šul-gi lugal Úrim$^{ki}$-ma-ke$_4$ gána níg-ŠID šag$_4$ é $^d$En-líl $^d$Nin-líl-lá-ke$_4$ si bí-sá-a, "the year Ninurta, the 'great governor' of Enlil, pronounced an ominous decision in the

4. The creation of a unified administrative system for southern and northern Babylonia.
5. The introduction of the bala taxation system, coupled with the creation of a chain of redistribution centers, such as Puzriš-Dagan, which served to collect, to process, and to distribute the state revenues.[7]
6. The creation of an enormous bureaucratic apparatus, as well as of a system of scribal schools that provided highly uniform scribal and administrative training for the prospective members of the bureaucracy.
7. The radical reform of the writing system.
8. The introduction of new accounting and recording procedures and of new types of archival records.
9. The reorganization of the system of weights and measures.[8]
10. The introduction of a new calendar, the so-called Reichskalender, which became the official calendar throughout the Ur III state.[9]

In addition, there are strong reasons to believe that the so-called Ur-Nammu Code, which, as its name shows, has traditionally been attributed to Ur-Nammu, was in reality Šulgi's creation.[10]

In the economic sphere the most significant of Šulgi's reforms was that the possessions of the temple households, as well as the temple households themselves, all now became the de facto property of the state. The way in which Šulgi brought this about was quite ingenious: while preserving the original system of temple households, which, in theory at least, continued to function as the domains of individual gods, he placed all of the households located in one province under the control of that province's governor, a royal appointee. The surplus revenues of the temple households, which in the past had been retained in the province, were now delivered to the central government.

Reviving a policy first introduced by the Sargonic kings, Šulgi also created a new category of land, the crown land or royal domain. This land was distributed in the form of allotments among the members of the military organization and among other types of royal dependents in exchange for services.

A significant innovation of Šulgi's reign was the creation of huge industrial complexes devoted to highly specialized commodity production and run directly by the central government.

In terms of the resources concentrated and the level of governmental control exercised in their management, the Ur III state constitutes a unique phenomenon in the history of ancient Mesopotamia. Though later Mesopotamian rulers proved by no means immune to the enticements of "totalitarian temptation" and tried many times to unify Babylonia and to impose a centralized government on it, never again did centralization reach such a high degree. It is this uniqueness or, one might say, abnormality of the Ur III state that warrants the historian's interest in it. By identifying the factors which rendered the

---

temple households of Enlil and Ninlil, (and) Šulgi, king of Ur, put in order the fields (and) the accounts/management in the temple households of Enlil and Ninlil" (A. Goetze, "The Chronology of Šulgi Again," *Iraq* 22 [1960] pl. 18 5N-T490:12–20; see ibid., p. 153).

7. See below.
8. Sollberger, *AfO* 17, p. 18 and n. 34.
9. See most recently R. M. Whiting, *ZA* 69 (1979) 27–31.
10. Šulgi's authorship of the code is virtually assured by data provided by the Sippar fragment (see n. 1 above). For the arguments in favor of this interpretation, see J. van Dijk, *apud* F. Yildiz, *Or.* n.s. 50, pp. 93–94 n. 20a; Kramer, *Or.* n.s. 52, pp. 453–56. Assuming with Yildiz, pp. 93–95, that lines 125–95 of the prologue are to be translated in the first person singular (for a different opinion, see Kramer, *Or.* n.s. 52, pp. 455–56), the reorganization of the system of weights and measures (lines 136–50 in the Sippar fragment) would have to be ascribed to the author of the code. This, conversely, would yield yet another argument in support of the Šulgi attribution, because the only Ur III king for whom such a reform can be documented so far is Šulgi.

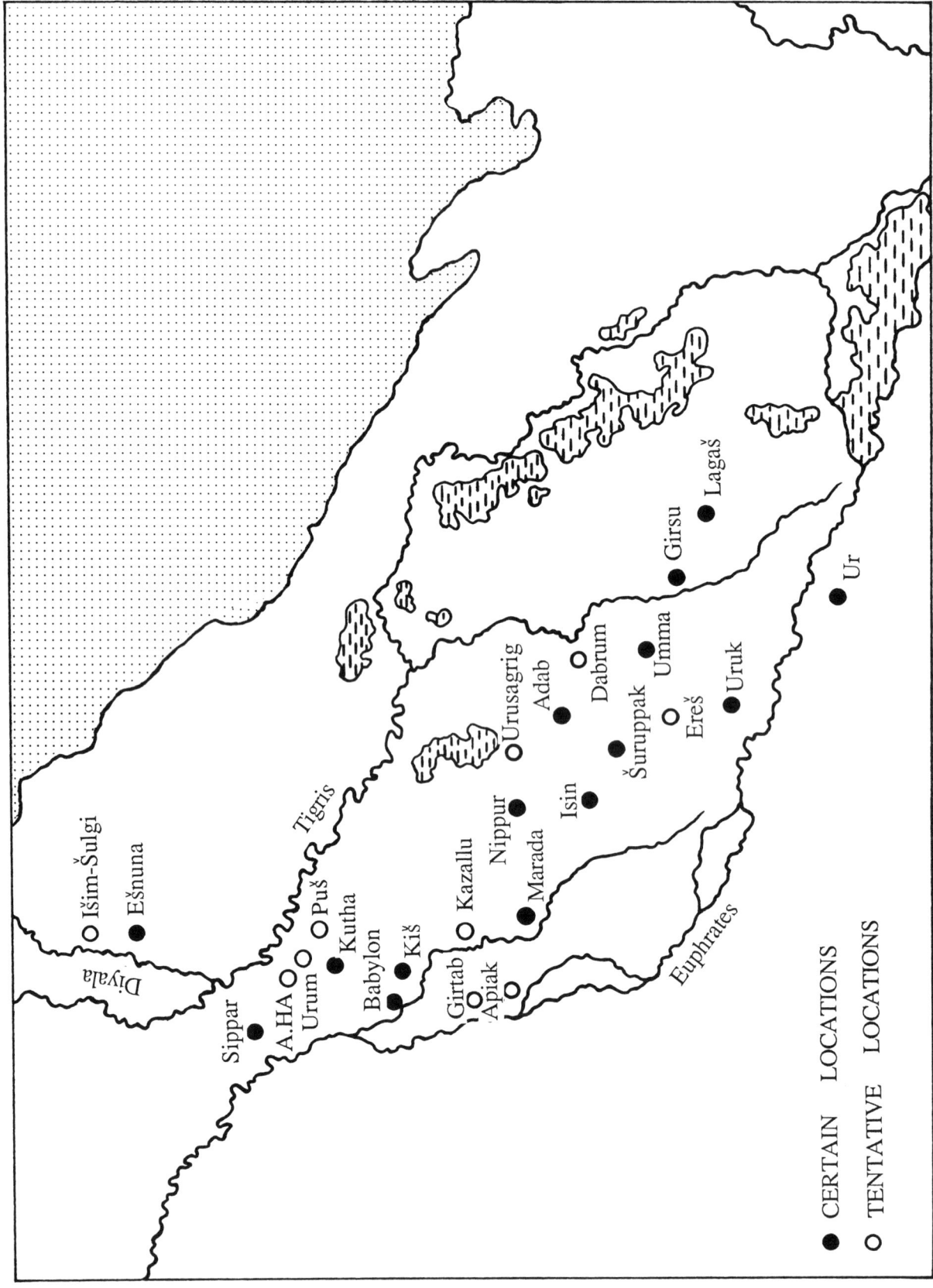

Figure 1. Core Area of the Ur III State

Ur III experiment such a complete failure, one can gain important insights into what the dominant and enduring traits of Mesopotamian history were.

The task of presenting a concise description of the administrative and economic organization of the Ur III state is not an easy one. As long as the many thousands of Ur III economic and legal documents are not adequately analyzed, such an attempt can only be provisional and highly speculative. The sketch offered below does not differ in that respect; I cannot emphasize too strongly its provisional character and must at the same time apologize for the limited use of documentation in asserting certain points. However, the format of this study has made it impossible to include all the supporting evidence; this will be done in a much larger work now in preparation.[11]

In trying to offer a description of the Ur III administrative and economic system, the first necessary step is to draw a distinction between the core and the periphery of the Ur III state, since important differences existed in the way each of these two areas was organized and managed. In view of these differences, each area needs to be considered separately.

The core, which comprised the lands of southern and northern Babylonia and the lower section of the Diyala region (with Ešnuna as its focal point) was subdivided into over twenty provinces. In terms of their number and territorial extent, these provinces corresponded very closely to the former city-states.

So far as the extant information permits us to ascertain, the core included the following provinces: Adab, A.HA, Apiak, Babylon, Dabrum, Ereš, Ešnuna, Girsu/Lagaš, Isin, Išim-Šulgi, Kazallu, Kiš, Kutha, Mar(a)da, Nippur, Puš, Sippar, Šuruppak, Umma, Ur, Uruk, Urum, and Uru-sagrig.[12] See figure 1 for a map of the core area, showing the locations of the provincial capitals. Except for a few possible additions,[13] this list appears to be virtually exhaustive.

Besides the main city—formerly the capital of the city-state, now the seat of the provincial government—each province also included the surrounding hinterland with its towns, villages, and hamlets. Thus, for example, the province of Umma encompassed the city of Umma (modern Tell Jogha) as its administrative center, as well as close to fifty towns and smaller settlements. Of these the most important were Amrima, Apišal, Asarum-dagi, Dintir, Garšana, Garkuruda, Girgiš, Id-dula, Kamari, K/Hardahi, Karkar, Maškan, Nagsu, Šarbat, and Zabalam.[14]

The provinces themselves were administered by governors (Sumerian énsi), who were royal appointees and could in theory be removed from office or transferred to other posts at the king's pleasure. In practice, however, the office of the governor tended to be hereditary, especially in the latter part of the period.[15]

11. "Economic Exchange within Greater Mesopotamia during the Ur III Period" (provisional title).
12. The administrative status of Ešnuna and Išim-Šulgi, both of which were situated in the Diyala region, remains somewhat uncertain. This is due to the fact that, on the one hand, Ešnuna and Išim-Šulgi seem to have been part of the bala-system, characteristic of the core area (see below pp. 22–24); but, on the other hand, they are known to have paid the gún ma-da tax, which was restricted to the periphery of the Ur III state (see below pp. 24–28). At the moment I have no explanation for this discrepancy.
13. One might consider here IŠ.SU (see YOS 4 66:4: énsi IŠ.SU$^{ki}$, mentioned together with the governors of Adab, Kazallu(?!), Mar(a)da, Babylon, and A.HA), Kuwara (see Sauren, NY Public Library 287:5 = Oppenheim, Eames W 13: bala énsi Ku$_6$-a$^{ki}$—unless HA.A$^{ki}$ stands here for the northern Babylonian A.HA$^{ki}$), and Maškan-puša (see Ist. Mus. L30232, cited by D. I. Owen, JCS 33 [1981] 259: énsi Maš-gán-pu-[ša$^{ki}$]).
14. See my forthcoming article "Population Density and Settlement Patterns in Southern Babylonia under the Ur III Dynasty: The Case of the Province of Umma."
15. The hereditary nature of the governorship can be demonstrated for Nippur (R. L. Zettler, AfO 31 [1984] 1–9), Babylon (cf. Ab-ba dub-sar dumu I-dur-DINGIR énsi KÁ.DIN[GIR(.RA)$^{ki}$] attested in BIN 2, p. 48 seal, and Ab-ba énsi KÁ.DINGIR$^{ki}$, found in Sauren, NY Public Library 215:5–6 = Oppenheim, Eames L 6), Mar(a)da (see the references to Lišānum, governor of Mar(a)da, son of Šu-ilī, governor of Mar(a)da, in Rép. géogr. 2, p. 117), and Šuruppak (see Da-da énsi Šuruppak$^{ki}$ Ha-la-ad-da énsi Šuruppak$^{ki}$ dumu-ni in

There are strong indications that the Ur III governors stemmed by and large from the local population, probably from the descendants of those aristocracies that ruled the individual city-states prior to the unification of Babylonia by the House of Ur. Assuming that this situation was the result of a conscious policy, the practice of recruiting governors from local families, rather than from the circle of the king's relatives and followers, can be interpreted as a calculated attempt to placate the local elites and to win their support for the concept of a unified Babylonia.

This policy, though, proved to be a double-edged sword, for it inadvertently contributed to the fostering of individualistic ambitions within the provinces. Throughout the whole of the Ur III period, the office of the governor remained the focus of such sentiments, and, however circumscribed its powers, it always posed a potential threat to the central government. Naturally, this threat became especially real if the governor's office was kept within a family. We have reason to believe that the Ur III kings were well aware of this danger and that they took various measures to prevent the governorships from becoming hereditary. To some extent these efforts may have been successful during the reigns of Šulgi and Amar-Sin, when the power of the central government was at its peak. But as conditions began to deteriorate with the accession of Šu-Sin, the preservation of the state became progressively dependent upon the continued support of local elites. In this way the king's capacity to control the selection process was greatly diminished, and the hereditary character of the governor's office seems to have become the rule.

Apart from the governor, each province had a district military commander, or general (Sumerian šagina), who, like the governor, resided in the province's capital.[16] In some provinces there was more than one general. For example, the province of Umma had, in addition to the general of Umma, generals at Maškan, Nagsu, and Zabalam, and possibly also at Garšana.[17]

As far as one can tell, the generals enjoyed full independence from the governors and remained under the direct orders of the chancellor (Sumerian sukal-mah) and of the king himself. Although the lines of authority between the governor and the general are not entirely clear, it is reasonably certain that the former controlled all the temple households and their employees, both in the capital and in the provincial towns and villages,[18] while the latter was in charge of military personnel and other types of royal dependents settled in the province on crown land.[19]

---

*SAKI*, p. 150, iii lines 1–7). The same was argued by P. A. Parr, "Ninhilia: Wife of Ayakala, Governor of Umma," *JCS* 26 (1974) 90–91, for Umma, but the evidence, though suggestive, is inconclusive. One of the provinces where the governorship definitely was not hereditary was Kazallu. See P. Michalowski, "The Royal Correspondence of Ur" (Ph.D. diss., Yale University, 1976), pp. 43–44.

16. In the case of the general of Umma, we find a specific reference to his Umma house, which was located near the "Gate of Šara" and measured seven sar (= ca. 245 m$^2$) in size (*YOS* 4 300:21).

17. See A-bu-ni šagina (*YOS* 4 208:48; *MVN* 4 263:3; *BIN* 3 374:2; Genouillac, *Trouvaille* 83:13; Oriental Institute, unaccessioned tablet, iii 6) (the general of Umma from the contexts), Hu-un-$^د$Šul-gi šagina Umma$^{ki}$ (*AUCT* 3 325, seal, ll. 1-2); Pù-pù šagina Umma$^{ki}$ (*RT* 19 [1897] 62–63; *RA* 12 [1915] 155 no. 13:9), Ur-šag$_5$-ga šagina Umma$^{ki}$ (Buchanan, *Early Seals*, p. 215 no. 562 i 1-3), Puzur$_4$-$^د$[X] šagina Maš-gán$^{ki}$ (M. Sigrist, *Tablettes du Princeton Theological Seminary époque d'Ur III* [Philadelphia, 1990], No. 394:6), Lú-$^د$Nanna šagina Nag-su$^{ki}$ (*TCL* 2 5488:7; *TIM* 6 36:5), and Da-da šag[ina] Zabalam$^{ki}$ (Sigrist, *NSAT* 26:2). Whether there was a separate general in Garšana depends on whether Garšana is the same place as Ušar-Garšana which is known to have had a general (see *SAKI*, pp. 148–50 22:15–16).

18. That the provincial temple households were administratively subordinate to the governor can best be demonstrated by the examples of Girsu/Lagaš and Umma. See, for example, the Umma texts *BIN* 5 277, Forde, *Nebraska* 37, and *Nikolski* 2 236, which prove that the Umma administration controlled temple households in such towns and villages as Aʾebara, Amrima, Dintir, Dukarsag, Garšida, Garšana, Id-sala, Kamari, K/Hardahi, KI.AN, Maškan, Šunamugi, and Ašarum-dagi.

19. A good illustration of the conflicts that resulted from such a division of authority is offered by the legal text *YOS* 4 208 (= Falkenstein, *Gerichtsurkunden* 2 212), which concerns a dispute between the civil administration of Umma and the military over the status of several individuals. The people in question had been claimed by the subordinates of the general Abuni on account of their alleged "soldier" status (nam-

In this arrangement the office of the general was clearly intended to counterbalance the position of the governor and to serve as an important check on his powers. Institutional arrangements of this type were not uncommon in the ancient Near East. The organization of the Persian satrapies, where the secretary of the satrap, his chief financial official, and the general of the satrapal capital all operated independently of the satrap and reported directly to the king, is perhaps the best-known example.[20]

In contrast to the governors, who appear to have come from local families, the generals were *homines novi* par excellence (as seems to have been true of the officers in general). Indeed the overwhelming majority of Ur III generals bore Akkadian names. Yet even more striking is the preponderance of foreign names (Elamite, Hurrian, Amorite, etc.) over Sumerian ones. Also, a surprisingly large number of generals were related to the royal family, either by blood or through marriage. All of these are unmistakable characteristics of a new upper class which owed its position to its loyal service to the king. Not unexpectedly, the generals' careers were characterized by a very high degree of mobility, both in the core and in the periphery, as shown by the numerous cases of generals being transferred from one post to another.

Both the governors and the generals were directly subordinate to the chancellor, the highest official of the realm after the king, exercising full authority in matters pertaining to the civil administration, the army, foreign relations, and the conduct of law. It appears that the chancellor was particularly involved in the administration of the peripheral territory, and that he even functioned as a sort of viceroy over that whole region.[21]

Due to the virtual absence of documentation from sites other than the provincial capitals,[22] the administration of smaller settlements is not known well. What is known is that towns and villages were run by officials called *hazānum*, "mayor." For the province of Umma, for example, there are references to the mayors of (Du-)Gišabba, Garšana, Maškan, and Nagsu.[23] The evidence indicates that the mayor exercised the highest legal authority in a given place.[24] Whether the mayors operated as subordinates of the generals or of the governors remains unclear; in legal matters, at least, they were subject to the governor's jurisdiction.[25]

---

érin), but the subsequent legal proceedings established that they actually were slaves. They were accordingly transferred by Abuni to the governor of Umma.

20. A. T. Olmstead, *History of the Persian Empire* (Chicago, 1948) 59.
21. This last aspect of the chancellor's office is borne out by the manifold titles of the chancellor Arad-Nanna (see *SAKI*, pp. 148–50 22 reign of Šu-Sin), among which one finds the generalships of Pašime, Urbilum, Nihi, (the land of) lú-SU, and the land of Karda, and the governorships of Sabum, the land of Gutibum, Āl-Šu-Sin, Hamazi, and Karhar. The geographical distribution of these places shows that, at least during the reign of Šu-Sin, the chancellor exercised control over most of the peripheral area—from Urbilum in the northwest to Pašime in the southeast. For a discussion of the territorial extent of the periphery of the Ur III state, see below and n. 57. At the same time, however, it cannot be excluded that these broad powers were given to the chancellor only in the reign of Šu-Sin as one of the remedies intended to check the collapse of Ur's rule over the peripheral zone.
22. Excluding here, of course, Puzriš-Dagan, which, due to its special character (see below), cannot be considered a subordinate settlement. The only sizable assemblages of Ur III economic tablets that seem to have originated in places other than the provincial capitals are the SI.A-a archive, possibly coming from Maškan-puša (see Steinkeller, "On Editing Ur III Economic Texts," *JAOS* 102 [1982] 643), and the Tell al-Wilayah texts, published by J. N. Postgate, *Sumer* 32 (1976) 77–100. Note, however, that the case of the SI.A-a archive is complicated by the fact that Maškan-puša may have had an énsi (see n. 13 above).
23. For (Du-)Gišabba, see Falkenstein, *Gerichtsurkunden* 2 120b:17; for Garšana, see Forde, *Nebraska* 1:14; for Maškan, see n. 25 below; for Nagsu, see Falkenstein, *Gerichtsurkunden* 2 120a:10, 120b:14, 21.
24. See the legal texts *TIM* 3 145:14–15 and *TIM* 5 12:6, belonging to the SI.A-a archive, both of which are witnessed by a mayor and sealed with his seal.
25. The text Sigrist, *Tablettes du Princeton Theological Seminary époque d'Ur III* (Philadelphia, 1990), No. 394, in which a mayor of Maškan, acting on behalf of the general of Maškan, borrows barley from the

The dual character of the Ur III administrative organization which we have stressed repeatedly, with the governor and the general occupying two independent and to a large degree antagonistic positions, is indicative on a broader scale of the basic configuration of political forces that existed in the core area of the Ur III state. The sphere controlled by the governor, essentially the old city-state cumbersomely tailored to fit the framework of a centralized empire, represented a force that was inherently hostile to the central government and to the king of Ur. In contrast, the general's domain, namely the dependents of the king living on crown land, was by its very definition pro-central-government and pro-king. To put it in even simpler terms, one could say that in the core the lines of political conflict were drawn between the cities and the countryside, between the opponents of the king and the king's power-base, respectively.

In terms of its economic organization, the core comprised the following three basic sectors:

1. Temple domain: landed and other property held nominally by the temple households and managed by the provincial administration (ensi).
2. Royal domain: land distributed among the dependents of the king (primarily military personnel) in exchange for services and certain taxes (Šagina); industrial complexes run directly by the central government (e.g., the weaving establishments at Ur, the workshops at Puzriš-Dagan); royal flocks and herds.
3. Private sector: land held in private possession; merchants; independent craftsmen, shepherds, fishermen, etc.

Of these, the least known is the private sector. While there is sufficient evidence to demonstrate that land could be held in private possession in Ur III times,[26] it is clear that this type of holding did not play a significant role in the economy. The same seems to be true of the private sector as a whole.

All three of these sectors contributed to the central government, though in a different form and to a different degree. From a quantitative point of view, the most important were the contributions of the temple domain, consisting primarily of agricultural and industrial products. The contributions of the royal domain were of two kinds; (1) services and certain taxes; (2) goods produced by the royal industrial complexes and other state-run operations. Practically nothing is known of the contributions made by the private sector.

In view of the dominant position of the temple domain in this picture, we shall concentrate on it in this paper. As already mentioned, in the Ur III period temple households and their possessions became the de facto property of the state, with their surplus revenues being delivered to the central government. This unprecedented concentration of economic resources, distributed over a wide and ecologically diversified geographical area, made it possible for the Ur III kings to institute a purposeful policy of regional specialization, with each major region concentrating on the production of different staples and goods.

Such a highly centralized and regionally diversified economy necessitated very efficient redistributive mechanisms, which could ensure the movement of products throughout the country. In the core, this need was met by the so-called bala institution. W. W. Hallo, the first scholar to study the bala, interpreted it as a pan-Babylonian organization, whose function was to supply the major temples of

---

governor of Umma intended for 840 "soldiers" (érin) of Maškan, seems to indicate that the mayors were administratively subordinate to the generals. For the mayor's being subject to the governor's jurisdiction, see the Umma legal texts Falkenstein, *Gerichtsurkunden* 2 120a and 120b, recording the cases which involved the mayors of (Du-)Gišabba and Nagsu.

26. I. J. Gelb, "On the Alleged Temple and State Economies in Ancient Mesopotamia," *Studi in onore di Edoardo Volterra*, vol. 6 (Florence, 1969) 146–52.

Nippur, the religious capital of Babylonia.[27] As such, he identified the bala as a form of amphictyony, comparable to that of Delphi in Greece. However, a re-examination of this problem, made possible in part by evidence that has become available since the publication of Hallo's article, reveals that the bala institution functioned as a central redistribution system, integrating all the provinces into one interdependent whole. Though Hallo's conclusion that the bala contributions were used to supply the temples of Nippur is a valid one, it is clear that this obligation was only one aspect of the total picture.

The key elements of the bala system were the centrally situated redistribution centers, created especially for this purpose by the Ur III kings. The one we know most about among these centers is Puzriš-Dagan (modern Drehem) near Nippur, which served as a collection place for livestock and animal products. Another such center was probably Dusabara, also located in the vicinity of Nippur, which appears to have specialized in agricultural products.[28]

Insofar as our present knowledge of the bala institution allows us to ascertain, the basic principles of its organization and operation were as follows:

1. The amount of goods and services supplied by a given province depended on its size and economic capabilities. Basically, the bala contributions consisted of those goods in whose production a particular province specialized. For example, it can be demonstrated that the province of Girsu/Lagaš paid its bala primarily in cereals,[29] whereas the contributions of Umma consisted, apart from cereals, of reeds, timber, and related products.[30]

2. The value of the contributions made by a province constituted its bala fund. Once the province met its obligations, it could then use this fund to obtain other goods or services as needed.

3. The bala contributions were delivered either to redistribution centers or directly to the interested parties, especially if neighboring provinces were involved.[31] If the contributions were sent to redistribution centers, their destination depended on the nature of the goods delivered. A substantial portion of the bala contributions was withdrawn by the central administration within the provinces themselves, mostly in the form of provisions for various types of royal dependents.[32]

Contrary to the conclusion of Hallo, who believed that "with some exceptions, the bala consisted of livestock,"[33] it can be shown that livestock did not play a significant role among the bala contributions. The picture that emerges from the Puzriš-Dagan texts is quite consistent and unequivocal: there are no records of livestock being delivered as the bala of individual Babylonian provinces to Puzriš-Dagan; on the contrary, it was the Babylonian governors or their representatives who *withdrew* livestock from

---

27. *JCS* 14 (1960) 88–114 (especially pp. 93, 96).
28. Whiting, *ZA* 69, 16 n. 19. In *JAOS* 102, pp. 640–42, I discussed a group of tablets associated with a person named Guzana (to be added to the list given there is *JCS* 19 [1965] 28), which seems to have originated in a redistribution center processing cereals, wool, and sesame. Though the origin of these texts could very well be Dusabara, it is equally possible that they derive from still another redistribution center.
29. According to the Lagaš text *CT* 7 pl. 8, which is a record of the total revenue and expenditure of barley in the province of Girsu/Lagaš for the year Amar-Sin 2, in that year the province expended as its bala almost exactly half of the barley produced. See K. Maekawa, "Agricultural Production in Ancient Sumer," *Zinbun* 13 (1974) 51–53 n. 24; T. B. Jones, *Sumerological Studies Jacobsen*, pp. 58–59.
30. For barley, see, for example, *Nikolski* 2 264:1–2; Contenau, *Contribution* 5:1–4; *MVN* 4 36:1–7, 55:1–2; for reeds, see, for example, *Nikolski* 2 193:1–6; *BIN* 5 84:1–17, 22; Contenau, *Umma* 52:1–3; *SACT* 2 151:1–6; for timber, see, for example, *BIN* 5 84:18–22, 345:1–13.
31. See, for example, *MVN* 1 198 and *YOS* 4 70, recording the expenditures of various staples made by the governor of Umma to the representatives of the governors of Šuruppak and Girsu/Lagaš respectively.
32. See, for example, Fish, *Catalogue* 354, 649; *Nikolski* 2 340; *YOS* 4 114 (= *TCS* 1 1).
33. W. W. Hallo, "A Sumerian Amphictyony," *JCS* 14, p. 91.

Puzriš-Dagan as their bala.[34] While some of the withdrawn animals were used locally to meet the obligation (also called bala) of supplying the temples of Nippur,[35] the rest (probably the majority of them) were transported to the respective provinces.[36] In this light, the bala of Puzriš-Dagan must be seen as a livestock fund, to which each Babylonian province was entitled in exchange for its own specific bala contributions.

As a matter of fact, the livestock originating in the core area does not seem to figure importantly among the Puzriš-Dagan deliveries. The only group of people who made significant and regular deliveries of livestock to Puzriš-Dagan were the herdsmen of royal herds and flocks. But even in this case, the quantities of livestock withdrawn by these individuals vastly exceeded those of the deliveries.[37] The Puzriš-Dagan livestock came by and large from the peripheral area of the Ur III state, to which we shall turn our attention below.

To conclude this part of our discussion, one must emphasize that the above sketch takes into consideration only the contributions of the temple domain, and incompletely at that, since we know that all major categories of people employed by the temple households were themselves required to pay various types of personal taxes.[38] A full treatment of the contributions made by the core would also have to include the manifold imposts, taxes, and services paid by the royal domain and the private sector, of which unfortunately considerably less is known.

Leaving the core area behind, we now pass to the periphery of the Ur III state. Although it is known that the Ur III kings (especially Šulgi) campaigned extensively in the region to the north and northeast of

34. See especially the following examples: 360 sheep were transported to Girsu by Intaea, the scribe of the "man" of Girsu, and received by Aradmu, the governor of Girsu/Lagaš (Legrain, *TRU* 81); 963 sheep were transported by the fattener Kamu (a well-known official from Girsu/Lagaš), and received by Aradmu, the governor of Girsu/Lagaš (*MVN* 11 195); 17 oxen and 414 sheep were transported by Lu-šaga, and received by Aradmu, the governor of Girsu/Lagaš (*PDT* 205); 100 oxen and 978 sheep were received by the above-mentioned Kamu on behalf of Ur-Lama, the governor of Girsu/Lagaš (*PDT* 425); 149 oxen and 1,336 sheep were received by Ur-Lama, the governor of Girsu/Lagaš (A. 663-1982, unpublished, courtesy of W. Horowitz); 10 oxen and 530 sheep were transported by Abba-šaga, and received by Ur-Lama, the governor of Girsu/Lagaš (*BIN* 3 373); 710 sheep were received by Ur-Ninkara, the governor of Šuruppak (AUAM 73.3010, unpublished, courtesy of M. Sigrist); 20 oxen and 100 sheep were received by Ititi, the governor of Kazallu (*PDT* 516); 79 oxen and 1,408+[x] sheep were received by Is(su)-ariq, the governor of Kazallu (*YOS* 4 75); 42 oxen were received by Arši-ah, the governor of Babylon (*MVN* 8 31); 51 oxen were received by Gudea, the governor of Kutha (AUAM 73.3184, unpublished, courtesy of M. Sigrist).

35. See for example, Genouillac, *Trouvaille* 79; Jones-Snyder, *SET* 57, 58; *PDT* 342; *BIN* 3 586; *MVN* 8 139.

36. K. Maekawa, "The Management of Fatted Sheep (udu-niga) in Ur III Girsu/Lagash," *ASJ* 5 (1983) 93–96, has recently claimed that Girsu/Lagaš delivered to Puzriš-Dagan large quantities of livestock as its bala. The extant sources, however, show that the movement of livestock took just the opposite course: from Puzriš-Dagan to Girsu/Lagaš This point is made particularly clear by the following pieces of evidence: 1) Legrain, *TRU* 81 (cited n. 34 above), which specifically states that the animals in question were transported "to Girsu" (Gír-su$^{ki}$-šè, line 5); 2) the Lagaš text Barton, *Haverford* 2 pl. 75 no. 57, recording the delivery of 51 oxen and 1,136 sheep "[from] Nippur" (Nibru$^{ki}$-[ta], iv 4; for the reconstruction, see ii 2, 12); 3) the Puzriš-Dagan text Limet, *TSDU* 65, recording the receipt of 900 sheep by Ur-Lama, the governor of Girsu/Lagaš, and the Lagaš text Reisner, *Telloh* 60:1–4, 12–14, containing the record of the same transaction. For other evidence see n. 34. I wish to stress here that I am not aware of any evidence which would indicate that Girsu/Lagaš made any significant contributions of livestock to Puzriš-Dagan.

37. See the projected deliveries of sheep from (the shepherds of) Maškan-DU.DU, Dēr, Maškan-šapir, Uru-sagrig, and Isin, which were intended for the governor of Sippar, and which amounted to 2,920 animals (*JCS* 14, p. 111 no. 14), as compared with 10,992+[x] sheep that were withdrawn by the shepherds of Maškan-DU.DU, Maškan-šapir, Isin, and Šuruppak (*MVN* 11 210). Several of the shepherds listed in the latter text (Bēlum-ilī, Abba'a, Ur-zikuma, Ur-alla, Abī-ṭāb, Abba, and Ur-lugal) also received large numbers of sheep in *TCL* 2 5498 i–iii.

38. Such as, for example, the gún tax paid by the "major-domos" (šabra) of temple households (see, for example, Contenau, *Contribution* 46:6).

Babylonia, achieving substantial territorial gains there, the scarcity of historical information has made it virtually impossible until now to determine the geographical extent of those territories, not to mention their political and economic status. Fortunately, there survives a group of Ur III economic texts from Puzriš-Dagan, known for some time but never studied systematically, which throws important light on these problems.

The texts I have in mind concern the delivery of a tax, called gún ma-da, "tax of the provinces," which was paid in livestock and delivered to Puzriš-Dagan. As far as I know, the existence of this tax was first noted by Hallo, who, in 1960, suggested that it represented a "territorial tribute," for which a given geographical area was collectively responsible.[39] In 1973, the gún ma-da was briefly discussed by I. J. Gelb, who saw it as a tax paid by the military settlers living outside of the core area of the Ur III state.[40] Five years later, some twenty gún ma-da texts were collected and studied by P. Michalowski.[41] Michalowski interpreted the gún ma-da as a tribute or impost paid by the unincorporated territories of the Ur III state. In his view, these territories represented the buffer zone of the empire, which served as the "defense line as well as the staging area for military expeditions against the enemy."[42]

About the time Michalowski's article was published, I became interested in the question of the gún ma-da myself. As a result of my work on this problem, I was able, first of all, to identify numerous other Puzriš-Dagan texts, both published and unpublished, which deal with the delivery of this tax; the total number of such documents presently known to me exceeds one hundred. The reason many of these texts were not recognized earlier as pertaining to the gún ma-da is that the term gún ma-da began to be used only in the third year of Šu-Sin's reign; in earlier texts, the deliveries of this tax usually appear without any special designation or, in some isolated instances, are identified simply as gún, "tax."

Secondly, and more importantly, I discovered that the entries recording the gún ma-da follow a standard sequence. In its most complete form this sequence begins with the delivery of ten oxen and one hundred sheep,[43] almost without exception by a general (šagina).[44] Listed next are the individuals bearing the title nu-banda, "captain," paying either two oxen and twenty sheep or one ox and ten sheep each. The unnamed ugula-géš-das, "officers in charge of sixty men," follow, paying the tax jointly, in the amount of one-twentieth of an ox and one-half of a sheep per ugula-géš-da. The sequence concludes, then, with a group of unnamed people identified as érin GN, "soldiers of GN," delivering collectively varying numbers of livestock, but also usually at the ratio of one ox to ten sheep.[45] See figures 2, 3, and 4 for examples of such sequences.

This evidence demonstrates quite clearly that the payers of the gún ma-da were military personnel, with the amount of livestock delivered dependent on the payer's military rank. Further, it is apparent that the given sequence of payers of the gún ma-da consists of the members of one military settlement, from its top commander down to the common soldiers. Along with the fact that the places mentioned in this connection are always foreign (i.e., non-Babylonian) localities, this shows, in agreement with Gelb's

---

39. *JCS* 14, pp. 88–89.
40. I. J. Gelb, "Prisoners of War in Early Mesopotamia," *JNES* 32 (1973) 85.
41. P. Michalowski, "Foreign Tribute to Sumer during the Ur III Period," *ZA* 68 (1978) 34–49.
42. Ibid., p. 46.
43. "Oxen" and "sheep" are used here (in agreement with the Sumerian practice) as the inclusive categories for large cattle (oxen and cows) and small cattle (sheep, goats, and gazelles) respectively.
44. Occasionally, the person appearing in this position can be identified as a governor (énsi). In either case, however, one finds here the chief administrator of a peripheral province, who exercised both civilian and military powers. The term that would best describe such an official is "general-governor."
45. Apart from these categories, in some rare instances the taxpayers also include such people as àga-uš, "gendarme," *hazānum*, "mayor," sipad, "shepherd," and ab-ba(-uru), "city elder."

earlier interpretation, that the gún ma-da represented a tax paid by the military personnel living in the periphery of the Ur III state.

Although the numbers of soldiers (érin) paying the gún ma-da are never specifically stated, the cases in which the numbers of the ugula-géš-das, "officers in charge of sixty men," are recorded (as in the text tabulated in fig. 2), make it possible to calculate the respective numbers of soldiers and consequently the tax paid by one soldier. By using this tax rate, one can in turn estimate the soldier populations of other settlements.

Since the prices of livestock were standard in Ur III times (ten shekels of silver for an ox and one shekel of silver for a sheep), it is possible to calculate silver equivalents of the gún ma-da. See figure 5 for the reconstructed sequence of taxpayer categories, with the corresponding tax rates.

Incidentally, the soldier's tax of twelve grains of silver corresponds almost exactly to that paid by the same category of people in the core area of the Ur III state. This, according to the Umma text *TCL* 5 6166, was either four or twelve grains of silver.[46]

After listing the taxpayers, the gún ma-da texts name the official responsible for collecting the tax and delivering it to Puzriš-Dagan.[47] The person who acted in this capacity was either the top commander of a given settlement (and thus the top taxpayer from that place) or, in the case of smaller settlements, the commander under whose jurisdiction that settlement fell.[48]

The available evidence demonstrates that the gún ma-da was paid yearly, and that it was usually delivered during the period from the middle of September to the middle of December.[49] In some instances the deliveries of livestock were made in two or more installments during the same tax year; there are even documented cases of taxpayers who, having failed to pay the tax in full one year, delivered the balance, together with a new tax, during the following year.[50]

A comparison of the gún ma-da texts shows that a given settlement generally paid the same tax through the years.[51] Further, there is unmistakable evidence that the administration of Puzriš-Dagan knew exactly how many animals were due from particular settlements each year,[52] demonstrating that the amounts of the tax must have been assessed beforehand.

46. See my article cited in n. 14 for a detailed discussion of this text.
47. He is described as ugula PN, "under the supervision of PN."
48. That the person designated as the official responsible for the collection and delivery of the tax paid by a given place was identical with that place's chief administrator is, in many instances, corroborated by outside evidence. For example, the chancellor Arad-Nanna (also known as Aradmu), who was in charge of the tax from Nihi (Jean, *ŠA* 36 1e lines 1–3; Šulgi 48), Pašime (see n. 57 below), Urbilum (Contenau, *Contribution* 6 i 1– iv 2; Šu-Sin 7), and Šabum (A. 5170:1–5, unpublished; Ibbi-Sin 1), is otherwise known to have held the generalships of Nihi, Pašime, and Urbilum, and the governorship of Šabum (see n. 21 above). In the same way, the general Enni-ili, who was responsible for the tax of BÀD.AN-kizi and was the top taxpayer there (unpublished tablet in private collection, lines 11–19), is documented in another source as a general of BÀD.AN-kizi (Owen, *NATN* 612 seal: Na-bí-$^{d}$En-líl / dumu En-ni-lí /šagina BÀD.AN-[ki-zi$^{ki}$]; cf. also *MVN* 3 294 seal: Na-bí-$^{d}$En-líl / dumu En-ni-lí / šagina).
49. This particular timing of the deliveries was probably due to climatic considerations, as the fall months would have offered the most favorable conditions for the transfer and foraging of livestock.
50. See, for example, *CT* 32 pls. 19–22, recording the remainder of the tax for the year Ibbi-Sin 1, due from the captains of Abibana, Kakkulatum, Išim-Šulgi, Tutub, and Kiškati (i 1–21), together with the tax paid by the same individuals in Ibbi-Sin 2 (ii 13–15, iii 27– iv 1, iv 6–8, v 16–22, v 32– vi 1).
51. Thus, for example, the soldiers of Gar-NE-NE delivered 4 oxen and 300 sheep both in Šulgi 48 and in Amar-Sin 5 (see fig. 4), while the soldiers of Puhzigar, whose tax is attested for the years Šulgi 47, Amar-Sin 2, and Ibbi-Sin 2, each time paid 1 ox and 10 sheep (see fig. 3; note that in Amar-Sin 2 the tax of Puhzigar was combined with that of Kakkulatum).
52. This is shown by the texts which record the failure of some places to deliver their tax during a particular year, with the figures indicated matching the numbers of livestock usually paid by these places. See, for example,

| Tax ||  Taxpayer | Place | Supervisor (ugula) |
|---|---|---|---|---|
| Oxen | Sheep | | | |
| 10 | 100 | Zé-lu-uš-ᵈDa-gan | I-šim-ᵈŠul-giki | Zé-lu-uš-ᵈDa-gan |
| 1 | 10 | Ì-lí-TAB.BA | | |
| 2 | [20] | [ ... ]-a | | |
| 1 | 10 | Puzur₄-A-bi-iḫ | | |
| 1 | 10 | ᵈŠul-gi-ì-lí | | |
| 1 | 10 | Ì-lí-zi-lí | | |
| 1 | 10 | Nu-úr-ᵈAdad | | |
| 1 | 10 | A-gu-a-lí | | |
| 1 | 10 | Za-rí-iq | | |
| 1 | 10 | Za-a-lum | | |
| 1 | 10 | Ì-lí-TAB.BA | | |
| 2 | 20 | IGI-ḫa-lum nu-banda-me-éš | | |
| 17 | 170 | érin I-šim-ᵈŠul-giki | | |
| 2 | 20 | Lú-ᵈNanna Z[i-mu-darki] | Ša-miki | Lú-ᵈNanna Zi-mu-darki |
| 1 | 10 | DI.TAR-ì-lí | | |
| 1 | 10 | Puzur₄-Ḫa-ìa | | |
| 1 | 10 | I-ku-mi-šar nu-banda-me-éš | | |
| 1 | 10 | ugula-géš-da-bi 20-me-éš | | |
| 4 | 40 | érin Ša-miki | | |
| 2 | 20 | Lú-ᵈNin-šubur nu-banda | Tum-ba-alki | |
| 3 | 30 | érin Tum-ba-alki | | |

Figure 2. Tax Paid by Išim-Šulgi, Šami, and Tumbal in the Year Ibbi-Sin 2 (*CT* 32 pls. 19–22)

Although the earliest attestations of the gún ma-da come from the forty-third year of Šulgi,[53] the actual date of its introduction should probably be placed somewhat earlier, around the year Šulgi 39, when the complex of Puzriš-Dagan was built. The very reason for creating Puzriš-Dagan obviously was to process this and related types of livestock imposts.

The dated records of the gún ma-da deliveries cover a period from Šulgi 43 to Ibbi-Sin 2.[54] Their breakdown according to the particular reigns is as follows: Šulgi: 35 texts; Amar-Sin: 35 texts; Šu-Sin: 19 texts; Ibbi-Sin: 3 texts. As shown by this distribution, during the reigns of Šulgi and Amar-Sin the deliveries of the gún ma-da remained at the same level; they decreased markedly under Šu-Sin, ceasing completely in the first years of Ibbi-Sin.[55]

---

Langdon, *TAD* 66, stating that (the soldiers of) Zatum did not deliver their tax of 10 oxen in Šu-Sin 9, as compared with *JCS* 31 (1979) 166–67 line 16 (Amar-Sin 8), where the tax paid by the soldiers of Zatum is likewise 10 oxen. Another such text is Langdon, *TAD* 54 (undated), recording 1 ox and 18 sheep that were not delivered as the tax of (the soldiers of) Tiran. This figure corresponds exactly to the tax paid by the soldiers of Tiran in Amar-Sin 7 (*BIN* 3 139:10).

53. *MVN* 11 212; A. 2870 (unpublished).
54. The earliest dated text is A. 2870 (Šulgi 43/vii/2); the latest is *CT* 32 pls. 19–22 (Ibbi-Sin 2/iv/29).
55. Highly informative of the political situation that existed in the periphery around the end of Šu-Sin's reign are the texts Langdon, *TAD* 66 and Genouillac, *Trouvaille* 50, both dated to Šu-Sin 9, which record the non-payment of the tax by Zatum and Arman respectively. An identical record, concerning the tax of Tiran, is

The above picture accords well with what is known about the history of the periphery based on other sources: its relative stability during the reigns of Šulgi and Amar-Sin, the growing unrest in the time of Šu-Sin, and, finally, the total collapse of Babylonian rule over the whole region at the beginning of Ibbi-Sin's reign.

At this time we can identify ninety settlements that paid the gún ma-da.[56] Since the locations (either certain or approximate) of many of them are known, it is possible to draw a general map of the gún ma-da territory (see fig. 6). This territory formed a large belt extending southeastward from the left bank of the Tigris and running parallel to the Zagros range. In the northwest its farthest extensions appear to have been Assur and Urbilum (modern Erbil), while in the southeast it reached as far as Sabum, Susa, and Adamdun.[57]

Given the fact that the gún ma-da clearly represented a personal income tax, with the amount dependent on the taxpayer's military rank and correspondingly, we may assume, on the size of his land allotment,[58] there can be little doubt that the gún ma-da territory had actually been incorporated into the Ur III state.

In this light, the payment or non-payment of this tax provides us with a useful criterion for determining a given locality's political status. The examples of such places as Anšan, Huhnuri, Marhaši, Šimaški, and Zabšali in the east, Nineveh and Simanum in the north, and Abarnium, Ebla, Madaman, Mari, Mukiš, Tutul, and Urkiš in the west, which both did not pay the gún ma-da and are positively known to have never become part of the Ur III state, confirm the validity of this observation.

A look at the map of the gún ma-da territory, when coupled with the knowledge of its highly militarized character, shows that this region served as a strategic buffer zone protecting the northeastern flank of Babylonia, in many respects comparable to the Roman *limes*.

To the north and east of the gún ma-da territory, there extended in another belt the vassal states of Ur, such as Anšan, Nineveh, Pašime, Šimanum, and Šimaški. The degree of dependence of these states on Ur varied from place to place and from one reign to another.[59]

Passing now to the question of the administrative organization of the periphery, it can be shown that the gún ma-da territory comprised settlements of three types: (1) large settlements run by the generals

---

Langdon, *TAD* 54. Though the latter document lacks a date, the fact that its formulary matches that of the earlier two texts suggests that it belongs to roughly the same time.

56. They are: Abal, Abibana, Adamdun, Agaz, Arami, Arman/Armana, Arraphum, Assur, Azaman Baʾa-NE, BÀD.AN-kizi, Badariš-⌈x⌉, Balue, Barman, Bidadun, Daltum, Dašinewi, Dēr, Duribla, Durmaš, Ebal, Eduru-Šulgi, Erud, Ešnuna, Gablaš, Gar-NE-NE, Gu-⌈na(?)⌉-rašina, Habura, Hamazi, Harši, Huʾurti, Hubiʾum, Hubni, Iaʾamiš, Innaba, Ilšu-rabi, Išim-Šulgi, Išim-Šu-Sin, Išum, Kakkulatum, Kakmum, Kismar, Likri, Lulubu, Lululu, Māhāzum, Marman, Mašatum, Maškan-garaš, Maškan-kallatum, Maškan-šarrum, Nēbir-Amar-Sin, Nēbirum, NI-darašwi, Nihi, Nugar, PI-il, Puhzigar, Pūt-šadar, Pūt-tuliʾum, Ra-NE, Sabum, Sallanewi, Simurrum, Siʾummi, Susa, Šami, Šanidat, Šetirša, Šuʾahi/Šuʾah, Šuʾirhum, Šumtiʾum/Šunti, Šurbum, Šu-Sin-nihi, Tablala, Tabra, Tašil, Terqa, Tiran, Tumbal, Tutul, Ú-⌈ra(?)⌉-e Urbilum, Urguhalam, Urua, Wanum, Zababa, Zatum, and Zimudar.

57. It appears that, sometime during the reign of either Amar-Sin or Šu-Sin, the southeastern section of this territory was extended farther east to include Pašime on the Persian Gulf. See Steinkeller, "The Question of Marhaši," *ZA* 72 (1982) 241–42. However, no records of the gún ma-da paid by Pašime are known thus far. (For the tax of Pašime, see now *TLB* 3 34, dated to Šu-Sin 6 I [x], which records the delivery of udu Pa-šim-e^ki, "sheep of Pašime," from the "chancellor" [i.e., Arad-Nanna]. For Arad-Nanna as the general of Pašime under Šu-Sin, see n. 21 above.)

58. See below, pp. 30–31 and n. 64.

59. For Anšan, see M. Lambert, "Le Prince de Suse Ilish-Mani, et l'Elam de Naramsin à Ibisîn," *JA* 1979, pp. 29–38; M. W. Stolper, "On the Dynasty of Šimaški and the Early Sukkalmahs," *ZA* 72, p. 50; for Nineveh, see Whiting, "Tišatal of Nineveh and Babati, Uncle of Šu-Sin," *JCS* 28 (1976) 174–78; for Pašime, see Steinkeller, *ZA* 72, pp. 240–43; for šimanum, see Michalowski, "The Bride of Simanum," *JAOS* 95 (1975) 716–19; for Šimaški, see Stolper, *ZA* 71, pp. 43–45.

or, in some instances, by the governors; (2) medium-size settlements, run by the senior captains (i.e., the ones paying two oxen and twenty sheep each); (3) small settlements, run by the junior captains (i.e., the ones paying one ox and ten sheep each). Whereas in settlements of the first two types the person in charge of the tax was the highest military/civilian official of a given place, in the case of settlements of the third type that person was an outsider who can always be identified as one of the officials associated with the higher-ranking settlements.

| Tax Oxen | Tax Sheep | Taxpayer | Place | Supervisor (ugula) | Date | Text |
|---|---|---|---|---|---|---|
| 1 | 10 | érin Bu-úḫ-zi-gàr$^{ki}$ | Bu-úḫ-zi-gàr$^{ki}$ | A-mur-É-a | Šulgi 47 | PDT 15 |
| 5 | 50 | I-ri-bu-um | A-bí-ba-na$^{ki}$ | I-ri-bu-um | Amar-Sin 2 | YBC 3635 (unpubl.) |
| 4 | 40 | érin A-bí-ba-na$^{ki}$ | | | | |
| 4 | 40 | érin Gag-gu-la-tum$^{ki}$* | Gag-gu-la-tum$^{ki}$ | | | |
| 1 | 10 | I-gi₄ nu-banda | (A-bí-ba-na$^{ki}$, | | | |
|   | 6 | Lú-ša-lim nu-banda | Bu-úḫ-zi-gàr$^{ki}$, | | | |
|   | 6 | SUḪUŠ-ki-in nu-banda | and Gag-gu-la-tum$^{ki}$) | | | |
| 2 | 20 | A-ḫu-ni dumu I-ri-bu-um | A-bí-ba-na$^{ki}$ | A-ḫu-ni dumu I-ri-bu-um | Ibbi-Sin 2 | CT 32 pls. 19–22 |
| 1 | 10 | [Nu-úr-Eš₄-dar nu-banda] | | | | |
| 4 | 40 | érin A-bí-[ba-na$^{ki}$] | | | | |
| 1 | 10 | Na-bí-$^d$EN.[ZU nu]-banda | Bu-úḫ-zi-gàr$^{ki}$ | | | |
| 1 | 10 | érin Bu-úḫ-zi-gàr$^{ki}$ | | | | |
| 3 | 30 | érin Gag-gu-la-tum$^{ki}$ | Gag-gu-la-tum$^{ki}$ | | | |

*Include the érin of Bu-úḫ-zi-gàr$^{ki}$

Figure 3. Tax Paid by Abibana, Kakkulatum, and Puhzigar in the Years Šulgi 47, Amar-Sin 2, and Ibbi-Sin 2

From this one may infer that the gún ma-da territory was subdivided into autonomous provinces, which, depending on their size, were administered either by generals (or governors) or senior captains. Each such province included a major settlement which served as the province's administrative center, and a number of smaller, subordinate settlements which remained under the charge of junior captains.

The province which during the years Amar-Sin 2 to Ibbi-Sin 2 was controlled in succession by the general Iribum and his son Ahuni, a senior captain, may serve as an illustration of this administrative principle (see fig. 3). This province comprised at least three separate settlements: Abibana, Kakkulatum, and Puhzigar. Since Iribum (and subsequently Ahuni) was the top taxpayer at Abibana and at the same time supervised the collection of the tax of Abibana, Kakkulatum and Puhzigar, Abibana was that province's capital, with Kakkulatum and Puhzigar sharing a subordinate status. The latter two settlements were run by junior captains and had considerably smaller soldier populations: an estimated 900 soldiers in the case of Kakkulatum, and 300 soldiers in the case of Puhzigar, against a figure of 1,200 men that can be obtained for Abibana.[60]

60. These estimates assume that the tax paid by a single soldier was twelve grains (= 1/15 of a shekel) of silver (see fig. 5). The taxes of the soldiers of Abibana, Kakkulatum, and Puhzigar were 4 oxen and 40 sheep (= 80

Similarly, the province supervised by the general Niridagal (Šulgi 48 to Amar-Sin 5) included the settlements of Gar-NE-NE and Tablala (see fig. 4). While Niridagal is listed as the official in charge of the tax of both Gar-NE-NE and Tablala, he does not figure among the taxpayers from either place; in each case, the top taxpayer was a different junior captain. This demonstrates that Gar-NE-NE and Tablala were subordinate settlements and that the capital of Niridagal's province was situated somewhere else. Unfortunately, the name of that place remains unknown.

| Tax Oxen | Sheep | Taxpayer | Place | Supervisor (ugula) | Date | Text |
|---|---|---|---|---|---|---|
| 4 | 300 | érin Gàr-NE-NE$^{ki}$ | Gàr-NE-NE$^{ki}$ | Nir-ì-da-gál | Šulgi 48 | SACT 1 65 |
| 2 | 120 | érin Tab-la-la$^{ki}$ | Tab-la-la$^{ki}$ | | | |
| 1 | 10 | Šu-$^d$Nin-šubur nu-banda | Gàr-NE-NE$^{ki}$ | Nir-ì-da-gál | Amar-Sin 5 | Jones-Snyder 10 |
| 4 | 300 | érin Gàr-NE-NE$^{ki}$ | | | | |
| 1 | 10 | Ḫu-un-ḫa-ab-bur nu-banda | Tab-la-la$^{ki}$ | | | |
| 2 | 60 | érin Tab-la-la$^{ki}$ | | | | |

Figure 4. Tax Paid by GAR-NE-NE and Tablala in the Years Šulgi 48 and Amar-Sin 5

| Oxen | Sheep | Silver Equivalent | Taxpayer |
|---|---|---|---|
| 10 | 100 | 200 shekels | "general" (šagina) |
| 2 | 20 | 40 shekels | "captain" (nu-banda) |
| 1 | 10 | 20 shekels | "captain" (nu-banda) |
| 1/20 | 1/2 | 1 shekel | "officer in charge of 60 men" (ugula-géš-da) |
| 1/300 | 1/30 | 12 grains | "soldier" (érin) |

Figure 5. Taxpayers and Tax Rates

Although most larger settlements were administered by generals, some of them, such as Adamdun, Hamazi, Sabum, Simurum, Susa, and Urua, had governors. This distinction appears to have been merely a matter of terminology, since we know that both offices had both military and civilian authority. The case of the administrator Zariqum, who is documented both as a general and as a governor of Assur,[61] offers a good illustration of this point.

---

shekels of silver), 3 oxen and 30 sheep (= 60 shekels of silver), and 1 ox and 10 sheep (= 20 shekels of silver) respectively (see fig. 3).

61. General: *KAH* 2 2:13; governor: see the references listed in *Rép. géogr.* 2, p. 19.

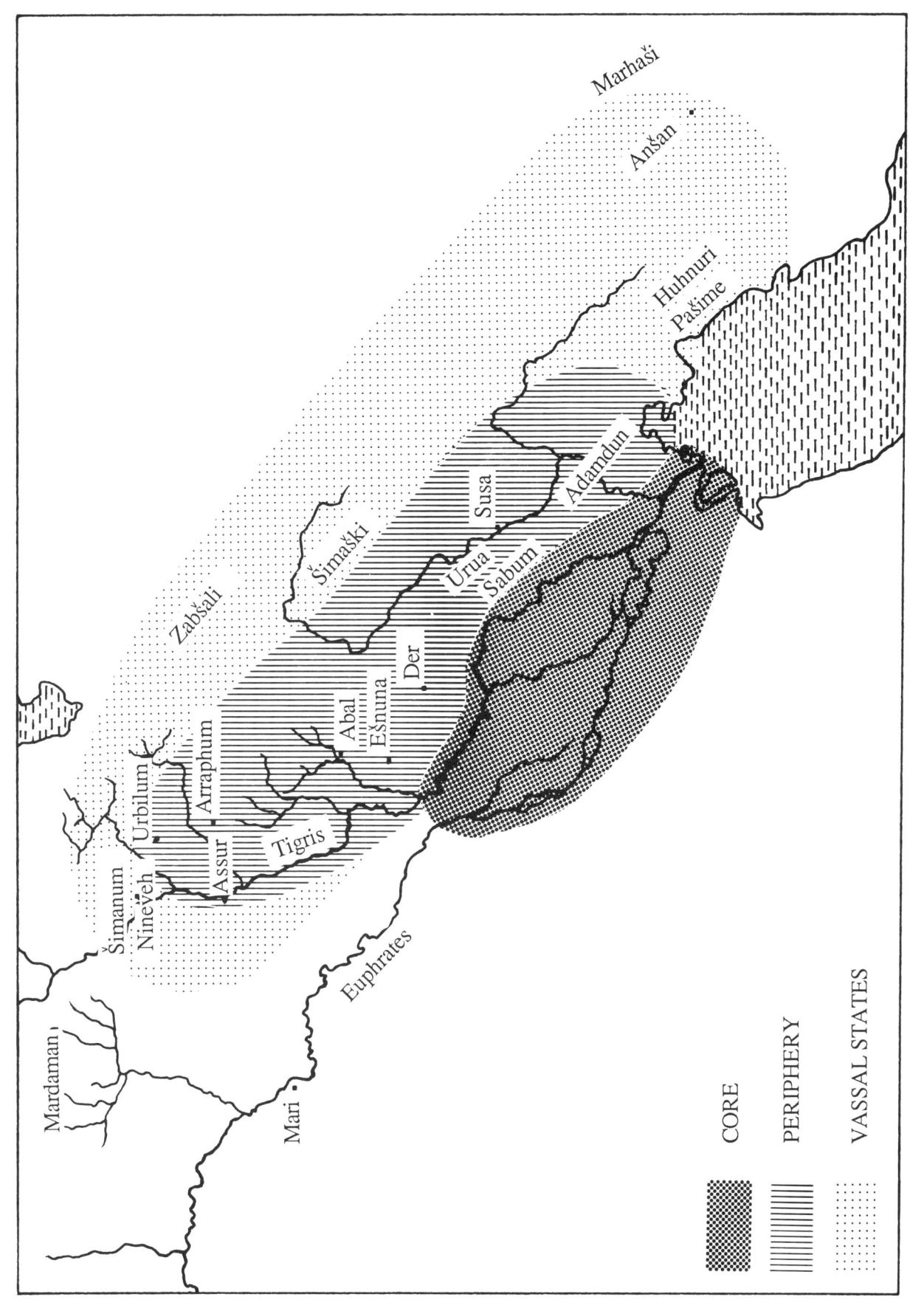

Figure 6. Territorial Extent of the Ur III State

Like their counterparts in the core area, the chief officials of the periphery were royal appointees. As shown by the example of Zariqum, who served as a general/governor of Assur and then assumed the post of the governor of Susa,[62] these officials could be dismissed or transferred to other positions. However, there is also evidence that in certain provinces the office of the general/governor passed from father to son.[63] Whether there was a tendency for the peripheral offices to become hereditary (as seems to have been the case in the core area) is uncertain.

When it comes to evaluating the economic organization of the periphery, we are unfortunately on considerably less certain ground. This is due primarily to the absence of textual information pertaining to the economic activity of that area. By extrapolating from what is known about the status of military settlers in the core area, however, we are justified in assuming that those residing in the periphery derived their livelihood from the land allotments that had been granted to them by the crown.[64] Although we lack any direct information concerning how these people utilized their land allotments and what type of economy they had, one point at least seems certain: since they paid their tax in livestock, animal husbandry must have been a major, if not the dominant, source of their subsistence. It may not be coincidental, therefore, that geographically the gún ma-da territory corresponds very closely to the region extending between 400 and 200 mm isohyets, within which rain agriculture is something of a gamble (the risk increasing the closer one gets to the 200 mm isohyet). This region, which was dubbed the "dimorphic zone" by M. B. Rowton,[65] is characterized by a symbiosis of rain agriculture and pastoral nomadism, with the amount of grazing land significantly exceeding that of agricultural land.

In this paper, we have restricted our discussion of the economic contributions of the periphery to the gún ma-da tax. It needs to be stressed, however, that the periphery also paid several other imposts or taxes, such as šu-gíd and máš-da-ri-a.[66] The latter usually consisted, like the gún ma-da, of livestock, but could also be paid in silver, timber, sesame, wine, etc.[67] One cannot exclude the possibility that these contributions were in fact more important than the gún ma-da, and that they were the equivalent of the bala taxes in the core area. Moreover, we know that the periphery not only made contributions to the

---

62. Hallo, "Zāriqum," *JNES* 15 (1956) 220–25; R. Kutscher, "A Note on the Early Careers of Zariqum and Šamši-illat," *RA* 73 (1979) 81f.

63. See, for example, Iribum and his son Ahuni, who governed in succession over Abibana, Kakkulatum, and Puhzigar, discussed above. Another such instance is provided by the general Hašip-atal and his son Puzur-Šulgi, who exercised control over Arraphum in Amar-Sin 5 (*PDT* 16:1–14) and in Amar-Sin 8 (*JCS* 31, pp. 166–67 lines 1–2) respectively. Hašip-atal is attested as a general in *TCL* 2 5488:2 (Šulgi 46).

64. Thus far, we find no mention of grants of land for any of the places appearing in the gún ma-da texts. There survives, however, a Puzriš-Dagan tablet which alludes to such a grant made in a place called Ahuti, which quite likely belonged to the gún ma-da territory. The text in question records an issue of 10 sheep to two men from Mari (lú Ma-ri$^{ki}$-me), named Amir-Šulgi and Šulgi-pālil, in Šulgi 47. According to lines 18–20 of this document, the sheep "were loaded for them into a boat, when they went to Ahuti to take possession of the fields" (ud A-hu-ti$^{ki}$-<šè> a-šag$_4$ dab$_5$-dè ir-ri-eš-ša-a má-a ba-ne-gub; Kelsey Museum 89125, unpublished, courtesy of D. Owen, collated by P. Michalowski). The location of Ahuti, which occurs also in the Abu Salabikh/Ebla geographical list (G. Pettinato, *MEE* 3, p. 239, line 273), is unknown. However, it seems virtually certain that it is a non-Babylonian toponym. In this connection, note that the same Amir-Šulgi and Šulgi-pālil appear among various "foreigners" in the Puzriš-Dagan text *TCL* 2 5500 ii 6–7, written nine years later.

65. M. B. Rowton, "Dimorphic Structure and Topology," *Oriens Antiquus* 15 (1976) 17–31.

66. For the šu-gíd, see, for example, *PDT* 234; Genouillac, *Trouvaille* 69; *Nikolski* 2 483; for the máš-da-ri-a, see, for example, *BIN* 3 18; *TCL* 2 5502/5503 ii 1–5.

67. For silver, see, for example, *TCL* 2 5515:1–3; for timber, see, for example, *ITT* 3 5114:1-2; Nesbit, *SRD* 4; for sesame, see Steinkeller, *JAOS* 102, pp. 641–42.

central government, but also that it received certain goods (mostly cereals) from it.[68] These facts can be taken as an indication that the Ur III economic system was a highly symmetrical one, with the core and the periphery mirroring each other in a relationship of interdependency.

68. For example, there is evidence for deliveries of grain to Susa and Adamdun. See E. Carter, "Elam in the Second Millennium B.C.: The Archaeological Evidence" (Ph.D. diss., University of Chicago, 1971), pp. 179–81; Michalowski, ZA 68, p. 47 and n. 40. For the shipments of grain to Adamdun, note also the Lagaš text ITT 2 763, which records an expenditure of one hundred bushels of barley intended for the "rations of the citizens of Adamdun" (še-ba dumu A-dam-dun^ki, line 2); the recipient of the barley was a royal messenger named Šulgi-bani, son of the general Kurub-Šamaš. For similar shipments to Susa, see especially the Susa text MDP 27 205, whose preserved section records the delivery of over 2,600 bushels of barley, wheat, and flour from the governors at Umma, Kutha, Kazallu, and Mar(a)da.

# CHAPTER 3

# UR III BUREAUCRACY: QUANTITATIVE ASPECTS

MIGUEL CIVIL
*University of Chicago*

### 1. INTRODUCTION

In this paper I will assume that "bureaucracy" is simply another term for "administration," adding to the latter such pejorative connotations as rigidity, slowness, lack of realism, proliferation of useless rules, etc. A bureaucracy can be studied from a structural point of view or in its quantitative aspects. In an economy a bureaucratic system, by definition, adversely modifies the flow of goods. In this paper I will attempt to answer the question of whether it is possible, with the available evidence, to conduct quantitative studies of the administration of the Ur III empire. Only when the question has been answered will it be possible to say in what measure the bureaucracy—if it turns out that the Ur III administration deserves this label—hindered the flow of goods or diverted them from their reasonable destinations. Note that only the role of bureaucracy in the production and distribution of goods will be considered here, leaving aside its legal and political functions. In the present state of the art it seems wise to limit the inquiry to the possibility of conducting quantitative studies in a productive and meaningful way.

The reader is asked to keep in mind, in the first place, that this is a methodological essay and not a study *per se* of the flow of goods as such. As well, he should be aware that there is more to a quantitative analysis than drawing a pie chart. The textual data are to be viewed as more or less representative samples of the actual circulation of goods.

The administrative archives of Ur III appear very promising both in the extent of information and in precision of detail. Three years ago—the last time I made a count—there were 22,980 documents published for a period that covers a little over four decades at the end of the third millennium. The texts available today certainly exceed 25,000. Mesopotamia has a long and fascinating administrative tradition, but nowhere is the accounting so fastidiously detailed and explicit as in the Ur III archives. One can find many references to collecting and using reeds—a traditional Mesopotamian activity—in most periods, but nowhere else do we have over 600 texts dealing with reeds which in one case are weighed with a precision of one part in 48,000. This is thus a preliminary exploration of the archives to see in what measure the size of the economy and of the institutions that controlled and recorded it can be reconstructed.

I am not aware of any formal discussion of this problem among Sumerologists. There are examples, of course, of quantitative evaluations, but none with explicit statistical justification. Tom Jones, a historian, sensed the importance of numerical data and gave some examples in a brief essay,[1] but he concluded—with a priori pessimism it would seem—that of the bodies of documents from different sites "none can be called representative of Ur III." Whether the label "representative," in its technical, statistical sense, can be applied to these archives is the subject of this inquiry.

## 2. SAMPLES FROM THE SAME ARCHIVE

The following discussion starts with the hypotheses (1) that Ur III administrative texts were preserved in large archive rooms of the type found, for instance, in Ebla, or discarded en masse in a single fill or dump, and (2) that the clandestine diggers of the texts did their best to get all of them out of the ground. I selected three independent samples of the same Drehem archive: (1) all tablets published before 1954 as listed by Fish, *MCS* 5/4, (2) tablets published in Çığ-Kızılyay-Salonen, *Die Puzriš-Dagan-Texte* (Helsinki, 1954), and (3) tablets published in Keiser, *BIN* 3 and Kang, *SACT* 1. Plotting the number of dated tablets for each year (fig. 1), the graph shows[2] that the samples are not random and that the dispersal of the tablets at the hands of the dealers and in the museums did not disrupt their chronological distribution to any large degree. In the counter example of the Tello archive that led Jones to his pessimistic conclusion, the second initial hypothesis does not hold. The native diggers removed most of the texts from Šulgi 44 to Amar-Sin 5, the French excavators the rest.

## 3. SAMPLES FROM DIFFERENT ARCHIVES

Figure 2 shows the chronological distribution of dated tablets from Djoha, Drehem, and Tello, three independent sites, up to the fifth year of Amar-Sin. Once more the distribution is not random. Considering how many factors are in operation here, the trends are remarkably similar. One can conclude that the samples are sufficiently representative so that global factors affecting the bureaucratic output show through. Before further discussion, the main factors of variation in the yearly number of tablets should be mentioned.

1. Factors affecting the number of tablets drafted:

   a. Changes in the level of business activity, due to climatic (e.g., drought) or political (e.g., war or civil strife) reasons.

   b. Changes in accounting practices either global, affecting the whole of the Ur III empire and presumably emanating from directives from the central administration, or local (perhaps this is the case of the cadaster texts from Tello, which date from Šulgi 47, Amar-Sin 7–8, or Ibbi-Sin 2–3, with apparently no texts from intervening years).

   c. Changes due to the nature of particular subsections of a general archive (as in the just mentioned case of cadaster texts or the artisan archives in the capital, Ur), or to the presence of texts autonomous to a certain degree from the central bureaucracy (family archives in Nippur).

---

1. Tom B. Jones, "Sumerian Administrative Documents: An Essay," *Sumerological Studies Jacobsen*, pp. 41–61.
2. The years marked by an asterisk have been omitted because of ambiguities in their date formulas.

# UR III BUREAUCRACY: QUANTITATIVE ASPECTS

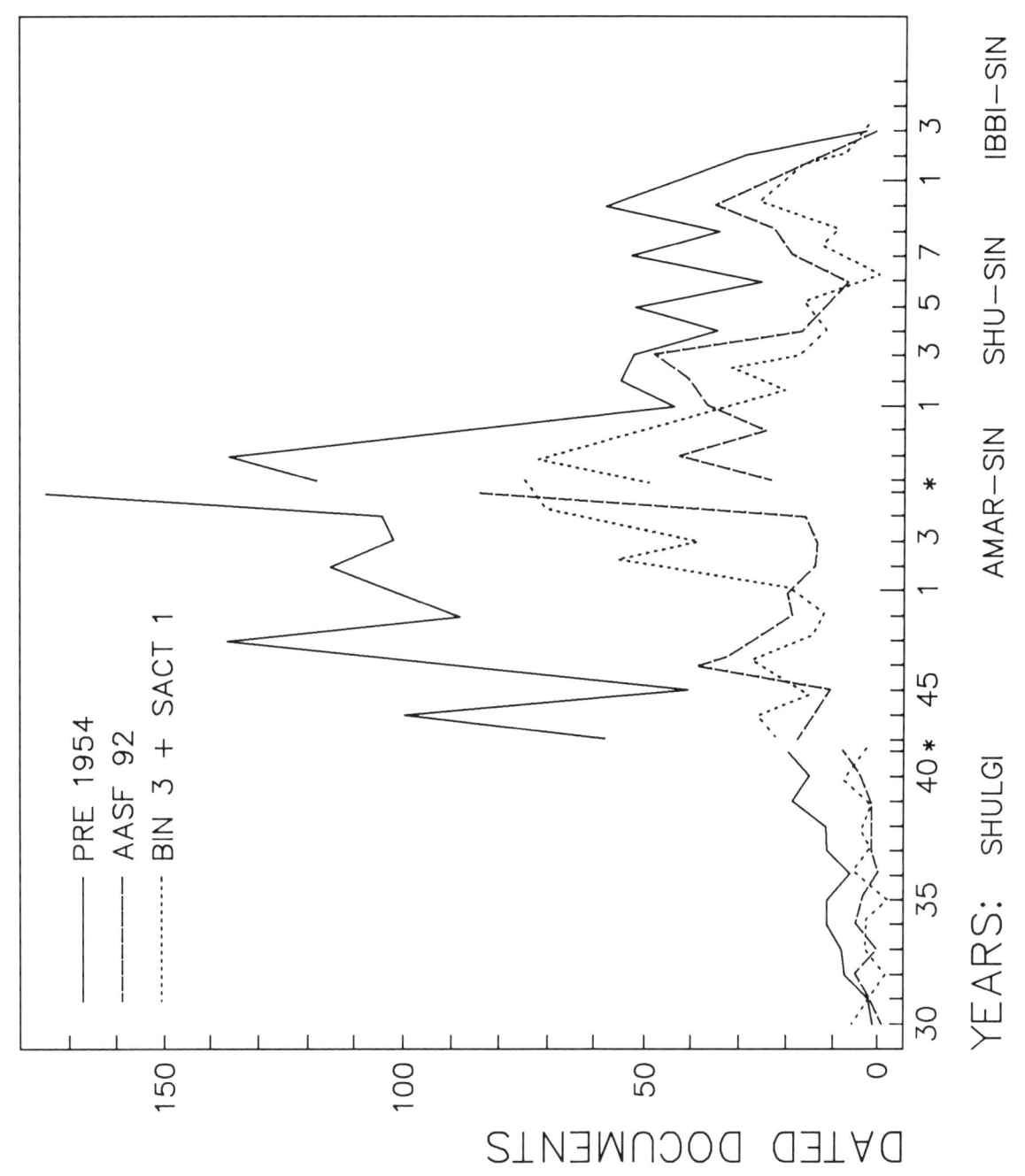

Figure 1. Chronological Distribution of Three Groups of Dated Tablets from Drehem

2. Factors affecting the number of tablets preserved:

   a. Purposeful destruction of documents in antiquity, required by the nature of the text (e.g., loan tablets) or due to the disposal of obsolete documents (the rules for discarding tablets in general are not known; see also b).
   b. The "catastrophe" factor: the greater number of recovered texts from a given archive date always to the time immediately preceding the destruction or conquest of a town (Pre-Sargonic Lagash, Ebla, Old Babylonian Nippur).[3] Two explanations may account for the

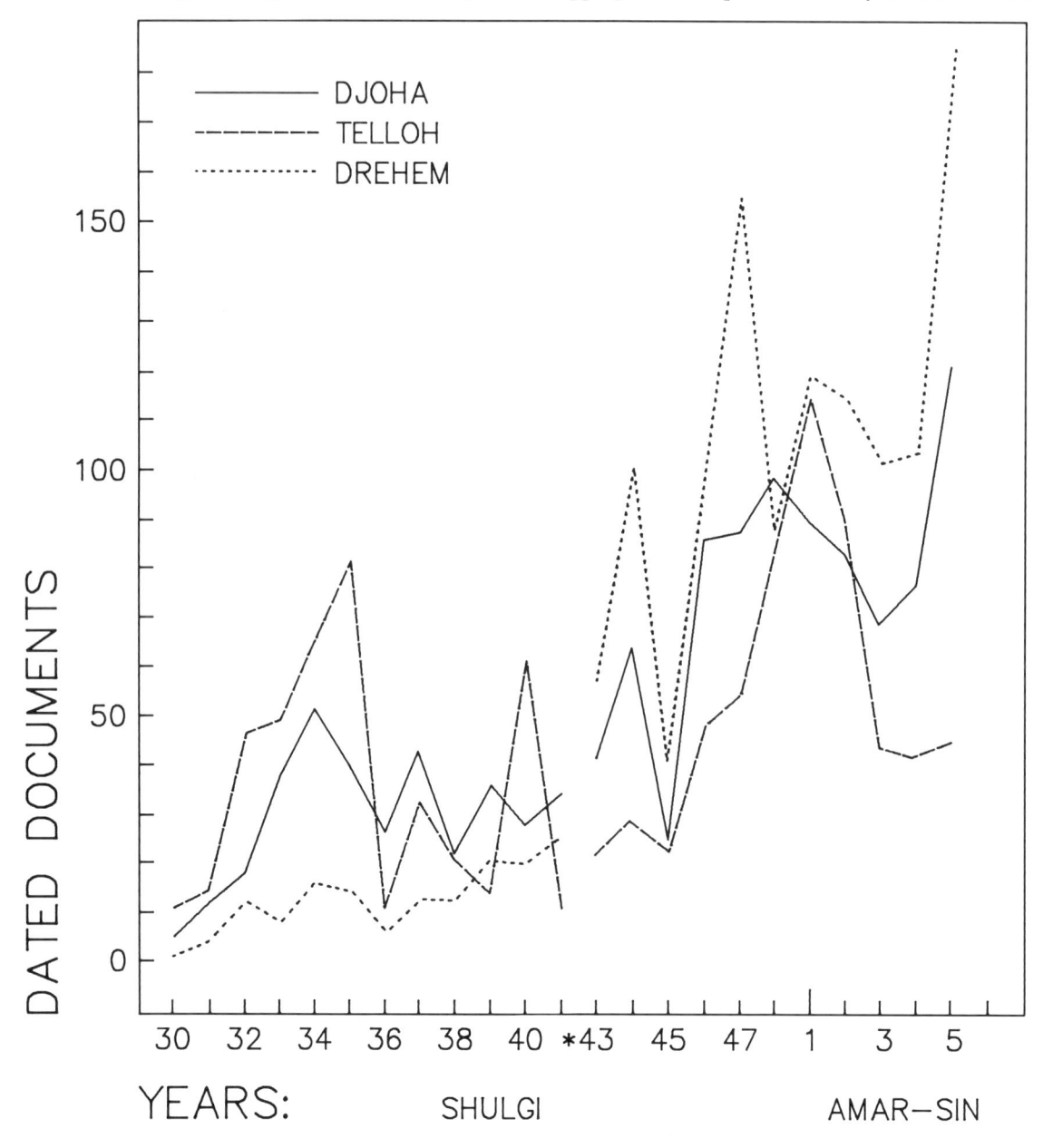

Figure 2. Chronological Distribution of Dated Tablets from Three Different Sites

3. See my remarks in *MSL* 14, p. 7.

latter factor. First, the number of old documents in an archive declined gradually through the years by elimination of valueless documents; there are more texts from the final period because this process of attrition had not yet had time to operate. Second, there exists something which could be called "bureaucratic cycle"; it starts with a moderate amount of document drafting but then the number of documents increases through the years until the sheer weight of the bureaucracy chokes the economy that crumbles when faced with a political or economic crisis.

c. Loss of documents after excavation. Some tablets were broken and therefore discarded by the clandestine diggers or by the dealers; others have disappeared into private collections or small museums and can be considered temporarily lost.

The interpretation of time series is a notoriously difficult task. Note that the sign of a variation is more important than its size. What is attempted here is only to investigate the possibility of this type of study and I cannot possibly go into details of interpretation. Points to keep in mind for further research include an evaluation of the error size (obviously one cannot define a "depression" by an average drop of only three tablets), an analysis of the local variations and possible correlations between sections (e.g., agriculture and river traffic) within the same archive, and studies of documents that would seem to be particularly sensitive to economic changes (e.g., loan documents).[4]

Figure 3 gives a comparison between two geographically close sites, Nippur and Drehem, to illustrate the importance of local factors; note, among other points, 1) how the Drehem expansion at the beginning of Amar-Sin's reign fails to affect Nippur, 2) the remarkable agreement between the sites for the years 4 to 9 of Amar-Sin, and 3) the influence of the "catastrophe factor," moderately visible in Drehem, very marked in Nippur.

The inclusion of texts from the capital—the space and time allocated to this paper do not allow a necessarily long discussion of them—would be still more instructive and illustrate at the same time some of the problems. Besides the effects of the "catastrophe factor," relatively trivial from a methodological point of view, but of very large size and historical significance, the peaks and dips during the reign of Šu-Sin lag one year behind those detected in Nippur and Drehem, either due to accounting delays in the administrative center or to the more likely possibility that economic changes in the periphery affected the capital only some time later.

Before ending this discussion of the chronological distribution of documents, I would like to stress that in the available text editions there are a relatively large number of mistakes both in the dating and in the attribution to sites. Nippur, for instance, has tablets dated by the Drehem calendar, a fact that went unnoticed until recently. Once again, the reader is asked to keep in mind that this is an exploratory essay and that a more rigorous and detailed examination of the data is needed before drawing conclusions for economic or political history.

### 4. FIELD SIZES AND AGRARIAN REFORM

On three occasions that we know of, extensive field surveys were conducted in the Lagash region during the 47th year of Šulgi, the 7th and 8th years of Amar-Sin, and the 2d and 3d years of Ibbi-Sin.[5]

---

4. If the loan documents were destroyed after repayment, the number of preserved documents would indicate not the number of loans made, but the number of unpaid loans. Could the debtor keep a copy after payment? Could the creditor?

5. The reasons for these particular dates are not known. If the field surveys were conducted every seven years, we should have some traces of such surveys around the 5th year of Šu-Sin. Possibly they were reforms with no periodicity.

The pertinent documents are conveniently collected by Pettinato, *An Or* 45 (1969). Examining first the plot sizes in the Amar-Sin surveys (fig. 4), it is obvious that the size distribution does not follow a normal, random distribution. The sizes cluster with a frequency much higher than expected[6] around a central value of about 100 ikus. The conclusion that the administration assigned plots of an ideal size of 100 ikus is a legitimate one. The other values represent odd-sized plots resulting from the physical configuration of the fields, possibly taking into account not only geometry but also other factors such as access to water. The conclusion about the "standard" size of 100 ikus is reinforced by a comparison with the average plot size in the Šulgi cadaster: its plots are on the average twice the size of those in the Amar-Sin cadaster. A comparison between Ibbi-Sin's field surveys and previous ones (fig. 5) gives information of another nature. The graph gives the amount of fallow land (sù) in each plot. One can detect a change from larger plots with about 2/3 of the land left fallow (Šulgi), to smaller plots with between 1/3 and 1/2 left fallow (Amar-Sin), and finally to plots of the same size but with only 1/5 (sometimes nothing) left fallow. This suggests an intensification of cultivation, the reasons for which are left to the historian to investigate. A demographic increase of the whole population of the empire or perhaps only of the number of persons eligible to receive land could account for the changes. An alternative, or perhaps concurrent, factor would be a decrease in land available for cultivation due to a shrinkage of the borders under pressure from neighboring powers (at least in Ibbi-Sin's time). One may ask as well why these "agrarian reforms" are attested only in the Lagaš-Girsu region. In any case, a quantitative study of the cadasters gives some hints about the administrative decisions that governed land distribution. The decisions themselves were either never written down or are lost.

## 5. OTHER APPLICATIONS

Quantitative studies can help not only economic and administrative history but also assist in the lexicographer's task, thus increasing our understanding of the texts. The article "Hacke" in the *Reallexikon der Assyriologie* explains that "working with the hoe" was called either al—ak (often abbreviated to al) or al—dù. If one reads the texts with numbers and sizes in mind, however, it appears that al—ak is done on areas of from 3.3 to 10 sar at a time (the average being 5.5 sar) while al—dù is done on areas of from 10 to 30 sar (average 15.5 sar) and thus the two verbs must designate two different tasks, the latter three times less time consuming than the first.

A feeling for numbers and sizes can prevent mistranslations such as "large container" for an object (al-la-LUM) that weighs 3 shekels and 12 grains (ca. 13.85 gr.),[7] or "nail tip" for an object (kun-KAK) that weighs 1 mina and 17 shekels (ca. 641.4 gr.).

An Umma text from the fourth year of Šu-Sin about agricultural work provides information about the relative extent of weed infestation ("weed" is perhaps not the best word since some of these plants were used for fodder or fuel); see table 1. Comparison of the ancient data with present-day weed cover confirms the identification, obtained by other means, of the first listed plant with *Prosopis farcta*, "mesquite" or "false carob," and of the second with *Alhagi maurorum*, "camel thorn"; see Civil, "Feeding Dumuzi's Sheep: The Lexicon as a Source of Literary Inspiration," in F. Rochberg-Halton, ed., *Language, Literature, and History: Philological and Historical Studies Presented to Erica Reiner*, AOS 67 (New Haven, 1987) 41.

---

6. Skewness = 1.478, kurtosis = 4.688.
7. Read *al-la-núm* "acorn-shaped bead." The examples are taken from H. Limet, *Le Travail du métal au pays de Sumer au temps de la III<sup>e</sup> dynastie d'Ur* (Paris, 1960), a book that attempts to study the terminology of metal objects with no recourse whatsoever to archaeology.

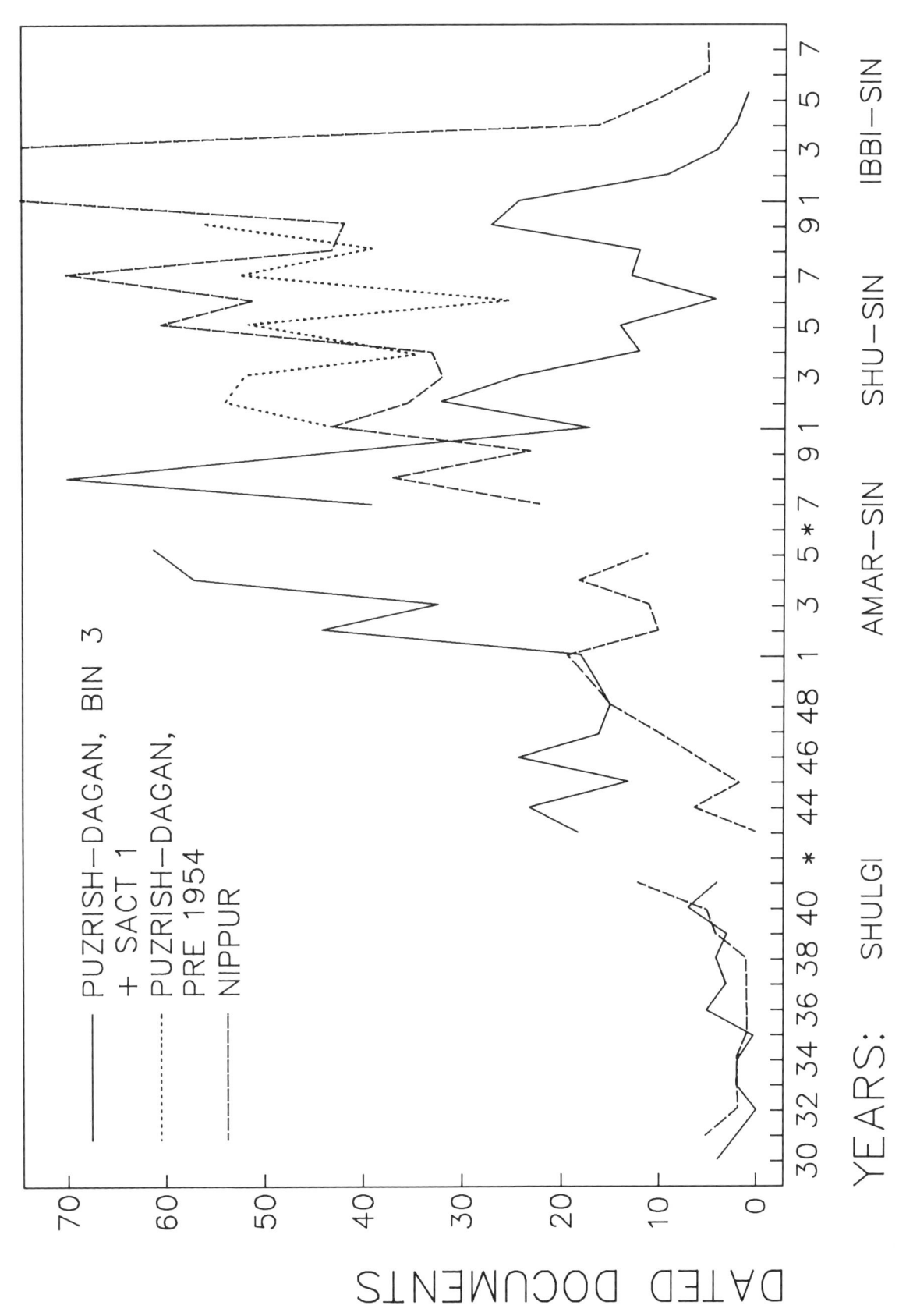

Figure 3. Comparative Chronological Distribution of Dated Tablets from Nippur and Drehem

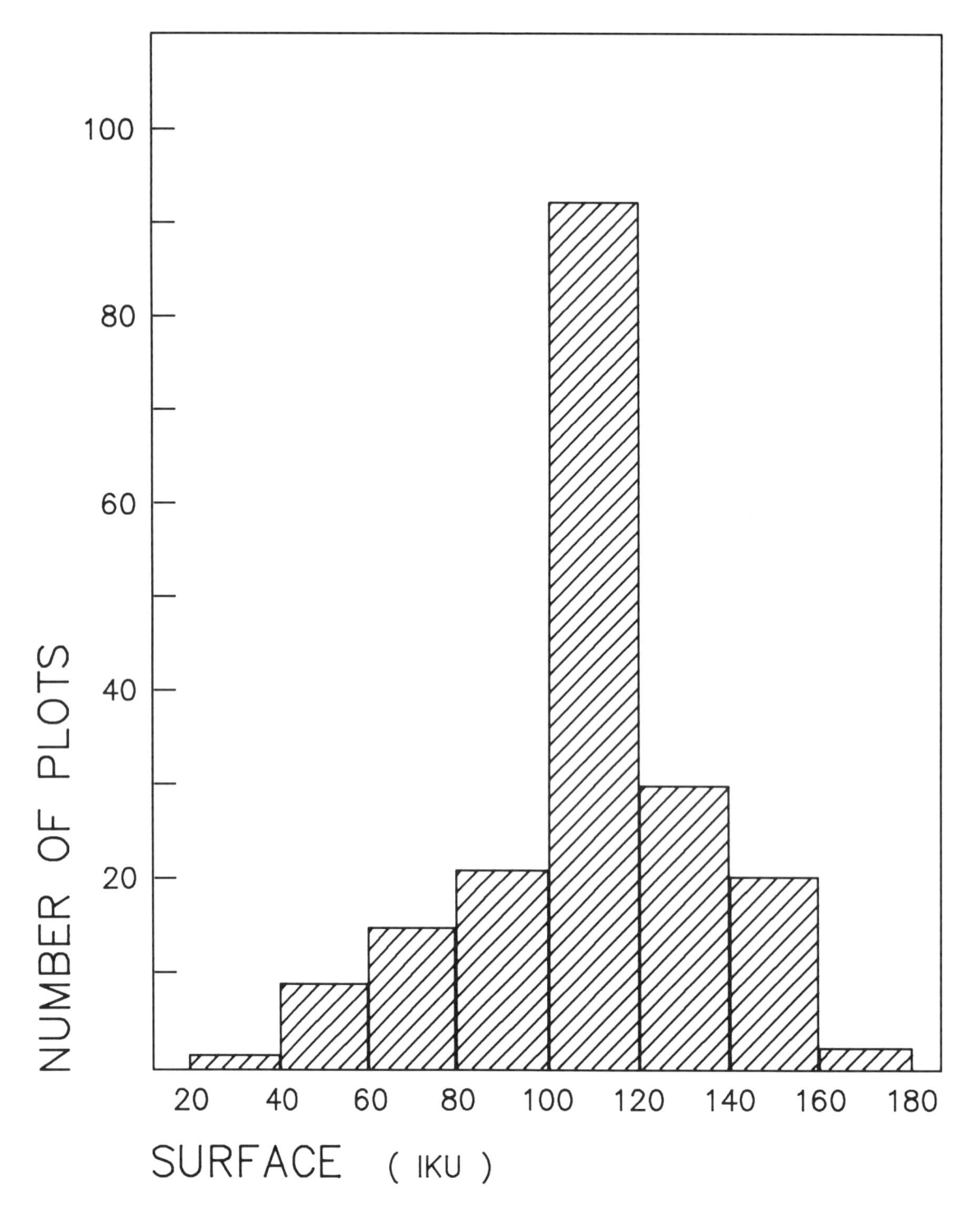

Figure 4. Plot Sizes in Land Surveys in Years 7 and 8 of Amar-Sin

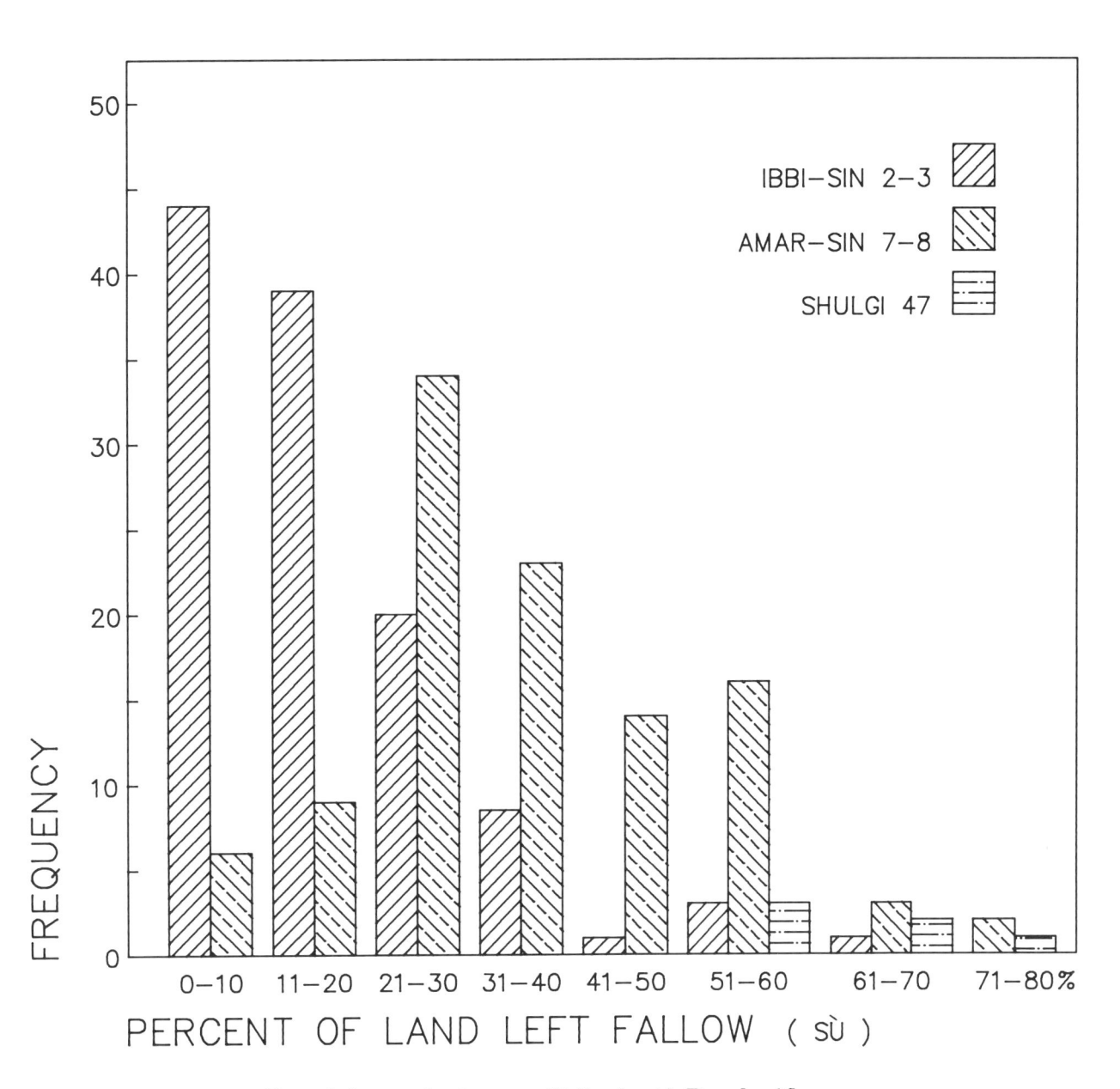

Figure 5. Comparative Amounts of Fallow Land in Three Land Surveys

Table 1. Weed Coverage of a Field in Umma in the 4th Year of Šu-Sin (*TCL* 5 5675)

|    | Plant | Surface |     | Percent |
|----|-------|---------|-----|---------|
| 1. | ᵘkiši₁₆ | 6,115 | sar | 45.3 |
| 2. | ᵍᶦšdìh | 3,120 |     | 23.1 |
| 3. | ᵘ ᵍᶦšhašhur | 590 |     | 4.3 |
| 4. | ᵘLAK175-na | 1,082 |     | 8.0 |
| 5. | ú-kul | 1,120 |     | 8.2 |
| 6. | Mixture of 1–4 | 660 |     | 4.8 |
| 7. | Mixture of 3–4 | 807 |     | 5.9 |

## 6. FINAL CONSIDERATIONS

One important matter relevant to the study of bureaucracy which could not be discussed here is the determination of the extent of coverage of any particular activity. Often we have documents covering a very concrete type of production or service involving specific individuals, but only for a very restricted period or periods of time. For instance, for ten months of the first year of Šu-Sin there is a text (*YOS* 4 301) that lists—in order to compute wages—the amount of gi-zi-reeds (a particular stage in the growth of the common reed fed to sheep and goats) collected at the Tell of Murula (du₆-mu-ru-la$^{ki}$). There is one text (Nesbit, *SRD*, no. 26) for the second month of the following year. There is nothing before these dates, and the subject does not reappear until eight years later: two texts in Ibbi-Sin 1 (*BIN* 3 329 and 465), and one text the following year (*BIN* 3 265). In this case the relatively sudden retreat of the central administration at the beginning of Ibbi-Sin's reign is sufficient explanation for the ensuing silence, but the sudden appearance of the account and the eight-year-gap remain unexplained. One could quote many more similar cases in which the cessation of bureaucratic control cannot be explained by the decline of the Ur III empire. Besides the obvious, but hardly satisfying, assumption that other documents relating to the matter in question have been lost, one could reasonably ask whether the bureaucracy did not constantly try to expand its control over more and more activities of the population, but often had to desist due to practical difficulties or the resistance of the parties involved. The matter deserves careful investigation. The cadasters discussed above were almost certainly activities that took place only at distant intervals.

In conclusion, the application of quantitative methods in general and statistical analysis in particular to ancient administrative texts is not only possible but is the only way of extracting meaningful data in order to reconstruct the economic institutions. As a side benefit we would also gain a better understanding of the vocabulary. The meticulous accounting of the ancient scribes deserves a proper quantitative treatment. It is not an easy task. Tables and graphs are only a way of presenting raw data. To interpret the information statistically, finding probabilities and margins of error, is another matter. Quantitative methods, being in a sense more powerful than philological ones, require an explicit analysis of basic assumptions and demand rigorous methods coupled with common sense lest we be accused of "counting without thinking" after being guilty of "thinking without counting."

# CHAPTER 4

# CHARISMA AND CONTROL: ON CONTINUITY AND CHANGE IN EARLY MESOPOTAMIAN BUREAUCRATIC SYSTEMS

PIOTR MICHALOWSKI
*University of Michigan*

## 1. INTRODUCTION

The study of ancient bureaucratic systems is still in its infancy. The many reasons for this state of affairs need not be enumerated here; suffice it to say that a reluctance to indulge in theoretical speculation, combined with an overwhelming amount of data from a variety of textual types from different societies and many historical periods have provided obstacles to the understanding of the functioning of ancient Near Eastern bureaucracies. There is a pressing need for detailed studies of a variety of basic problems bearing on the matter. In this paper, rather than a full-scale study of any one issue, I shall present some general remarks on a series of interrelated topics, ranging from problems of political domination to issues associated with the socialization of bureaucrats in early Mesopotamian states. Due to the nature of the preserved documentation, as well as my own interests, I shall concentrate primarily on the period of the Third Dynasty of Ur.

## 2. BUREAUCRATIC SYSTEMS AND THE PROBLEM OF POLITICAL DOMINATION

The study of bureaucracy owes much to the pioneering work of Max Weber. I shall not attempt to discuss here in full Weber's concept of bureaucracy and the literature which it has spawned, but I would like to draw attention to certain matters which are of relevance to the present discussion.[1] Weber's ideas concerning bureaucracy were closely related to his famous tripartite division of types of political domination and their related forms of legitimacy: traditional, charismatic, and legal-rational or bureaucratic. The traditional type, which is of most interest to us, is further subdivided into patriarchal, patrimonial, and feudal domination. As summarized by Frank Parkin, patrimonial legitimation is based on:

> ... the 'loyalty and fidelity' felt by subjects towards their master. Patrimonial rulers foster the same relationship with their political subjects that they enjoy with members of their household.

---

1.  Some of the most important passages from his work can be found conveniently in S. N. Eisenstadt, ed., *Max Weber: On Charisma and Institution Building* (Chicago, 1968).

While in theory they have absolute powers of command over their followers, in practice they are held in check by the limits laid down by custom and convention.[2]

While there is some resemblance to bureaucracy, the differences between the two systems are instructive for an understanding of Weber's concept of bureaucracy. To quote Parkin once again:

Patrimonial administration knows no clear separation of private and official spheres. The ruler governs his political territory by personal fiat and draws upon wide discretionary powers. His officials are charged simply with the task of faithfully doing his bidding. There are none of the statutory practices and formal procedures of rational bureaucracy. The bureaucrat owes his allegiance to the rules, not the ruler.[3]

This distinction between patrimonialism and bureaucracy should give us much to think about. For how would we classify early Mesopotamian states in accordance with these distinctions? And if we should find that these descriptions will simply not do then why is it that they do not fit? Can we speak of bureaucracy at all and if so in what contexts? Weber's ideal types of domination cannot be applied without qualification to any society and the Mesopotamian social landscape may in fact prove to be much too complex to be encompassed by such definitions. But while the invocation of such a meta-language often carries with it the danger of blindness and simplification, the posing of questions in a particular manner may lead to interesting results. In order to analyze some of the questions which arise in the study of ancient officialdom, it will be advantageous to discuss certain aspects of the historical contexts of the various centers of power and authority in early Mesopotamian states.

## 3. THE DISCONTINUOUS NATURE OF EARLY MESOPOTAMIAN STATE FORMATIONS

There has been a strong tendency to view Mesopotamian history as a continuous affair, one in which better and ever bigger "empires" followed one another, teleologically focused on achieving national greatness. This continuum was broken by a number of "Dark Ages" which were overcome and after a period of reconstruction, progress marched on. I think that it is fair to say that currently few scholars would identify with such a position. As became evident in the criticism of the concept of the "Zweite Zwischenzeit," which was used to designate the early Old Babylonian period, the norm of political organization during the third and early second millennia was the city-state and the so-called empires of the Dynasties of Akkad and Ur III, as well as the short period of glory of Babylon under Hammurabi and Samsu-iluna, lasted in each case for no more than a few generations.[4] In fact, the whole time of unity of Sumer and Akkad up to the end of the Old Babylonian period consisted of two hundred and thirty years, at the most. The dynasties by which we traditionally designate historical periods are likewise imprecisely defined. Some of them may be considered true dynasties—here one may mention the successors of Sargon, Ur-Namma or Sumu-abum. Others are historical fictions, as in the case of the so-called Larsa dynasty, which, in fact, consisted of at least three distinct lineages. It is true that the modern terminology defining changes of dynasties is roughly equivalent to certain ancient categorizations but this does not necessarily make matters easier for the historian.[5] The overt recognition of these ruptures and discontinuities is of crucial importance for the study of bureaucratic systems, for each of these states had

---

2. Frank Parkin, *Max Weber* (Chichester, 1982) 81.
3. Ibid., p. 82.
4. See the review of D. O. Edzard, *Die "Zweite Zwischenzeit" Babyloniens* (Wiesbaden, 1957) by W. W. Hallo in *BiOr* 16 (1959) 234–38 and idem, "Royal Hymns and Mesopotamian Unity," *JCS* 17 (1963) 112–18.
5. See J. J. Finkelstein, "The Genealogy of the Hammurapi Dynasty," *JCS* 20 (1966) 95–118.

to be created anew, at least to a certain extent, and the sad fact is that we know next to nothing about the important early years of their formation.

Thus, while we speak of political changes, it is impossible to establish the effect that such occurrences had on the various levels of bureaucracy. To cite some examples: there are almost no economic documents from the time of Sargon of Akkad and thus, except for the names of a few local rulers who were kept in power by the new king, we know nothing of the continuity, or lack of it, among other echelons at the local level nor of the methods of recruitment which the new dynasty may have had in order to create its own officialdom. The same holds true for the first two decades of the Ur III state. While apparently there are economic texts from Girsu which may span the reigns of Gudea to Ur-Namma, at present they have not been made available for study. The transition between the Ur III and Isin dynasties is likewise undocumented in the published records, although a few unpublished tablets from Nippur, as well as an unpublished private archive of a merchant by the name of Turam-ili from Isin, may provide some information on these matters.[6]

The case of Isin is of particular interest for there is good evidence that Išbi-Erra and Šu-ilišu, the first two rulers of the dynasty, made considerable efforts to maintain a continuity with the house of Ur. In the aftermath of the fall of Ibbi-Sin's kingdom, the new ruler of Isin, himself a high official in the latter's employ, instituted a system of organization which appears to have mimicked that of the Ur III state, albeit on a smaller scale. He did not attempt the drastic reforms of writing and bureaucracy which Šulgi utilized to such great advantage when he made his mark on the social landscape of Sumer. On the contrary, he maintained the writing system, the metrology, and possibly even the organizational hierarchy of the Ur III state. A study of the early Isin texts reveals that the titulary and responsibilities of officials must have changed very little, if at all, during the reign of Išbi-Erra. Even the institution of the sukkal-mah, the "chancellor," and highest military commander of the state, appears to have been maintained.[7] Ideology and propaganda followed suit as can be seen by the fact that the Isin rulers formulated a set of literary texts which bound them to the rulers of Ur—"The Lament over the Destruction of Sumer and Ur," "The Tummal Chronicle," and, perhaps most importantly, the so-called Sumerian King List.[8] There is even a possibility that the cult of the deceased rulers of Ur was continued under the Isin kings.[9] The identification with the house of Ur was further fostered through the cult, as can be observed in a literary text which identifies the dead monarchs of Ur and Isin with Damu and lists the places where they were buried.[10]

This historical discontinuity, and the attendant lack of documentation on the early periods of the consolidation of larger state formations such as those of the Sargonic and Ur III kings, deserves some attention. If we are to follow the model of patrimonial domination then we could posit an initial period when the trusted families which were closely tied to the new ruling house would aspire to the higher ranks of the bureaucracy while their own followers, in turn, filled the middle ranks. On the local level, on the other hand, some kind of continuity must have existed. Important examples of such respect for

---

6. A. Goetze, review of *UET* 3 in *JCS* 7 (1953) 30–32. (This archive has now been published by Marc van de Mieroop, "Tūram-ilī: An Ur III Merchant," *JCS* 38 [1986] 1–80. Unfortunately, the extant texts span only the period between ŠS 3 and IS 3.)

7. For a study of the early texts from Isin see M. G. van de Mieroop, *Crafts in the Early Isin Period: A Study of the Isin Craft Archive from the Reigns of Išbi-Erra and Šū-ilišu* (Leuven, 1987).

8. P. Michalowski, "History as Charter: Some Observations on the Sumerian King List," *JAOS* 103 (1983) 237–48.

9. See ki-a-nag ⌜ma-aḫ-ku-um⌝ lugal-lugal-e-ne-šè, in *BIN* 9 440:31, a text dated to the reign of Išbi-Erra, hence the "libation place of the spirits of the (dead) kings" would probably include the rulers of Ur.

10. Genouillac, *TRS* 8: 198ff.

traditional local authorities may be found in the royal correspondence of Šulgi and Šu-Sin and in the later omen literature.[11]

## 4. BUREAUCRACY AND STATE FORMATION

The higher strata of the bureaucracy may have arrived with the new kings. There can be little doubt that they did form the core of the higher echelons of the ladder of authority. There is enough evidence from the Ur III period to indicate that during the rule of that dynasty, many official positions became hereditary. First of all, it is clear that the large extended family of the kings themselves played a crucial role in the administration of the state. Children of the kings filled many high positions and we find them in strategic positions in the military as well as in the civilian and temple administrations. Many of the provincial civilian governors came from the local population, but the military authorities were often members of the royal family, either through direct descent or through marital alliances.[12] Priests and priestesses were appointed from the royal brood and princesses were married to kings of allied border territories. The cities of Ur and Uruk were not part of the normal provincial administration but were most probably ruled directly by members of the royal family. Uruk, the ancestral home of the dynasty, was for a short time administered by the crown prince Šu-Sin and later most probably by the dowager queen Abi-simti.[13] Her brother, Babati, controlled many functions in the military and civilian parts of the bureaucracy.[14] Many of the important officials of the realm intermarried with the royal family. Among the most telling examples one may list the family of the chancellor Arad-Nanna,[15] the important generals Huba'a, Hašib-atal, Šarrum-bani, Lugal-magure, and Lu-Nanna,[16] the well-documented priest Dada,[17] as well as Lu-Ninšubur, the high priest of An.[18]

11. P. Michalowski, *JAOS* 103 (1983) 244; J. Bottéro, "Le Pouvoir royal et ses limitations d'après les textes divinatoires," in A. Finet, ed., *La Voix d'opposition en Mésopotamie* (Brussels, 1973) 119–65.
12. See, for example, the šakkanas who were most probably royal sons listed by A. Goetze, *JCS* 17 (1963) 30.
13. P. Michalowski, "Dūrum and Uruk During the Ur III Period," *Mesopotamia* 12 (1977) 83–96.
14. R. M. Whiting, "Tiš-atal of Nineveh and Babati, Uncle of Šu-Sin," *JCS* 28 (1976) 173–82.
15. geme₂-é-an-na é-gi₄-a arad₂-mu sukkal-mah A. 5426:7 (unpublished, courtesy P. Steinkeller); [geme₂]-é-an-na é-gi₄-a arad₂-mu sukkal-mah FLP 277:11 (unpublished, courtesy D. I. Owen). Geme-Eanna is listed as a royal daughter in Metropolitan 11.217.29 ii 1 (unpublished, courtesy M. Sigrist) and in *CT* 3 21335:175.
16. For the former, see: níg-MUNUS-ús-sá KA-ᵈnanna dumu lugal é hu-ba-a-šè *TCL* 2, 5563: 9–10; for the latter: nin-hé-du₇ é-gi₄-a ha-ši-ba-tal *TRU* 110:7. Hašib-atal is the šakkana associated with Arrapha (e.g., *PDT* 166); Nin-hedu is a royal daughter in the Metropolitan tablet cited above, i 29. Šarrum-bani was at one time ensi of Abiak and then was put in charge of the building of the Muriq-Tidnim wall. Lugal-magure is well attested with the title šakkana (A. Goetze, *JCS* 17 [1963] 10–12), as is Lu-Nanna, son of Ur-nigar (ibid., p. 24). Metropolitan 11.217.29 lists dam lugal-má-gur₈-re (ii 7), dam šar-ru-um-ba-ni (ii 13), and dam lú-ᵈnanna dumu ur-ni₉-gar (ii 16) among other princesses (dumu-munus lugal-me, ii 17).
17. níg-MUNUS-ús-sá a-mi-ir-ᵈšul-gi dumu lugal é da-da gala-šè Sigrist, *AUCT* 1 418:2–3.
18. níg-MUNUS-ús-sá ur-ᵈba-Ú dumu lugal é lú-ᵈnin-šubur šabra an-na-šè *MVN* 3 232:3–4. Still another marriage into the royal family is documented in *MVN* 11 155:3–4, níg-MUNUS-ús-sá ᵈen-líl-al-šu dumu nu-úr-ᵈutu é ša-at-ᵈen.zu-šè (ŠS 7). Note that a recently published text lists animals which were the property of one Šat-Sin, most probably the same princess, which were in the trans-Tigridian city of Kakkulatum: níg-gur₁₁ ša-at-ᵈen.zu (l. 6) ... šà kak-ku₈-la-tumᵏⁱ (l. 10), J.-M. Durand, *Documents cunéiformes de la IVᵉ Section de l'Ecole Pratique des Hautes Etudes* 1 (Geneva and Paris, 1982) no. 267 (ŠS 9). Is it possible that she herself was married to the military governor of this outpost? In *CT* 32 pl. 12 ii 6, dated ŠS 3, a woman by the same name is nin-dingir [ ... ]. There is good reason to believe that all these references concern the same person. (In this study dumu lugal and dumu munus lugal have been taken to be sons and daughters of kings. Should it be that the Sumerian kinship system belongs to the Hawaiian type, however, these terms could refer to all children of the extended royal family. See my article "Thoughts about Ibrium," in H. Waetzoldt and H. Hauptmann, eds., *Wirtschaft und Gesellschaft von Ebla*, Heidelberger Studien zum Alten Orient, vol. 2 [Heidelberg, 1988] 267–76.)

In addition to the royal family we have some evidence for other lineages in the higher strata of the bureaucracy. The best known of these was the family of Arad-Nanna, which held the post of sukkal-mah for at least four generations, most probably during the whole Ur III period. The sukkal-mah was in charge of overseeing the administration of the conquered territories on the eastern and northeastern frontiers.[19] No wonder that when Elam regained its independence, the local rulers assumed the title of sukkal-mah. But other families also consolidated their power. Besides such well-known examples as the family of Ur-Meme of Nippur, which held many of the highest "secular" and "religious" offices in Nippur, including leading positions in the Inanna Temple as well as the governorship of the city,[20] we know of families of temple officials as well as at least seven hereditary governorships, the case of the city of Umma being most prominent.[21]

So much for the higher levels of the administration. But what of the lower ranks of the bureaucracy? Surely, when a new dynasty came to power, it could not abruptly replace all the officials throughout the state. This would require massive training of new administrators, producing chaos during a delicate period of the consolidation of power. But local officials have local habits and if one is to coordinate a uniform administration throughout the state some changes have to be made.

## 5. LANGUAGE AND POWER

In the case of the Akkadian and Ur III dynasties, administrative reforms were not brought about by the founders but by the consolidators, Naram-Sin and Šulgi. Both kings changed standards of measures and reformed the administration of the provinces of their kingdoms. These and other changes could only have been achieved after a period of consolidation. But other changes in bureaucratic practices may also have been instituted. The Ur III period has often been called, quite unfortunately, the Neo-Sumerian period—even the Neo-Sumerian renaissance. This terminology originated at a time when history was considered very much an ethnic, or even racial chronicle, but it has stayed with us, partly as a stylistic alternate, but also as an unfortunate relic of certain ideas of history. There is another reason for this term, however, which is of some interest, namely language policy. Before the dominance of the Sargonic kings, Akkadian had been the primary language of writing in the north while Sumerian dominated in the south. During the time of the Sargonic kings, Akkadian was used alongside Sumerian throughout the "empire" as the language of administration and of propaganda. With the ascent of the Ur III dynasty, Sumerian became the primary written language, at least in the south.[22]

---

19. D. M. Scharaschenidze, "Die sukkal-mah des alten Zweistromlandes in der Zeit der III. Dynastie von Ur," in J. Harmatta and G. Komoróczy, eds. *Wirtschaft und Gesellschaft im alten Vorderasien* (Budapest, 1976) 103–12.

20. See W. W. Hallo, "The House of Ur-Meme," *JNES* 31 (1972) 87–95 and R. Zettler, "The Genealogy of the House of Ur-Me-me: A Second Look," *AfO* 31 (1984) 1–9. An earlier example of such a combination of power at Nippur is represented by an Akkad period stamped brick of Lugal-nigzu who was the governor (ensi) of the city and chief administrator (sanga) of the Enlil temple, *PBS* 15 82. See my remarks in *RA* 75 (1981) 175, n. 14.

21. D. M. McGuiness, "Studies in the Neo-Sumerian Administrative Machinery," Ph.D. diss., University of Minnesota, 1976. For another example of a hereditary office in Ur III Umma, see D. M. McGuiness, "The Family of Giri$_x$-zal," *RA* 76 (1982) 17–25.

22. The limited attestation of Ur III documents may account for this fact although texts from Umma, Girsu, Dusabara, Adab, Drehem, Ur, Tell al-Wilayah and Ešnunna are all written in Sumerian, there are a few Akkadian texts from Nippur in addition to the predominantly Sumerian documentation from that city. The private "SI.A-a archive," most recently discussed by P. Steinkeller, *JAOS* 102 (1982) 643, includes a few texts written in Akkadian, as are a few documents from unknown sites which use northern calendars. The only Ur III text supposedly from northern Babylonia, published in Genouillac, *PRAK* 2 D. 49, cannot have

This turn of events can hardly be ascribed to preference for the vernacular; there is in fact very little evidence that Sumerian was a living language during this time.[23] Moreover, the situation in Sumer was hardly unique for there seems to be an almost universal preference for the use of foreign, often dead, languages in societies with restricted literacy. Walter J. Ong has described this phenomenon, noting the metaphorical use of the term "mother tongue" and the consequences of the distancing effect of the combination of a foreign language and the medium of writing.[24] The changes in written languages were not dictated by the ethnic makeup of the ruling classes. Something else was at play here and I can only suggest some of the ramifications of the matter. The use of languages which were primarily written, and I mean here not only Sumerian but also literary Akkadian ("Standard Babylonian") as well as possibly such languages as Eblaite, have direct social consequences. Let us turn to Ong.

> There are, however—or have been—languages, and extraordinarily influential languages, which have existed as no one's mother tongue, languages learned by males from other males, always as second languages acquired by those who already have other mother languages. Such languages are indeed spoken and hence are acoustic and "oral" phenomena. But they depend on writing rather than on oral speech for their existence. Writing establishes them at a distance from their immediate interpersonal human lifeworld where the word unites one human being with another, and particularly infant with mother. These sex-linked male languages have distanced their users very often from their fathers, too, for they have been acquired normally not from the learner's father at all but from some more distant males, such as schoolmasters or their equivalents.[25]

One could discuss many of the social and psychological consequences of the use of non-mother tongues in written communication in Mesopotamia as well as in other ancient Near Eastern societies.[26] What interests us here, however, are the consequences of this state of affairs for the analysis of bureaucracy in early Mesopotamia. First of all, I think one should point out the political ramifications of the switch to Sumerian accounting during the Ur III period. Granted, we have little or no documentation from the time of Ur-Namma and the earliest years of Šulgi but certain hypotheses may be offered. The organizational reforms of the latter king included not only standardization of weights and measures but also the establishment of scribal schools. We have hardly any contemporary evidence for this nor are the details known to us, but there is enough material available to indicate that that king did indeed reorganize education.[27] The combination of educational policy and what must have been a centrally directed revamping of local accounting procedures was facilitated by a standardization of the written language. This was achieved not only by a directive which must have mandated the use of Sumerian in accounting, but was in all probability accompanied by a reform in the writing system resulting in a relatively uniform use of sign values and sign usage in the Ur III state. The "non-standard" Nippur texts from private archives, which do not always conform to the normal orthographic rules of the period, are a

---

been excavated at Kish and undoubtedly belongs to the so-called early Drehem series for which see, most recently, D. I. Owen, ZA 71 (1981) 46.

23. There has been much discussion on this point but no one has as yet proposed a set of criteria which could be used to establish the time when Sumerian died out as a spoken language. Whatever the case may be, the rough estimate of the demise of Sumerian is not relevant to this discussion.
24. Walter J. Ong, *Interfaces of the Word* (Ithaca, 1977) 22–34.
25. Ibid., p. 25.
26. The use of Akkadian and Sumerian for only specific types of texts in the West, for example, is still in need of study.
27. See Å. Sjöberg, "The Old Babylonian Eduba," *Sumerological Studies Jacobsen*, pp. 159–79.

vivid reminder of the extent of this phenomenon.[28] Hence, one can propose to see language policy as independent from "ethnic" political movements and population change. Language can be an important instrument of power; the state that controls the dissemination of information maintains a strong hold, practical as well as ideological, upon its literate classes. Moreover, the change of official language provides an excellent opportunity for the reform of local accounting practices and channels of responsibility since it allows the central government to do away with certain residual survivals of previous patterns.

I have sketched here some of the problems which arose from the discontinuous patterning of third and second millennia state formations in Mesopotamia. The next matter which I would like to take up is the perpetuation of the system and the recruitment of new members of the middle and lower levels of the administration.

## 6. RECRUITMENT AND SOCIALIZATION OF BUREAUCRATS

The term that is most commonly encountered in discussions of Mesopotamian bureaucracy is dub-sar, traditionally translated as "scribe." Landsberger, Goetze, and others, however, have questioned this rendition, and have shown that in many cases this title did not refer to a specific occupation but simply denoted a graduate from a scribal school.[29] In Ur III times dub-sar was a general term for low and middle level bureaucrats. This can be demonstrated on the basis of the impressions of inscribed cylinder seals found on numerous administrative tablets from that period. Quite often we find that the tablet itself lists the sealing official as holding a specific office but the seal inscription designates him simply as a dub-sar. The titles which were held by "scribes" include i-rá-rá, ka-gur$_7$, kuš$_7$, má-lah$_4$-gal, nu-banda$_3$, sa$_{12}$-du$_5$ and even *hazānum* and sanga.[30] The sheer number of "scribes" also supports the hypothesis that the title covered a variety of occupations—for the Ur III period alone we know the names of over 1,560 dub-sars.[31] Often, future members of the highest levels of the administration used the title "scribe." A good example of this is the case of Ilšu-iliya, son of Ituria, the governor of Ešnunna. On his seal he was called dub-sar but he succeeded his father as the highest authority in his city.[32]

If dub-sar was a general word for bureaucrat then one should be able to conclude logically that literacy was one of the prerequisites for administrative service. This may appear redundant but it must be noted that there is, in fact, very little other evidence to support the hypothesis that a majority of bureaucrats could read and write. One could very well have otherwise suggested that officials themselves could not write but that they had scribes who did it for them. This may very well have been the case in many instances, but the important matter here is that middle and even lower echelon bureaucrats passed through the eduba, commonly translated as the "scribal academy," before they could aspire to any office. The consequences of this fact should not be underestimated. Often students of Mesopotamian literary and administrative texts proceed as if the two worlds had little to do with each other, but in the period we are discussing, at least, the two are inseparable. Admittedly, only a very few Ur III literary texts have been published to date and our knowledge of the literature is based primarily on

---

28. On the spellings in these texts see H. Sauren, "Untersuchungen zur Schrift- und Lautlehre der neusumerischen Urkunden aus Nippur," *ZA* 59 (1969) 11–64.
29. See, most prominently, B. Landsberger, "Scribal Concepts of Education," in Carl H. Kraeling and Robert M. Adams, eds., *City Invincible* (Chicago, 1960) 94–102.
30. The conventional translations of these terms are: perfume maker, herdsman/groom, granary superintendent, chief sailor, military lieutenant, recorder, mayor, and chief temple administrator.
31. The material on this subject has been collected in Hartmut Waetzoldt, "Das Schreiberwesen in Mesopotamien" unpublished Habilitationsschrift, University of Heidelberg, 1972.
32. R. M. Whiting, "The Reading of the Name DINGIR-šu-i-lí-a," *JAOS* 97 (1977) 171.

Old Babylonian copies. Nevertheless, I would suggest that one can venture some hypotheses on the matter. The Old Babylonian literary texts, primarily from Nippur, Ur, Isin, and Sippar, are almost without exception the exercises of schoolboys. As such they represent the curriculum of the scribal academy during a relatively short period of time. Most of the Nippur texts must have originated in the middle of the reign of Samsu-iluna while some of the Ur texts were written a generation or so earlier, during the time of Rim-Sin of Larsa.[33]

The content of this curriculum has little to do with practical administrative matters. Starting with basic exercises which were meant to facilitate the learning of cuneiform signs, the students proceeded to learn royal and divine hymns, debates, literary letters, myths, epics, and other literary compositions—all of them, in the south at least, in Sumerian. There is little evidence, among the actual school texts, of any training in practical matters; the model contracts, the mathematical exercises, and the Akkadian school letters constitute the only known remnants of such schoolwork.[34] Most of our evidence for administrative instruction comes only from idealized descriptions of school work found in the literary debates and in the post-Old Babylonian "examination texts."[35] What, then, was the purpose of drilling native speakers of various Semitic languages and dialects in the intricacies of the Sumerian language and literature? The answer, I think, is quite clear. The school was an ideological molder of minds, the place where future members of the bureaucracy were socialized, where they received a common stock of ideas and attitudes which bound them together as a class and in many ways separated them from their original backgrounds. Seen in this light, the literary texts acquire their proper ideological significance. The royal hymns celebrated the magnificence of the ruler and the myths perpetuated certain concepts of eternal cosmic order. I shall return to these specific ideas below; for the time being, however, I think it will suffice to say that the content of the texts is in many ways irrelevant to the main point of my argument. It does not really matter what they learned as long as they learned it and it made them different. The conceptual dimensions of literacy literally made them different human beings; they knew of matters that others only imagined existed, they even knew what year it was. In such a context the perpetuation of a dead literary language—Sumerian—has a definite function which helped to define membership in an exclusive club— the world of the bureaucracy.

It is impossible at present to trace the history of the uniformity of the school tradition and to discover the changes which were made in the curriculum within particular historical periods. Certainly it appears that some texts were widely distributed as early as the Early Dynastic period. The first true indication of conscious state reform of the schooling system most probably took place during the reign of Šulgi of Ur, who, in addition to practical administrative reforms, claims to have established schools in Nippur and in Ur. The royal hymns of the same king extol for the first time the writing of literary texts in honor of the ruler, and the sheer number of Šulgi hymns, combined with their unparalleled political rhetoric, suggests that this sovereign of Ur consciously reformed the school system in order to indoctrinate future bureaucrats with the propaganda of empire and of the charismatic force of the king.[36]

Very few Ur III literary texts are available for study, but the content of even this little group deserves attention. Already in this period there existed manuscripts of "Lugalbanda-Hurrum," which

---

33. M. Civil, *MSL* 14, p. 7.
34. See my remarks in *JCS* 35 (1983) 226.
35. Thus one must view with some caution the reconstruction of the school curriculum described by Å. Sjöberg, *Sumerian Studies Jacobsen*, pp. 159–79.
36. It is always difficult to determine which royal hymns were contemporary and which were composed later in a similar style. Some of the Šulgi texts definitely have traces of earlier writing practices. Royal hymns began with Ur-Namma, Šulgi's father, a fact documented by the discovery of an Ur III fragment of Ur-Namma hymn B; see M. Civil, "On Some Texts Mentioning Ur-Namma," *Orientalia* n.s. 54 (1985) 33–36. This article also contains an argument for the reading Ur-Namma rather than Ur-Nammu.

celebrates a hero from Uruk, the ancestral home of the dynasty, of the "Temple Hymns," which describe the shrines of a unified Sumer and Akkad and, perhaps most interesting of all, of the "Curse of Agade," a completely fictitious poetic depiction of the fall of the Akkadian state, an event which took place at most one generation or so before the beginning of the Ur III period.[37] The events which were distorted in this text were well within the reach of human memory and it is therefore particularly interesting that the school tradition was already manipulating history for propagandistic purposes, imposing the big lie upon the future officials of the state. But the "Curse of Agade" is in many ways the story of a doomed king, of excessive hubris on the part of the ruler. As such it also functions as a form of antidote against the bombastic claims of the rulers and provides us with a glimpse of another function of the school—the role of fashioning a permanent bureaucracy which would be independent of the figure of the ruler. Akkad was gone, but the story lingered on, distorted and manipulated in writing. The traditions fostered through the schools provided an ideological continuity for a bureaucratic class, independent, to a degree, from the vagaries of power at the top.

## 7. IDEOLOGY, CHARISMA, AND CONTROL

The justification of power and authority in early Mesopotamia was constantly threatened by the unstable nature of the political system. Local power in city-states had traditional justification, but the intermittent attempts at forging larger territorial states were confronted by the need for different forms of legitimacy. The constant rebellions against the Akkadian kings were symptomatic of the difficulties which were encountered by those who tried to counter the localistic, centrifugal forces of power in Sumer and Akkad. It was the Ur III dynasty, however, and more specifically its second king, Šulgi, which was responsible for the most systematic attempt to provide a reform of ideology for the purpose of legitimation of a new form of central power. Many of the elements of this new order had existed previously, but it was the combination and the new perspectives on these matters which distinguished it from the actions of earlier kings. Šulgi consolidated the military and organizational achievements of his father, Ur-Namma, by means of a series of practical reforms of the organization of the state, providing new standards of weights and measures, instituting a standing army, and inventing a new system of provincial structure and a standardized form of taxation.[38] These measures undoubtedly contributed to the short-lived success of the Ur III state, but they were also accompanied by other innovations which had wide-reaching ideological and economic consequences.

In every society there is a focal point where the central values which bind the community together reside. The existence of such a central value system has been argued by E. Shils in the following manner:

> There is a central zone in the structure of society. This central zone impinges in various ways on those who live within the ecological domain in which the society exists ... The center, or the central zone, is a phenomenon of the realm of values and beliefs. It is the center of the order of symbols, of values and beliefs, which govern the society.[39]

As Shils points out, this centrality is not geographical; it is found scattered in institutions and actions. Rather, as Clifford Geertz has phrased it, "It is a sign, not of popular appeal or inventive craziness, but of

---

37. For this composition see J. S. Cooper, *The Curse of Agade* (Baltimore, 1983). On the Ur III literary texts see my "On Some Early Sumerian Magical Texts," *Orientalia* n.s. 54 (1985) 217, n. 6.
38. These reforms are discussed in more detail by P. Steinkeller in his contribution to this volume.
39. E. Shils, "Center and Periphery," in *The Constitution of Society* (Chicago, 1972) 93.

being near the heart of things."[40] The varieties of charismatic acts and symbols of Mesopotamian royalty have yet to be analyzed in any detail and thus it is difficult to contrast the patterns established under Šulgi with those of his predecessors. It is possible, however, to delineate the areas in which the changes took place. The focus of the organization of charisma was unquestionably the deification of the king. The consequence of this act was to identify the ruler with the central zone of values of the society. A statue of the deified king now had a place in the temples of other gods, most notably in the central shrine of Enlil at Nippur.[41] Actual temples, or more precisely, temple estates of the divine king, were erected anew or were established in older places of worship in the major cities of the realm.[42] This allowed the crown to appropriate older temple estates in the name of the new god, thus scaling down the influence of local traditions and at the same time binding local elites to the new order. The extension of royal power to the temples, in economic as well as ideological terms, did not begin with the deification of the king. The tradition established by Sargon, according to which the ruling king of Sumer appropriated the office of high priestess of Nanna at Ur was continued for centuries and led to other such positions for royal children at Uruk, Nippur, Mari, Durum, and elsewhere.[43]

The propaganda of the ruler as the source of charismatic power and as the center of social values tied to a broader cosmic order was propagated by a wide-reaching cult of living and deceased rulers as well as through the new schools. For in the curriculum of the scribal academies, the indoctrination of the future bureaucrats now included in the curriculum not only myths, divine hymns, and lexical lists but also a new type of text—the royal hymn. This new "genre" consisted of a variety of thematic types, all designed to focus on different aspects of divine kingship. Public festivals, the open travels of the king, the majesty of royal buildings were all symbols of power to the majority of the populace, but for the scribes the school curriculum was a source of indoctrination in the values which were inherent in the sacred power of Šulgi and his successors. If it is indeed the case that Gilgamesh stories were made part of the school curriculum during the Ur III period, then one may be forced to see in this but an extension of the same idea. Gilgamesh, associated with Uruk, the home of the dynasty, provided these kings with an eponymous ancestor, a semi-divine hero who embodied the idea of this type of charismatic kingship and who became a god after his death.

---

40. C. Geertz, "Centers, Kings, and Charisma: Reflections on the Symbolics of Power," in *Local Knowledge: Further Essays in Interpretative Anthropology* (New York, 1983) 123.

41. *TCL* 2 5501 ii 9 and 24 mention the statues of Šulgi in the temples of Enlil and Ninlil, respectively. See R. Kutscher, "An Offering to the Statue of Šulgi," *Tel Aviv* 1/2 (1974) 55. The same sequence is attested in *MVN* 13 584:1'–2' and 8'–9'. It should be pointed out here that this practice antedated the deification of kings as is demonstrated, for example, in the case of Rimuš of Akkad who had a statue of himself placed before Enlil. See Rimuš b 12 xxvii 1–14 = xviii 1–17 (H. Hirsch, *AfO* 20 [1963] 68 and P. Steinkeller, *Oriens Antiquus* 23 [1984] 35). See also the studies listed in the following footnote.

42. See, in general, C. Wilcke, "Zum Königtum in der Ur-III Zeit," in P. Garelli, ed., *Le Palais et la royauté* (Paris, 1974) 180; J. Klein, *Three Šulgi Hymns: Sumerian Royal Hymns Glorifying King Šulgi of Ur* (Ramat-Gan, 1981) 31, n. 43. New evidence for the existence of a life-size statue of an Ur III ruler is presented by E. Sollberger, "A Statue for Šū-Suen," *Anatolian Studies* 33 (1983) 73–74. Most interesting, in this context, is the fact that the latter king also had a statue in the estate of the chancellor (alan ᵈšu-ᵈen.zu šà é sukkal-mah Kang, *SACT* 1 172:12). Most unusual is the occurrence of a statue of Kubatum, the wife of Šu-Sin, situated at the "gate of Enlil." See P. Steinkeller "More on Ur III Wives," *ASJ* 3 (1981) 80. Finally, we now have evidence for the transport of statues of kings to outlying regions of the empire upon their accession to the throne, as documented by B. Lafont, "Deux notes sur les règnes de Šu-Sîn et Ibbi-Sîn," *RA* 77 (1983) 69–71.

43. See W. W. Hallo and J. J. van Dijk, *The Exaltation of Inanna* (New Haven, 1968) 1–11; W. W. Hallo, "Women of Sumer," in D. Schmandt-Besserat, ed., *The Legacy of Sumer* (Malibu, 1976) 23–40, and P. Michalowski, "Tudanapšum, Naram-Sin and Nippur," *RA* 75 (1981) 173–76.

The cult of divine kings is also reflected in the naming patterns of the bureaucracy. Following upon a precedent already established under Naram-Sin, members of Ur III officialdom gave their children names which included the name of the king as a divine element.[44] More important, many lower and middle echelon officials changed their own names to include the divine royal element. This is clear from the fact that we have no names compounded with the elements Amar-Sin, Šu-Sin or Ibbi-Sin preceding the reigns of these kings. In each case the official in question had to be an adult at the time of the change of name, a fact which implies that this was a conscious, intentional act.[45] It is interesting that the *homo novus* Išbi-Erra, in clear imitation of his Ur III models, was a most popular figure in the naming practices of his officials.[46]

A peculiar case of the influence of this type of charisma is encountered in the relatively few cases in which individuals who were apparent outsiders, "foreigners" such as Amorites, bear names compounded with divine royal names.[47] Two places on the borders of the Ur III territory are the sources of such names, Marhaši[48] and Simanum.[49] Both cities were allied with the Ur government through diplomatic marriages: Liwwir-miṭṭašu, a daughter of Šulgi, became queen of Marhaši,[50] and Kunši-matum, Šu-Sin's child, was married to a member of the royal house of Simanum.[51] These are, admittedly, scant traces but one may suggest that these individuals changed their names to theophoric ones which included the deified rulers of Ur on the occasion of the alliances with the Mesopotamian state. A third example of this practice may perhaps be documented in the case of Mari. This state was independent of Ur and was allied with the south quite early in the Ur III period. The daughter of Apil-kin of Mari was married into the royal family of Ur.[52] The woman changed her name for the occasion to Taram-Uram but so far she has not been identified in any of the extant Ur III administrative texts. It may be only coincidence but there is a group of individuals from Mari, attested in documents from Šulgi 47 through the end of Amar-

---

44. Most conspicuous in this respect was the gala priest, Dada. Two of his children were named Hedut-Amar-Sin and Šu-Sin-migir-Eštar; see I. J. Gelb, "Homo Ludens in Early Mesopotamia," *Studia Orientalia* 46 (1975) 66.

45. See N. Schneider, "Herrschernamen als theophores Element bei Personennamen," *ArOr* 17 (1949) 351–58 and, more recently, I. J. Gelb, *Studia Orientalia* 46, p. 53. The sparse documentation from the time of Ur-Namma and the beginning of Šulgi's reign does not allow for any generalizations about these kings although it is significant that Ur-Namma, who was not deified, does not figure in personal names.

46. See the index of personal names in *BIN* 9.

47. To date all the attested examples include the name of Šulgi: hu-un-$^d$šul-gi (*TCL* 2 5505: 15); ša-at-$^d$šul-gi (*TRU* 267: 12); šul-gi-da (*ITT* 2 3470: 5); $^d$šul-gi-a-bí (*TCL* 2 5508 i 14; *HSS* 4 108 r. 5); $^d$šul-gi-ì-lí (*BIN* 5 119: 82; *Or* 47–49 21: 1; Buccellati, *Amorites* 10: 8); $^d$šul-gi-na-piš-ti (Buccellati, *Amorites* 14: 18); ur-$^d$šul-gi-ra (Falkenstein, *Gerichtsurkunden* no. 52: 18′–19′); šu-$^d$šul-gi (*MVN* 11 199: 6). hu-un-$^d$šul-gi lú-SU.A, mentioned in *PDT* 411: 9 and *PDT* 529 viii 15 may be the same person as the first one in this list; see *Rép. géogr.* 2 172.

48. *MVN* 13 lists four individuals from Marhaši whose names include the divine element Šulgi: me-ra-ah-$^d$šul-gi dumu ma-aš-hu-un-da-ah-li (l. 7, also in *PDT* 529 x 16), $^d$šul-gi-li-ba-ni dumu du-uk-ši (l. 21), a-ab-$^d$šul-gi dumu x [ ... ] (l. 22), and kàr-tab-$^d$šu[l-gi ... ] (l. 23).

49. $^d$šu-$^d$en.zu-PI-zu-um-i-šar-ri lú si-ma-[núm$^{ki}$] M. Sigrist, *Tablettes du Princeton Theological Seminary époque d'Ur III* (Philadelphia, 1990) no. 83:11.

50. Documented by the name of the eighteenth year of Šulgi's reign; see P. Steinkeller, "The Question of Marhaši: A Contribution to the Historical Geography of Iran in the Third Millennium B.C.," *ZA* 72 (1982) 259.

51. P. Michalowski, "The Bride of Simanum," *JAOS* 95 (1975) 716–19.

52. She is mentioned as é-gi$_4$-a of Ur-Namma in an Old Babylonian copy of a dedicatory inscription published by M. Civil, "Un Nouveau synchronisme Mari–III$^e$ dynastie d'Ur," *RA* 56 (1962) 213 (now fully available in M. Civil, "On Some Texts Mentioning Ur-Namma," *Or.* n.s. 54 [1985] 37–45).

Sin's reign, which includes five persons with Šulgi names.[53] One is tempted to propose that this group of officials from Mari was somehow connected with the presence of a princess from that city resident in Sumer, but one would have to further posit that they changed their names upon the accession, or more probably, upon the deification of Šulgi. It should be noted, however, that at least two other foreigners bore names compounded with royal theophoric elements, Dan-Amar-Sin, son of Gabadi of Tikitihum, and Šulgi-atal from Gumaraši.[54] However one chooses to interpret these facts, it is clear that the charismatic force of the deification of the Ur III kings had consequences which had effects outside the immediate circles of the central bureaucracy.

The charismatic aspects of early Mesopotamian kingship discussed above were undoubtedly part of the search for an ideological center which would provide an underpinning for the new concepts of "empire" arising as a result of the political innovations of the Sargonic and Ur III kings. It should be stressed, however, that often we can only guess at innovation for there is only a limited amount of direct evidence on the ideology of kingship in earlier periods. Much of what has been said on the subject in modern times is in fact extrapolated from later sources and it is doubtful that it has much bearing on the situation in the city-states of Mesopotamia preceding the attempts at unification which began with Lugalzagesi and Sargon. There can be little doubt that local traditions differed widely, although the written record, at least, provides some evidence of common textual sources dating back to the third millennium. The new concept of divine kingship, which began with Naram-Sin but which acquired new ideological features under Šulgi and his successors, was created in order to provide a broader vision of societal center, one which overcame localized forms which had been anchored in the city, the temple, and the city ruler. By displacing the ideational core through a variety of symbols centered around the figure of the divine king, the larger states gained access to allegiance and domination which could not have been theirs through force and economic power alone.

## 8. CONCLUSIONS

At the outset of this study I invoked the theories of Max Weber concerning the ideal types of political domination. The reason for this was not to ascribe certain Mesopotamian state formations to this or that category, but to open the way for discussion of officialdom within the context of domination, power, and charisma. It is clear that bureaucratic domination, with its reliance on strict rules and professional competence and training, never developed in these states; rather, they relied on traditional and charismatic forms of domination. The officials who worked within these frameworks were, in the loose sense of the word, bureaucrats, but this bureaucracy did not resemble the ideal type invoked by Weber, who based his definition on a study of contemporary Prussia.[55] In order to sketch out certain concepts of political control which need to be studied in this context I have, for the most part, centered my attention on the Ur III state. The reasons for this are not hard to define: the nature of the documentation, the central position in the development of crucial ideas in Mesopotamian ideology, as well as my own past interest in this particular historical period have led me to concentrate my attention on the time of this dynasty. This kingdom lasted only for a hundred years and the causes of its eventual

---

53. Amur-Šulgi, Šulgi-palil, Šulgi-abi, Šulgi-ili, and Hun-Šulgi; for references see A. Goetze, *JCS* 17 (1963) 18–19.
54. *TCL* 2 5500: 18 and 27. Gadabi and Šulgi-atal were most probably the rulers of their principalities. The latter name is Hurrian; for another possible example of such a mixed name see hu-ba-ᵈšul-gi-da, *BIN* 3 315: 2.
55. For Weber's conceptions of bureaucracy see "Bureaucracy," in S. N. Eisenstadt, ed., *Max Weber: On Charisma and Institution Building* (Chicago, 1968) 66–77.

decline and collapse were embedded within the structure of the state. Many, if not all, of the features described above were to be found in one form or another in previous historical periods, but it was Šulgi and his successors who combined these elements into a consistent form of influence and control and who set the pattern for dynasties to come.

# CHAPTER 5

## LEGITIMATION OF AUTHORITY THROUGH IMAGE AND LEGEND: SEALS BELONGING TO OFFICIALS IN THE ADMINISTRATIVE BUREAUCRACY OF THE UR III STATE*

IRENE J. WINTER
*Harvard University*

The Ur III period in Mesopotamia (ca. 2112–2004 B.C.) is generally recognized as marking a significant advance in the political organization of the territorial state and its attendant bureaucracy. At the same time, the period is characterized by major literary achievements: compositions that have themselves been seen as celebrations of the Mesopotamian polity.[1] The visual arts of the period, however, have been considered repetitive, formulaic, and lacking in richness when compared either to the art of the preceding Akkadian period or to the sister literary arts of the Third Dynasty of Ur.[2]

But, in fact, the single major artwork preserved, the Stele of Ur-Nammu, is a monumental undertaking in scale, quality of representation, and meaningful royal program.[3] Old Babylonian texts, preserving copies of descriptive epigraphs and inscriptions from Ur III monuments, provide evidence that there was once a considerable corpus of major representational sculpture.[4] It is rather the cylinder seals which seem less varied in subject matter and vitality.[5]

---

*The present article could not have been written without the help in its initial stages of Darlene Loding, Babylonian Section, The University Museum; and in its later stages of Piotr Steinkeller, Department of Near Eastern Languages and Civilizations, Harvard University—help gratefully acknowledged. My thanks also, for comments, conversations, and information to M.-Th. Barrelet, Hermann Behrens, Marc Cooper, Maria de J. Ellis, Robert Falkowitz, Robert C. Hunt, Mogens Trolle Larsen, Piotr Michalowski, Holly Pittman, Edith Porada, Norman Yoffee, and Richard Zettler.

1. See W. W. Hallo, "Royal Hymns and Mesopotamian Unity," *JCS* 17 (1963) 112–18.
2. See H. Frankfort, *Cylinder Seals: A Documentary Essay on the Art and Religion of the Ancient Near East* (London, 1939) 143 and Hallo in W. W. Hallo and W. K. Simpson, *The Ancient Near East: A History* (New York, 1971) 84.
3. A. Moortgat, *Art of Ancient Mesopotamia* (London, 1969), fig. 194 and J. Börker-Klähn, "Šulgi badet," *ZA* 64 (1975) 235–40.
4. These texts are to be the subject of a study by Miguel Civil, University of Chicago. For the present, see D. O. Edzard, "Neue Inschriften zur Geschichte von Ur III unter Šūsuen," *AfO* 19 (1959–60) 1–32, M. Civil, "Šū-Sîn's Historical Inscriptions: Collection B," *JCS* 21 (1969) 24–38, and idem, "On Some Texts Mentioning Ur-Namma," *Or.* n.s. 54 (1985) 27–45.
5. Frankfort, *Cylinder Seals*, p. 143.

However, it must be remembered that Mesopotamian seals are not only "works of art" according to modern designations; they were also functional "artifacts" within the Mesopotamian system, used to mark transactions in the very administrative and commercial spheres that were so highly developed in this period. It is at least a reasonable possibility, then, that we should view the limited repertoire of Ur III seals not as mechanically repetitive in a pejorative sense, but rather as *standardized*, much in the way of coinage and identity cards, in order to demarcate formally the place and/or authority of the seal owner within the administrative hierarchy. The legends inscribed on most seals clearly do just this by providing personal name (PN), patronym, and office of each individual. What I would suggest here is that, in the Ur III period at least, the imagery also conveyed general information regarding the place of the seal owner within the system, complementing the particulars of the legend in such a way that both text and image work together to provide a more complete context.

The present investigation of the combined verbal and visual message encoded on one particular set of Ur III seals is a direct consequence of a study of the iconography of Ur III "royal presentation scenes."[6] In those scenes, an individual, frequently bald and clean-shaven and often accompanied by an interceding goddess, is introduced into the presence of a seated figure, recognizable as a king by attributes of dress, headgear, seat, and object held in the extended right hand. These attributes differentiate the seated figure from similarly placed deities shown in related scenes.[7]

Results of that study suggest that the king functioned on a plane that is distinct from, yet parallel to, that of the gods similarly represented and that the king's distinguishing attributes are carefully and consistently maintained. The "deification" of kings in this period notwithstanding, neither the king's divine status per se nor his identity as a participant in the sacred marriage ritual[8] can account for his presence in the "presentation scene." Rather, the one primary role in which the king's function is exactly parallel to the gods'—a role that can be documented from petitions, legal, and literary texts—is that of giver of justice, maintainer of order in the land, and source of authority. This does not preclude attitudes of "worship" on the part of the standing individual toward the seated king, but in this light, one must see the presentation scene as part of a cultural system in which worship and audience, ritual and civil petition, sacred and secular, are not subject to modern divisions. Both primary actors in the scene are bound into mutual recognition and receipt-of-address, in a situation the context of which must include the full range of royal functions as described in contemporary texts.

It is my intention to pursue here the relationship between this imagery and the legends included on many of the seals—particularly those naming individuals holding office within the administrative bureaucracy of the state—as part of a lengthy dedicatory formula asserting the owner's service to the king. I shall argue that these seals represent an elaborate double-play on authority, understandable only when seal imagery and legend are taken together. On the one hand, the seal articulates the legitimate authority of the seal-owner, as granted by the king, to exercise his office within the Ur III bureaucracy; and on the other hand, the seal attests to the legitimate authority of the king, both to grant the particular seal and office, and, by implication, to exercise his divinely-sanctioned rule in the first place. I shall further suggest that these seals are restricted to a class of high public officials ranking just below the king in the administrative hierarchy, and that a public statement of legitimate authority in word and image is one of the seal's primary functions in the Ur III period.

---

6. I. Winter, "The King and the Cup: Iconography of the Royal Presentation Scene on Ur III Seals," in M. Kelly-Buccellati, P. Matthiae, and M. N. van Loon, eds., *Insight through Images: Studies in Honor of Edith Porada*, Bibliotheca Mesopotamica, vol. 21 (Malibu, 1986) 253–68.
7. See Moortgat, *Rollsiegel*, nos. 252 and 255–57 and Porada, *Corpus,* nos. 291–94 as contrasted with *Rollsiegel*, nos. 269–71 and Porada, *Corpus*, nos. 274–88.
8. E. Van Buren, "Hommage to a Deified King," *ZA* 50 (1952) 103.

The idea that there was a relationship between the legends and the imagery was pursued early on by Schneider,[9] but in most discussions of seals such as that of Frankfort, *Cylinder Seals*, this has not been taken into account. Van Buren gave examples of the types of inscriptions on the seals she discussed, but since her interests lay in demonstrating the connection of these representations to the role of the king in performing the sacred marriage, she did not investigate the legends with respect to the presentation scene itself.[10]

Barrelet touched on the subject in the context of her discussion of royal iconography, noting that the full nature of the relationship between the Ur III kings and their functionaries named on the seals had yet to be studied.[11] Franke, conversely, studied the inscriptions on seals actually presented to officials by various Ur III and Isin-Larsa period kings, but she did not differentiate among the various representational themes in her analysis.[12]

Essentially there are three descriptive categories for legends on Ur III seals showing seated kings (see the typology given by Gelb):[13] first, those marked by no inscription at all (e.g., Buchanan, *Early Seals*, nos. 230, 234, 269; von der Osten, *Newell*, no. 179), which tend also to be the poorest in quality; second, those that include only the name of the individual whose seal it is, his title/profession and/or his patronymic and occasionally the profession of his father (e.g., Buchanan, *Early Seals*, nos. 631, 640; Kang, *SACT* 1, nos. 42, 49, 108–16; Porada, *Corpus*, nos. 291, 294); and third, a group that includes not only the name and history of the seal owner, but also a lengthy dedication citing the name and titles of the current ruler in whose service the individual functions (e.g., our pls. 1–9). It is with these seals that we shall be mainly concerned here.[14]

9. N. Schneider. "Die *arad-zu-*, *dumu-ni-* und *in-na-ba-* Siegel von Ur III," *Or.* n.s. 5 (1936) 109–20 and idem, "Die Siegellegende der Geschäftsurkunden der Stadt Ur ... im 20. Jahrhundert v. Chr.," *Mededelingen van de Koninklijke Vlaamse Academie voor Wetenschappen, Letteren en Schone Kunsten, Kl. der Letteren* 12/6 (Brussels, 1950).

10. Van Buren, "Hommage to a Deified King," p. 105.

11. M.-Th. Barrelet, "La 'Figure du roi'" in P. Garelli, ed., *Le Palais et la royauté* (Paris, 1974) 52.

12. J. A. Franke, "Presentation Seals of the Ur III/Isin-Larsa Period" in *Seals and Sealing*, pp. 61–66.

13. I. J. Gelb, "Typology of Mesopotamian Seal Inscriptions" in *Seals and Sealing*, pp. 107–26.

14. An inventory of the seal legends citing each of the kings of Ur was first provided by Schneider, "Die *arad-zu-* ... Siegel von Ur III," and selected examples were included in Hallo "The Royal Inscriptions of Ur: A Typology," *HUCA* 33 (1962) 1–44. They have recently been the subject of a dissertation by D. McGuiness, "Studies in Neo-Sumerian Administrative Machinery," University of Minnesota, 1976. In addition, various sealings from Ur, Nippur, Drehem, Umma, Girsu/Lagaš, and Adab have been published as part of text corpora, as well as seals and sealings in several collections. This may well be the place to note how much more difficult the investigation of seal legends in relation to representations has been made by the manner in which most publications have divided the two subjects. M. T. Larsen, "Seal Use in the Old Assyrian Period" in *Seals and Sealing*, p. 93, lamented the tendency to isolate the study of seals from that of texts, and the situation has not improved since his writing. T. B. Jones, "Sumerian Administrative Documents: An Essay," *Sumerological Studies Jacobsen*, pp. 41–61, provided a history of the publication of Ur III economic and administrative texts to date. Of these, and several published since, many consistently leave out the seals on tablets entirely (Jones-Snyder); or publish only the seal legends, with either very poor and incomplete sketches (Kang, *SACT* 1 and 2) or no reference to imagery at all (Limet, *Textes sumériennes*; Pettinato, *MVN* 6; Owen, *NATN*). The joint publication of Sippar texts and sealings by M. Weitemeyer and E. Porada, *Some Aspects of Hiring of Workers in the Sippar Region at the Time of Hammurabi* (Copenhagen, 1962) provided a welcome exception to this, a model that unfortunately has not been followed. At the opposite extreme, most studies dealing with seals either did not include legends at all (Frankfort, *Cylinder Seals*), or included them in separate appendices, without taking the inscription into account in the analysis (Porada, *Corpus*, Buchanan, *Catalogue of Ancient Near Eastern Seals in the Ashmolean Museum* [Oxford, 1966]). Even the recent publication of the Yale Babylonian Collection seals and sealings (Buchanan, *Early Seals*) relegates the legends to the end in a separate section by W. W. Hallo, although at least sealings are included, and dating of tablets as well as ownership of seals is given in the main catalogue—but only as the author deems relevant, not as part of the consistent format of each entry. The whole category of sealings has

These longer inscriptions are generally written in two vertical columns perpendicular to the length of the seal. The left column provides the king's name and titles:

| | |
|---|---|
| RN | Royal Name |
| nita kalag-ga (Ur-Nammu or Šulgi), or lugal kalag-ga | powerful male, or powerful king |
| lugal Urim<sup>ki</sup>-ma | King of Ur |
| lugal an-ub-da limmu-ba | King of the four quarters |

The right column often begins a few millimeters lower than the left—presumably so that the individual's name is not on a level with that of the king.[15] The name of the seal owner is given; then, in varying order, one or more professions or titles of that individual, plus the name and sometimes the profession of his father; and finally, a formula of servitude to the king. This last portion takes two forms. One is the simple acknowledgment: arad-zu—i.e., the individual, having named the king, announces himself "your servant" (see caption, pl. 2a). The other form usually takes two lines, the first reading arad-da-ni-ir, the second in-na-ba—i.e., the king designates the individual as "his servant," to whom the king himself "has given" the seal:

| | |
|---|---|
| PN | Personal Name |
| dub-sar, ensi of GN, etc. | Scribe, governor of GN, etc. |
| dumu PN$_2$ | Son of PN$_2$ |
| (+ occasionally, profession of father) | |
| arad-zu, or arad-da-ni-ir in-na-ba | Your servant, or (To) his servant (the king) has presented (this) |

Whether the final phrase used follows the arad-zu or arad-da-ni-ir in-na-ba formula, a special relationship between the king and the owner of the seal is documented: the owner as the servant of that particular king, or, no less in service, as the recipient of the seal from the king himself.[16]

---

been much ignored—rarely included in text analyses, and rarely included in studies of seals. This last is particularly unfortunate, as the seals themselves, while sometimes preserved from good archaeological contexts (e.g., Frankfort, *Stratified Seals*), all too often occur in collections with no provenience. The papers presented in Gibson and Biggs, *Seals and Sealing*, particularly those of Franke and Whiting, mark a significant departure in this regard, as does the Yale catalogue (hampered only by the quality of the photographs and the absence of drawings in many cases). Ideally, one would envision a situation in which philologists would include drawings, if not photographs, of all their texts with sealings (as did Hussey in 1915, *Sumerian Tablets*, pt. 2, and Nies in 1920, *Ur Dynasty Tablets*; and as attempted by Sigrist for the Andrews University tablets [*AUCT* 3]—although there one has the impression that someone else has done the drawings, and signs in seal-legends are not always accurate). Conversely, one would envision a situation in which art historians and archaeologists would include legends as part of the primary catalogue entries, with both drawings and photographs (as in Moortgat, *Rollsiegel*), and make some reference to the nature of the texts on which sealings appear so that information is provided regarding the context of seal usage.

15. This is not always consistent, however. There are some instances where extended royal titles continue into the second column; others where the name of the seal owner begins at the bottom of the first column; and one case where the entire formula is contained in a continuous column of seven or eight lines. Nevertheless, the standard division of columns constitutes by far the majority.

16. It may be demonstrated further that the seals of the arad-da-ni-ir group belong to especially favored individuals, and tend also to be among those that are most elegantly cut and of the finest workmanship (see Franke, "Presentation Seals"). The simple formula of declaration by an individual as servant of a particular king in cylinder seal inscriptions is noted already in the Early Dynastic Period (ibid., 61). By the Akkadian

*Appendix 1* gives a list of seals with extended RN formulas that occur in conjunction with royal presentation scenes. The list has been generated by a survey of several seal and text publications. It is by no means complete; however, even with this partial list, certain patterns emerge which command our attention.[17]

All of the kings of the Third Dynasty of Ur are represented in inscriptions on seals with presentation scenes—from a single seal in the reign of Ur-Nammu (pl. 1a),[18] to a number from each of the subsequent reigns Šulgi, pls. 1b–2a; Amar-Suʾen, pls. 2b–3a and possibly pl. 4b; Šu-Suʾen, pls. 3b–6; and

---

period, the canonical formula of dedication is employed—especially by formerly independent rulers to acknowledge their subjection to the kings of Akkad (Frankfort, *Cylinder Seals*, p. 9). D. O. Edzard, "Die Inschriften der altakkadischen Rollsiegel," *AfO* 22 (1968) 12–20, has catalogued and discussed the various groups of formulas employed on Akkadian seal legends, in conjunction with Boehmer's publication of Akkadian seals, *Die Entwicklung der Glyptik während der Akkad-Zeit* (Berlin, 1965); the implications of this catalogue were subsequently discussed by Zettler, "The Sargonic Royal Seal" in *Seals and Sealing* (1977). Officials whose seals are presentation-scenes in the Akkadian period include one šabra-official (Boehmer, *Entwicklung*, no. 657) and one šakkanakku of Elam (ibid. no. 640); a scribe of Gudea of Lagaš also had such a seal (ibid. no. 439). Following the Ur III period, the dedicatory formula remained in use in the Isin-Larsa period, used by several servants of rulers of Ešnunna and Isin (see Frankfort, *Stratified Seals*, nos. 705, 709; Legrain, *UE* 10, no. 440; Nagel, "Glyptische Probleme der Larsa-Zeit," *AfO* 18 [1964] 319–27). By the Old Babylonian period, the formula had changed, giving the PN and patronymic first, then including the ruler's name in construct to the term "servant of ... " in the last line (e.g., Buchanan, *Early Seals*, no. 753). In Kassite times, the general Old Babylonian formula continued, with the profession of the individual sometimes following after the citation of service to the king and his titles (Limet, *Les Légendes des sceaux cassites* (Brussels, 1971) no. 2.16; or else, the profession itself is in construct to the king's name: i.e., lú-sag ("officer") (of) Burnaburiaš (ibid. no. 2.19). Like the representations, then, the formulas too are subject to stylistic changes which can be used for chronological purposes and also can be analyzed for cultural and historical implications.

17. It should be emphasized that the present discussion represents only a very cursory search through available publications. In the long term, what is needed is a careful compilation of all such examples, collating texts where only legends and no images have been published. In addition, a project such as this would lend itself well to quantitative analysis, seeking correlations between various titles of officials to variations in royal garb, or vessel held in the hand, stylistic differences on the basis of location (Umma, Drehem) or task named in legend or activity cited on tablet, etc. But this could only be effective if as complete a corpus of relevant exemplars were gathered as possible.

18. According to comments made by Giovanni Pettinato and David Owen at the meetings of the American Oriental Society, Baltimore, in 1983, there is a large corpus of unpublished Ur III texts in the Istanbul Museum, dated from the reign of Ur-Nammu into year 22 of Šulgi. If this is indeed the case, and if these tablets are sealed, it is possible we might add substantially to our catalogue, particularly as we have only a single example attributed to Ur-Nammu at present. It would certainly be welcome, as this one seal (Collon, *British Museum* 2, no. 469) is stylistically an anomaly in many ways: depth and hard edge of cutting; lack of cup in the king's hand; odd chair with high, curved back, and simple lines for seat and front legs but fully-modeled bull's legs behind. Since this seal does not come from a documented context, but was rather purchased by the British Museum (albeit quite early on), it seems wisest not to draw any significant conclusions from it. Conceivably our type of seal with RN-legend was not fully introduced until the administrative organization established by Šulgi after the death of his father. This would, in fact, make a great deal of sense. As Steinkeller (this volume) has argued, it is most likely that the rapid territorial and administrative expansion of the Ur III state (which included the creation of a unified administrative system for northern and southern Babylonia and an enormous bureaucratic apparatus plus the introduction of new accounting and recording procedures and new types of archival records) took place within a very limited period (about 10–20 years) under Šulgi, with all of the markings of a tightly-conceived and executed masterplan. This could well explain why our seals are so standardized in type—for perhaps the first and only time in Mesopotamian history—coinciding with Steinkeller's observation of the striking degree of overall "systemic cohesion that characterized the institutions of the Ur III state"; it would also explain why we have only one example (if that) of our seal type from the reign of Ur-Nammu.

Ibbi-Su'en, pls. 7–8). Both Hallo[19] and Barrelet[20] have suggested that representations of the seated king must be intentional references to the king cited in the accompanying inscription, since Ibbi-Su'en, apparently quite young at his accession to the throne, is shown in sealings from early in his reign as beardless, while later on he is fully bearded.[21]

The private individuals named on this particular group of seals represent the highest classes of government officials. *Appendix 2* lists the titles and offices mentioned on such seals, organized by reign. It will be noted that a seal of this type was held by the prince Šu-Su'en when he was šagina ("military governor") of Uruk under his father, Šulgi; and this is the seal type used also by the maternal uncle of both Šu-Su'en and Amar-Su'en, Babati, in his role as šagina of Maškan-šarrum and ensi ("civil governor") of Awal (see pl. 4b, a tablet found at Tell Asmar; the seal was also used on tablets found at Drehem = *BRM* 3, nos. 37 and 38). Indeed, we find a number of other šaginas having this type of seal, particularly individuals associated with provinces on the troubled northeastern and eastern frontiers, such as Simudar and Kazallu, (e.g., pl. 5a), as well as various ensis of formerly autonomous city-states, including Umma, Nippur, Adab, Marada, and Šulgi-Utu (e.g., pls. 1b, 2b, and 7).

For Umma, we now have a complete sequence of ensis from Šulgi to Ibbi-Su'en, and all would appear to have had this seal type: Ur-Lisi under Šulgi and Amar-Su'en, A'akalla under Amar-Su'en and Šu-Su'en, Dadaga under Ibbi-Su'en. Equally for Nippur, we have a sequence of three governors serving successive kings of Ur. Not only does each of them have a seal of this type, but also they are all related: Ur-Nanibgal under Šulgi; his elder son, Namzitarra, under Šu-Su'en; and his younger son, Dada, under Ibbi-Su'en.[22] And finally, in the highest office of the state, that of sukkal-mah ("chancellor"), we find the same family situation: the individual occupying that office under Šulgi, Ur-Šulpae, has this seal type, as does his son Arad-Nanna, sukkal-mah under both Šu-Su'en and Ibbi-Su'en. A third individual, one Nin-[ ... ], designated sukkal-[ ... ] on a damaged sealing, may in fact be Ninlil-amamu, sukkal-mah later in the reign of Ibbi-Su'en.

Also holding seals of the type under discussion are six sukkals, or couriers, of whom two are brothers, sons of a high-ranking judge (pls. 3 and 4a); three temple officials from Nippur, one of whom also holds the office of šà-tam-lugal, "royal clerk"; at least two šadubas (GÁ-du-ba), or highly placed official accountants, "chief comptrollers," (see pl. 8a and Goetze, *JCS* 17, p. 23); and two cup bearers of Šu-Su'en—a rank probably equal to the majordomo of the royal household. Finally, Šulgi's chief receiving officer for animals at Drehem, the kurušda, holds this type of seal; that he was a personage of considerable importance in the economic bureaucracy is clear when one considers that Šulgi established Drehem as a clearing house for animal distribution throughout the Ur III state.[23]

At least five of these individuals had their seals presented to them by the king (arad-da-ni-ir in-na-ba). They were associated with the full range of activities listed above, including the offices of šagina (Babati, pl. 4b), cupbearer (Abi-abih), sukkal-mah (Arad-Nanna), šà-tam-lugal and priest of Enlil (Lugal-azida), priest of Enlil (Sag-Nannazu), and šaduba (Ur-nigingar, pl. 8a).

Even the scribes cited on these seals seem to have held particularly high positions in their profession (see tabulation, *Appendix 3*): one became the ensi of Lagaš (Ur-Lama); another became the šagina of Simudar (Lu-Nanna): several held multiple offices; and there are family ties among many of them— either to other holders of this seal-type, or to persons of very high rank whose seals have not been preserved. For example, one scribe in the reign of Ibbi-Su'en was the son of a scribe of Šulgi (Nanna-

19. In Hallo and Simpson, *The Ancient Near East*, p. 86.
20. Barrelet, "La 'Figure du roi'," p. 52.
21. Ibid., fig. 1:100 and 101.
22. See R. L. Zettler, "The Genealogy of the House of Ur-me-me: A Second Look," *AfO* 31 (1984) 1–9.
23. See Hallo in Hallo and Simpson, *The Ancient Near East*, p. 81.

ludug, son of Lu-dingirra); both have presentation scene seals with seated king and extended RN formulas as legends. Another scribe, under Šu-Suʾen, was the son of the ragaba ("mounted messenger") of Šulgi; and his own son was a scribe under both Šu-Suʾen and Ibbi-Suʾen. All three generations of functionaries (Lu-Bau, Lu-Ningirsu and Ur-kugnuna-2) have this seal type. A third scribe under Ibbi-Suʾen was the son of the šaduba of that king (Ur-Šumah, son of Ur-nigingar, pl. 8b), while the seal of the father is of the in-na-ba type. A fourth scribe, having seals inscribed to both Šu-Suʾen and Ibbi-Suʾen, was the son of an ensi of Umma under Ibbi-Suʾen (Gududu, son of Dadaga); earlier in his career, the father had held the office of chief comptroller (šaduba) of Umma, to which the son subsequently succeeded,[24] and, at least once the father was made ensi, he too had this type of seal. A fifth scribe with this seal type was the son of the eventual šagina of Simudar under Šu-Suʾen (Nanna-kiag, son of Lu-Nanna).

The careers of at least twelve individuals span two or more reigns, and we can observe the changes in their seals, which were either completely reissued, or recut with a different royal name to acknowledge the new ruler: compare the seals of Ur-Lisi, ensi of Umma under both Šulgi and Amar-Suʾen and continuing into Šu-Suʾen,[25] replaced by Aʾakalla under Amar-Suʾen and continuing into Šu-Suʾen; Lu-Nanna, appearing as scribe under Šulgi and as šagina of Simudar under Šu-Suʾen; Babati-1, highly placed under both of his nephews (pl. 4b); Ur-kugnuna-1, sukkal under Amar-Suʾen and continuing into the reign of Šu-Suʾen, wherein he apparently was succeeded by his brother, Igi-annakezu (pl. 4a); Arad-Nanna, sukkal-mah under Šu-Suʾen and Ibbi-Suʾen; and finally, the scribes Babati-2, Ur-Šulpae and Lugal-ituda under Amar-Suʾen and Šu-Suʾen; Aham-arši, Gududu, and Ur-kugnuna-2 under Šu-Suʾen and Ibbi-Suʾen.

In each of these cases, while changes in the legends of the seals were made, the same imagery was kept or repeated in the new seal, suggesting that the particular presentation scene motif was meaningful for the individual. This hypothesis is further supported by the suggestion of Parr that while the two seals of Ur-Lisi with royal presentation scenes naming Šulgi and Amar-Suʾen mark the changes of reign that occurred while he was ensi of Umma, a third seal giving just his name and patronym is likely to be the seal used after Ur-Lisi was succeeded as ensi by Aʾakalla in Amar-Suʾen year 8.[26] In other words, once the official appointment was over, the seal and its official citation/affiliation with the king had to be relinquished.

At this point, two observations may be made regarding the holders of seals with extended RN formulas: first, all were generally very highly placed individuals within the administration of each Ur III king; and second, the use of the RN formula, and very possibly the royal presentation scene as imagery, was most likely not randomly distributed, but rather was appropriate to certain individuals and their rank.[27]

24. See P. Steinkeller, "The Foresters of Umma: Toward a Definition of Ur III Labor," in M. Powell, ed., *Labor in the Ancient Near East*, American Oriental Series, vol. 68 (New Haven, 1987) 73–115.

25. See P. A. Parr, "A Letter of Ur-Lisi, Governor of Umma," *JCS* 24 (1972) 135f.

26. Ibid.

27. It must be noted that not all seals of arad-zu or arad-da-ni-ir/in-na-ba type are restricted to representations of an individual before the seated king. One bulla from Drehem (Buchanan, *Early Seals*, no. 660) shows a man with long open skirt holding a lion-club and scimitar (Nergal?), yet the inscription of Šara-kam, sa$_{12}$-sug$_5$ lugal ("royal surveyor") cites Šulgi in the standard way. A tablet from Drehem showing a procession of two interceding deities and a king figure before a seated god includes the legend of a scribe, Lugal-[ ... ], who calls himself the servant of Amar-Suʾen (Grégoire, *MVN* 10, no. 245). And a text from Umma dated Šulgi year 46 has an RN-dedication to that king by Lugal-ezen, rá-gaba ("rider," "mounted messenger"), although the imagery on the seal is a presentation scene to a seated god (Buchanan, *Early Seals*, no. 606). In the in-na-ba- class, one seal of Ur-nigingar, šaduba ("comptroller") shows the king standing with a towel over his arm (Franke, "Presentation Seals," C5b; and see on this, Börker-Klähn, "Šulgi badet"); another seal,

One detail from the visual imagery tends to support the suggestion of purposeful distribution of these seals to officials with a close relationship to the king and a high position in the state, and that is the arrangement of figures on in-na-ba seals, those given to individuals by the ruler. Unlike most arad-zu seals showing an individual either preceded or followed by an interceding goddess, the arad-da-ni-ir in-na-ba seals generally include only two figures: the king and the individual; the interceding goddess is dispensed with (see esp. pl. 2b). Franke has argued that the individual depicted must be the seal owner himself, and, as these seals are given only to specially privileged individuals, their higher status is asserted visually through direct access to the king.[28] Those few arad-zu seals which also dispense with the interceding goddess and leave the individual face to face with the king, such as the second seal of Aʾakalla, ensi of Umma (see Buchanan, *Early Seals*, no. 652) and that of Naša, kurušda of Drehem, also belonged to the most highly placed officials, even if their seals were not explicitly a royal gift.

That this particular combination of imagery and legend may have been tailored to the rank or status of the individual is further suggested by cases in which it is *not* found: i.e., seals of scribes and other officials in the service of local ensis and šaginas rather than of kings. It will be remembered that Ur-Lisi, ensi of Umma, had a seal of this type. His own scribes, however, do not use the presentation scene with seated king as their image; nor do they cite the king in their dedicatory legends, but rather the ensi under whom they serve.[29] The same is true for the servants of Ur-Lisi or Aʾakalla (Kang, *SACT* 2, seal nos. 35, 68, 71, and 88); for a šabra-official of Ur-sagga, šagina of Umma (Buchanan, *Early Seals*, no. 562); for scribes of the ensi of Simurum (ibid., no. 679) and the ensi of Uru-sagrig (Sauren, *NY Public Library*, no. 281A); and for a number of servants of the ensis of Lagaš (Buchanan, *Early Seals*, no. 538; McGuiness, "Studies," pp. 239f.). The full implications of this difference in seals for social stratification in the Ur III period will be pursued below. However it may be suggested here that the absence of the presentation scene with seated king and extended RN formula in these cases corresponds to bureaucratic distance from the king, and thus supports the hypothesis that there was a positive correlation between the use of this particular seal type and proximity to the king through specific offices held by individuals in the state bureaucracy.[30]

---

      belonging to Ur-saga, sukkal ("courier"), has the king standing wearing a short kilt and facing a man holding a long stick (Franke, "Presentation Seals," C6c). Some sort of selection must be operating. Yet, whether this constitutes an aesthetic choice on the part of the king presenting the seal or the individual choosing it, or rather, if it is specifically tied to some consistent principle such as office, region, identity, etc. (as will be argued below for three sets of seals) is at present impossible to determine.

28. Franke, "Presentation Seals," pp. 64f.

29. See N. Schneider, *Or.* n.s. 5, pp. 114f. and D. McGuiness, "Studies in Neo-Sumerian Administrative Machinery," Ph.D. diss., University of Minnesota, 1976 (University Microfilms no. 77-19-062), 238.

30. Two exceptions to this are known to me. The first (A. Moortgat, *Vorderasiatische Rollsiegel* [Berlin, 1940] no. 252) includes a dedication to Dada, ensi of Nippur, by his scribe, Nanna-galzu; the second (ibid., no. 254) was given by Ur-Ningišzida, ensi of Ašnun, to Irrabani, his son. In *both* cases, the inscriptions run outside and beyond the neatly inscribed cases meant to hold the text (in the latter example, even running into the picture field, with signs both to right and left of the seated king), suggesting that the seal was cut and left blank, the inscriptions added secondarily. On the seal of Nanna-galzu, a male stands alone with clasped hands before a seated king, interceding goddess behind—a composition more common to arad-da-ni-ir/in-na-ba seals, and especially to highly placed individuals such as ensis and it is possible that in this case the ensi of Nippur provided a precut seal from his own store for his scribe. On the seal of Irrabani, a man with raised hand is led by an interceding goddess; however, before the goddess stands a second male with hands clasped, facing the seated king. Again, since the independent male figure fits the seals of several ensis, it is possible that both father and son are here represented—the father in effect introducing and preceding his son into the presence of the king. To pursue this issue of imagery reflecting relative distance from the king of Ur, it would also be extremely interesting to isolate seals of local ensis and rulers in regions *not* strongly tied to Ur in this period. For example, there is good evidence that the rulers of Mari were relatively independent at this time (A. Goetze, "Šakkanakkus of the Ur III Empire," *JCS* 17 [1963] 8; Kupper, "Rois et šakkanakku," *JCS* 21 [1967] 123). Six individuals are known who have the title šagina (*šakkanakku*), but it has been suggested that this

Three further sets of seals can be used to buttress the suggestion that there were meaningful correlations between seal imagery and the legends ascribing the seals to particular individuals. These include seals making reference to persons in the service of a particular god or temple, seals belonging to merchants, and seals belonging either to women or to individuals in the service of women.

For example, a tablet from Drehem includes the seal of a scribe, Lugal-[ ... ], whose standard RN formula cites Amar-Su'en, yet his seal shows a procession of two interceding deities and a king-figure standing before a seated god (Grégoire, *MVN* 10, no. 245). The tablet on which this seal is rolled deals with the delivery of animals for the festival of the god Ninazu, and it is tempting to speculate that the scribe in question is connected to the temple administration; hence, his seal shows a god. On the seal of one Ur-Lama, there is certainly a clear relationship between his profession as ka-gur of dNin-MARki and the representation of a deity on his seal (Pettinato, *MVN* 6, no. 216); while a second individual from Lagaš who calls himself a servant of the same deity also has a divine figure represented on his seal (ibid., no. 457). Two additional instances that belong in this group serve to demonstrate the range of variation in the standard RN formula as well as in imagery. The first is a sealing found on a bulla from Ur, dated Šulgi year 35, on which the owner's inscription cites Šulgi not by name, but by his title as Ennirzianna, priest of Nanna, while the scene shows a seated god with weapons, seated on an architectural facade throne, not a king seated on a fleecy stool (Legrain, *UE* 10, no. 403 = our pl. 9a). The inclusion of Šulgi's priestly title would seem therefore to correlate with the representation of the god (Nanna?). The second example is even more conclusive. The seal of one Lugal-engardu, prefect (ugula) of the temple of Inanna and priest of Enlil, is preserved on a tablet from Nippur (Buchanan, *Early Seals*, no. 681).[31] The dedication on the legend is to Amar-Su'en, with the king's standard titles, but an unusual epithet is added at the end: ki-ág ("beloved of") Inanna; and the seal itself shows a royal figure pouring a libation on a palm plant before the standing goddess (see partial representation of the seal, pl. 9c). Here, too, then, an official in temple service refers to the king by a religious title, and shows a religious scene related to the goddess he himself serves and whom he invokes for the ruler.

This last case is particularly interesting, as Lugal-engardu belongs to the same family as the ensis of Nippur, Ur-Nanibgal and his sons, all of whom had seals with the standard royal presentation scene (for example, the seal of Dada, pl. 7). However, as we now know from the work of Richard Zettler on the Inanna Temple archives at Nippur,[32] Lugal-engardu and Ur-Nanibgal represent two quite distinct branches of the family: the one monopolizing the civil office of ensi, the other engaged in the highest levels of temple administration.[33] It is therefore particularly important to note that the ensis utilize our seal type, while, with two exceptions, the temple administrators do not.

---

reflects not a position within Ur III officialdom, but rather subservience to the overlordship of the local god, Dagan, "king of the land" (ibid., p. 124). It is certainly to be expected that seals of such individuals (like those of the rulers of Ešnunna after Ibbi-Su'en year 2, discussed below) would not be our type for Mari, but would more likely show the individual before the god Dagan, or the goddess Ištarat, to whom we have several dedicatory inscriptions by rulers of Mari in this period (see Parrot, *MAM*, p. 21). In any event, one could conceivably plot seal types on a map of Mesopotamian city-states to have a sense of which areas were most tightly bound into the Ur III polity.

31. This seal, published by Buchanan, "An Extraordinary Seal Impression of the Third Dynasty of Ur," *JNES* 31 (1972) 96–101, and again in 1981, *Early Seals*, no. 681, has been redrawn by Zettler. See *JNES* 46 (1987) 60, fig. 1.
32. R. Zettler, "The Genealogy of the House of Ur-me-me."
33. Zettler argues elsewhere (this volume and "House of Ur-me-me") that these offices of temple administration also carried with them some ritual functions.

One of the exceptions is Sag-Enlil, son of Lugal-engardu, who succeeds his father as ugula of Inanna under Ibbi-Su'en; the other is Lugal-azida, priest of Enlil under Ibbi-Su'en,[34] who may have been related to this family, as a paternal uncle of Lugal-engardu bore the same name. While we have no explanation for the first case, we know that for the second, the presentation scene seal of Lugal-azida is an in-na-ba seal, presented by the king, and that, in addition to his priestly office, the seal-owner was also a šà-tam lugal ("royal clerk").[35] He thus held a high civil office as well, and so it is not impossible that other individuals with priestly titles could have had dual roles. In fact, of the more than seventy seals of this type which I have collected, only three belong to individuals with priestly titles (the two cited here plus the seal of Sag-Nannazu—see *Appendix 1*, V, n). All of the owners are associated with Nippur, and all three instances occur in the reign of Ibbi-Su'en. It may well be that this last king of the Ur III dynasty simply had a special relationship with Nippur, or employed its temple administrators in new ways. Apart from these, all known holders of royal presentation-scene seals seem to have had civil titles.

In general, then, if highly placed individuals related to temple activities and cult service were using religious scenes on their seals, appropriate to their temple functions, it would support the suggestion that seals showing officials before the king were purposely distributed among individuals holding secular office—civil and military governors, administrative officers, and functionaries of the royal household.

It must further be noted that not all secular professions are represented in the list of royal presentation-scene seal holders; and this, too, is likely to be significant. There is, for example, a marked absence of seals designating the owner as dam-gàr ("merchant"), despite the fact that mercantile activities constituted an essential and highly developed subdivision of economic life in the period.[36] A typical merchant's seal contains only the simple three-line legend: PN, son of PN$_2$, dam-gàr (Porada, *Corpus*, no. 277; Buchanan, *Early Seals*, nos. 520, 540), and will contain a presentation scene before a seated god or a heroic combat scene as image. Only one full RN-formula of a merchant is known to me: the seal of Aba-Enlilgin (Owen, *NATN*, no. 680). Unfortunately, when the sealing (UM 29–16-162) was collated in the University Museum, Philadelphia (with the help of Hermann Behrens), nothing of the imagery was preserved except the back of the head of a standing bald male. This would suggest a presentation scene, but whether royal or divine cannot be determined. The dedicatory formula can perhaps be understood in light of the activities of one merchant, named Ur-DUN, who on at least one occasion reported directly to the king on conditions in the eastern provinces.[37] In other words, there must have been instances in which a merchant acted politically for the king, and may well have enjoyed quite high status and royal favor. Nevertheless, since we have no merchant's seal preserved that shows an individual before a seated king, and only one with an extended RN-formula as legend, we must conclude that the lack of examples in our category is meaningful. It corresponds with what we know from other sources—that merchants were mainly of a rank below administrators,[38] and, unlike merchants in the succeeding Old Babylonian period, tended to act quite independently of the crown in Ur III times.[39] This case, too, then, would tend to substantiate our suggestion that royal presentation scenes in conjunction with extended dedicatory formulas on seals were reserved for individuals within the *state* bureaucracy.

---

34. E. Sollberger, "Three Ur-Dynasty Documents," *JCS* 19 (1965) 26–30 and Franke, "Presentation Seals," no. C-4b.
35. See also M. Gallery, "The Office of the *šatammu* in the Old Babylonian Period," *AfO* 27 (1980) 1–36.
36. See A. L. Oppenheim, "The Seafaring Merchants of Ur," *JAOS* 74 (1954) 6–17.
37. See P. Michalowski, "The Royal Correspondence of Ur," Ph.D. diss., Yale University, 1976, p. 40.
38. P. Steinkeller, personal communication.
39. See Oppenheim, "Seafaring Merchants of Ur," and N. Yoffee, *The Economic Role of the Crown in the Old Babylonian Period* (Malibu, 1977).

A parallel situation may be observed for seals related to women. An unusual amount of information exists concerning royal and highly placed women in the Ur III period,[40] including the seals of several individuals and their servants. In particular, we have two seals of Ninhilia, wife of Aʾakalla, ensi of Umma, and one seal belonging to the wife of the previous ensi, Ur-Lisi.[41] The husbands of both of these women had official seals with RN-formulas and royal presentation scenes; the women did not. The seals of Ninhilia are particularly interesting because the seated figures in the presentation scenes are in fact goddesses, not gods; and on one seal a woman is being led into the deity's presence. Similarly, on a sealing from Ur, the inscription again names a woman, Nin-addana, wife of Zi-lim, and the image again is that of a figure (unfortunately indistinguishable as to sex) before a seated goddess (Legrain, *UE* 10, no. 423 = our pl. 10b).[42] Once more, then, the imagery seems tailored to the owner.

For all three categories of seal holders just considered, temple officials, merchants, and women, it is likely that significant choices were operating with respect to seal imagery and legend, and that these choices were determined at least in part by the identity of the owner. It is not possible to demonstrate absolute consistency in this. However, as Kelly-Buccellati has shown with a group of Old Babylonian seals, there are high percentages of correspondence—in the case of her corpus, between god represented and god cited in legends,[43] and in the case of our corpus, between the profession of seal owner and the combination of seal image and legend. While the present analysis has not made use of quantitative methods, the examples gathered here suggest that there is indeed a compelling degree of correspondence between the figurative and epigraphic elements on the seals and the identity of their owners.

It also seems to be the case that the full RN-formula, with its canonical citation of king and official, occurs most frequently in association with the *royal* presentation scene. Earlier in the scholarly literature, when this motif was interpreted as "worship," Schneider noted the apparent disjunction between the essentially practical character of the legends and the so-called religious nature of the imagery.[44] But on the basis of what I have argued for the aspects of petition, judgment, and conferment of authority inherent in the presentation scene,[45] the imagery may be considered to be as appropriate to the official as the inscription. In short, I would suggest that use of the royal presentation scene is intended to convey the visual information that the individual is engaged in the royal service, just as the legend accomplishes this in words.

Thus far, we have discussed mainly the imagery and legends on these Ur III seals in terms of who owned them. Despite the fact that Franke has called "the attempt to formulate relationships between the owners of cylinder seals and the scenes depicted on them ... one of the most unrewarding aspects of the study of cylinder seals,"[46] I suggest that the glimmer of a rational system is there, pairing individuals with imagery appropriate to his or her position. Support for this statement, and further insight into the

---

40. See especially P. A. Parr, "Ninhilia: Wife of Ayakala, Governor of Umma," *JCS* 26 (1974) 90–111, P. Michalowski, "Amar-Suʾena and the Historical Tradition," in M. de J. Ellis, ed., *Essays on the Ancient Near East in Memory of J. J. Finkelstein* (Hamden, Connecticut, 1977) 155–57, and idem, "Royal Women of the Ur III Period, Part II: Geme-Ninlila," *JCS* 31 (1979) 171–76, and P. Steinkeller, "More on the Ur III Royal Wives," *ASJ* 3 (1981) 77–92.
41. See the article of Parr cited in n. 40.
42. The seal of a priestess from Assur apparently also contains the image of a seated woman, but without divine crown (Larsen, personal communication), and one wonders if this could represent the seated priestess herself.
43. M. Kelly-Buccellati, "Towards the Use of Quantitative Analysis in Mesopotamian Sphragistics," *Mesopotamia* 12 (1977) 41–51.
44. N. Schneider, "Die *arad-zu-* ... Siegel von Ur III," p. 109.
45. Winter, "The King and the Cup."
46. Franke, "Presentation Seals," p. 61.

importance of these seals, can be adduced from an investigation into how they were used within the context of Mesopotamian society.[47]

In a series of important papers presented at the University of Chicago symposium on seals and sealing in 1975, several scholars discussed the ways in which seals functioned in Mesopotamia.[48] As is commonly known, but all too commonly ignored in discussions of stylistic or iconographic properties of seals, these objects were intended to function in quite specific ways: as markers of their owners, they served to witness, guarantee, acknowledge receipt or confirm obligation when rolled on commercial or administrative documents, letter orders, envelopes, bullae, jar and door sealings.[49]

The power of a seal in obligating its owner is made clear in the few references we have to lost or contested seals. In one such case, copied in the Old Babylonian period from an Ur III text,[50] public announcement was made of the loss of the seal of Ur-DUN, merchant, to absolve him of any further obligation deriving from its use. The announcement was sufficiently important that it was witnessed and sealed by the current ensi. This Ur-DUN is presumably the same individual cited above, who acted on behalf of the king on at least one occasion; and he is also likely to be the author of a letter-prayer to Šulgi,[51] suggesting that he was a personage of some prominence, able to petition the king directly. In another case, the loss of the seal of a man named Lú-Ninšubur is announced; the kind of stone the seal was made of was indicated so that it might be recognized.[52] And from the Old Babylonian period there are instances in which seal cutters are called in to act as witness in disputes regarding the authenticity of seals cut for particular transactions.[53]

The degree to which the seal itself implies obligation and responsibility is further apparent in cases when an individual cited in the text of a tablet makes use of the seal of another person when "signing." Examples were collected by Schneider,[54] and include instances of individuals using brothers' or fathers'

---

47. An ideal study of how seals were used should investigate systematically not only seals and sealings, but the contents of tablets, bullae, and envelopes on which the seals were impressed—to see, for example, how often and in what circumstances seals of particular officials were used and what was the range of activities associated with the office. From this, one could expect to learn a great deal more about the administrative and control structures by charting domains in which certain officials functioned (as, for example, in the early Isin period where the sukkal-mah acted as comptroller in several transactions having to do with a workshop of wood-, leather-, reed-, and felt-workers, suggesting that at least some of their production was under royal control [M. Van de Mieroop in a paper at the meeting of the American Oriental Society, Baltimore, March 1983]). One would wish to know more as well about the frequency with which individuals used the seals of others, although I do cite a few instances here; and how often an individual's office as mentioned on the tablet does or does not correspond with his office as cited in the legend of the seal, given the fairly high degree of mobility for administrators from city to city (viz. Zariqum who apparently moved from šagina of Assur to ensi of Susa [Hallo, "Zāriqum," *JNES* 15 (1956) 220–25], or Apilaša, from special emissary in Nippur to šagina of Kazallu [Kutscher, "Apilaša"]), and from office to office within cities (as when Dadaga moves from head of the "fiscal office" at Umma to the office of ensi, succeeding A'akalla, some time late in the reign of Šu-Su'en or early Ibbi-Su'en [Steinkeller, "The Foresters of Umma,"] and see also the seal of his son, Gududu; see D. McGuiness, "The Family of giri$_x$-zal," *RA* 76 [1982] 17–25).

48. See especially the papers of Steinkeller, Zettler, Larsen, and Renger in *Seals and Sealing*.

49. See Steinkeller in ibid., p. 42 and Larsen, p. 98.

50. F. Ali, "Blowing the Horn for Public Announcement," *Sumer* 20 (1964) 66–68 and idem, "Sumerian Lectures: Two Collections from the Old Babylonian Schools," Ph.D. diss., University of Pennsylvania, 1964, text B-12, also Michalowski, "The Royal Correspondence of Ur," pp. 19–20.

51. W. W. Hallo, "Seals Lost and Found," in *Seals and Sealing*, p. 57.

52. Ibid., p. 55.

53. See Renger in ibid., p. 79.

54. N. Schneider, "Stellvertretende Siegelung der Vertragsurkunden in der Ur III-Zeit," *Or.* n.s. 16 (1947) 417–21.

seals, sometimes even after the original owner's death, presumably because the seal was known.[55] The practice is also seen in administrative contexts, where an official uses the seal of his predecessor because it is associated with the office;[56] or where, for some other reason, a substitute seal is used because the appropriate seal is not available.[57] Finally, we know that, at least in the Middle Assyrian period, a senior official could authorize the use of his seal by subordinates on official business.[58] In other words, the seal can stand not only for the individual, but also for the firm or office, carrying the same degree of obligation in all cases.

For high level political officials—ensis or šaginas—the seal of the individual would likely carry great weight in validating orders. On the basis of texts preserving some of the royal correspondence of the Ur III period, one can reconstruct most graphically the authority of the offices with which our seals would have been associated. An excellent example is contained in the correspondence concerning a man named Aradmu, who was sent by Šulgi to stabilize the taxes of the region of Subir.[59] In his report to the king, Aradmu recounts that he was received by Apilaša, the local šagina, or military governor, and complains:

> l. 11   The one who was sitting did not rise
>
> l. 16   He sat on a throne set with (a) quality cloth (cover)

—in other words, by retaining the socially dominant seated position, significant for the imagery of our seals as well, the local official was disrespectful, not only to the king's envoy, but, as implied by Aradmu, to the king himself. But the šagina's behavior is justified by the king in his response to Aradmu:[60]

> ll. 18–26   If my high commissioner had not ... sat on a throne set with quality
>             cloth ... (and) by his own authority removed ensis from office ... how
>             else could he have maintained order in the territory?

This exchange is significant since it documents the charge given by the king to officials acting on his behalf and allows us to judge just how important the seals of such officials would have been in issuing and implementing orders. It is all the more illustrative because a seal of Apilaša has been preserved, which identifies him as šagina of Kazallu in the reign of Šulgi's son, Šu-Suʾen; and it is precisely of the type we have been discussing (see pl. 5a).[61] The authority required by Apilaša as part of his continuing office, even in facing challenges to his activities by other royal envoys, is thus put together with his possession of this particular seal type. The combined evidence stands as a particularly vivid illustration of what we have suggested to be the power inherent in the seals themselves: they represent the concrete manifestation of the seal owner's authority to act within the royal bureaucracy.

That evocation of royal affiliation in the legend and representation of direct access to the king in the imagery was a substantial component of this authority may be demonstrated by material excavated at

---

55. See Larsen in *Seals and Sealing*, pp. 98f. and Oppenheim, *Eames*, p. 30, no. C16.
56. See Hallo, apud Buchanan, *Early Seals*, no. 452, with regard to the seal of Naša, chief receiving officer at Drehem, used by his successor, Abba-šaga.
57. See, for example, Oppenheim, *Eames*, p. 40, no. D24.
58. See W. Röllig, "Notizen zur Praxis der Siegelung in mittelassyrischer Zeit," *WO* 11 (1980) 113.
59. The texts are edited by P. Michalowski, "The Royal Correspondence of Ur," pp. 39f., corresponding to F. Ali's text A-1.
60. Michalowski, "The Royal Correspondence of Ur," pp. 155f. (Ali's text A-2).
61. See R. Kutscher, "Apillaša, Governor of Kazallu," *JCS* 22 (1969) 63–65. See Buchanan, *Early Seals*, no. 648x.

Tell Asmar, ancient Ešnunna. The city-state was under the domination of the kings of Ur from about Šulgi year 30 to Ibbi-Suʾen year 2.[62] Several seals belonging to officials from this period at Ešnunna were found;[63] they include examples from the reigns of Šulgi, Amar-Suʾen and Ibbi-Suʾen, and all use the RN-formula coupled with scenes representing the seated king. The last seal (= As.31-T.188) contains the standard dedication to Ibbi-Suʾen by a scribe, son of the ensi who had built and dedicated a chapel to king Šu-Suʾen of Ur at the site.[64] It is especially significant, therefore, that as soon as Ešnunna regained its independence from Ur, both legends and images on seals shifted markedly: replacing references to the king of Ur by verbal and visual citations of the local city-god, Tišpak.[65] The new legend formulation follows closely that of the former RN-citations, but now reads: "Tišpak / mighty king / king of the land of Warim," and then goes on to designate the seal owner. The new imagery substitutes the god Tišpak—recognizable by his attributes of twin dragon-headed *mušhuššu*-creatures issuing from the shoulders—for the seated king.[66] Since the owner of the seal illustrated here (Bilalama, to whom his father, the current ensi, presented the seal) is a political, not a temple official, these changes cannot be explained on the grounds of his professional ties. That the change is rather to be correlated with the political shift is corroborated by the fact that the dates on tablets also shift from year-names established by and referring to deeds of the kings of Ur to year-names relevant directly to Ešnunna. Clearly, both official state year-names and use of official state seals had been politically necessary during the hegemony of Ur, and ceased to be either necessary or desirable with independence. The situation at Ešnunna therefore underscores the political, official, and affiliative role of the RN-formula and the royal presentation scene on our seals within the Ur III network.

In sum, the Apilaša case cited above requires that we see the combination of legend and image on seals as functioning to confer legitimate authority upon the individual using the seal, and thereby upon any transaction in which he or she is involved. The Ešnunna case further indicates that, in return for office sanctioned by the crown, subservience and allegiance to the higher granting authority was expected.

Seals which make reference to the king, therefore, actually provide two messages simultaneously. Both verbally and visually, they act on the one hand as signifiers of status, office, legitimacy, and affiliation for the owner, calling upon the whole political hierarchy as party to the act for which the seal is being used; and on the other hand, they also acknowledge and affirm dependence upon the system which has granted the seal owner his office.

62. H. Frankfort, S. Lloyd, and T. Jacobsen, *The Gimilsin Temple and the Palace of the Rulers at Tell Asmar*, OIP 43 (Chicago, 1940) 3.
63. Ibid., nos. 1, 3, 5.
64. Ibid., pp. 134f. I do not feel qualified to enter into the discussion of the proper reading of the owner's name on seal no. 5 (see Whiting, "The Reading of the Name DINGIR-šu-ì-lí-a," *JAOS* 97 [1977] 171–77 and bibliography cited there). Yet, of course, were that name to be the same as that cited in OIP 43, nos. 6–8, it would make our case all the more striking, since in the first case (seal no. 5) the individual would be shown in a standard presentation scene, subordinate to the king of Ur, with a standard RN-formula in the legend, and would then subsequently shift (seals nos. 6–8) not only his titulary but also the representation once Ešnunna became independent of Ur. Nevertheless, given the philological arguments for reading that name as ᵈŠu-ilija, and the impossibility of checking the tablet containing the legend (Whiting, "DINGIR-šu-ì-lí-a"), I refrain from including that argument in the body of the present text.
65. H. Frankfort, *Stratified Cylinder Seals from the Diyala Region*, OIP 72 (Chicago, 1955), nos. 705 and 709. See our pl. 10c.
66. Edith Porada reminds me that this seal has actually been recut to accommodate both the legend of Bilalama and the *mušhuššu*-attributes of the seated god to conform to Tišpak. Another instance in which both representation and citation of the god appear on the same seal from Ešnunna occurs in the Akkadian period (Frankfort, *Stratified Seals*, no. 593), where an individual identified as the gal-sukkal of Tišpak has the god depicted on his seal, this time with the characteristic *mušhuššu* issuing from the hem of the god's skirt.

This is surely why individuals changed seals with the advent of a new ruler, or with a political shift; and why, by the same token, individuals might use seals other than their own, as long as they had the delegated authority to do so.

While all of this—the wedding of legend and image on seals to convey legitimacy of the seal owner, and the legitimation of the transaction by use of the seal—makes perfect sense on an ideal plane, actual practice, as is so often the case, is somewhat looser. In some cases, an official might use a seal citing one king on tablets dated well into the reign of the succeeding ruler (e.g., seals of Lú-Bau, Utu-GÍR-gal, and Ur-bagara[?] that name Šulgi, but are used in years 1 and 5 of Amar-Suʾen, respectively).[67] In others, although ideally legend and image should be seen as complementary and jointly conceived for each individual, the legend has clearly been added afterward, with portions of the inscription extending beyond the boxed lines engraved to contain the text.[68] It makes one wonder whether a stock supply of certain types of seals might not have been cut and kept in reserve—their meaning and ultimate use known and anticipated, the particulars of the inscription added as needed.

Also ideally there should be an exact correspondence between the individual and his official title(s) designated on the tablet as sealing the document (kišib PN, clearly indicated for example, on the tablet with seals of Babati, pl. 4b) and the same individual and title(s) on the seal impression on the tablet. But in fact, there are frequent discrepancies. We have noted above instances in which the seal of one individual is sometimes substituted for another.[69] But there are also cases in which an individual is cited on the tablet as holding one office, while the seal legend has him in another office—sometimes concurrently held, more often an earlier, less prestigious role (e.g., Utumu of Lagaš, nu-banda official on the seal, šabra ["chief steward"] on the tablet).[70]

Finally, the theoretical balance between inscription and image for which we have argued above is based upon the ideal visual impact of a complete rolling of the seal. This is certainly the way in which the ancient seal was conceived and executed, with an organized composition of elements; and it is the way in which seals are published in scholarly works, with illustrations of modern impressions (e.g., pls. 1a and 10c). Nevertheless, it is important to note that on the tablets, bullae, and sealings preserved from antiquity, the seals are not always rolled with an eye toward a complete and consecutive visual sequence. Rather, when one looks at original sealings, the central place is often given to the inscription (pls. 2a, 3a, 4a, 5a, 7, and 8b). Quite frequently the rolling was begun with the figure immediately to the right of the inscription on the seal, even if that figure was part of the far end of the visual sequence. It is likely that this was done to ensure that the legend would be impressed intact.[71] Once the legend was impressed, the rolling often did not continue around to a complete visual sequence on the far side, but rather stopped with the impression of the seated king immediately to the left of the inscription block.[72]

---

67. See Buchanan, *Early Seals*, nos. 639 and 642 and *Ashmolean*, no. 411; see also Steinkeller, "Seal Practices in the Ur III Period" in *Seals and Sealing*, p. 47. In one case, at least, the reverse occurs: Buchanan, *Early Seals*, no. 637 is a tablet dated in Amar-Suʾen year 9, but the seal of Babati impressed on it already names Šu-Suʾen as ruler.
68. As in Buchanan, *Early Seals*, nos. 649 and 650.
69. See also Steinkeller, "Seal Practices," p. 43.
70. Ibid., p. 47. The question must be raised whether these should be seen as consecutively held positions, or whether they could not be titles held concurrently—the seal having more relevance for one function than for another. In any event, there are a number of cases in which it would appear that a single individual had more than one seal (see Zettler, "House of Ur-me-me" in regard to Lugal-engardu; Franke, "Presentation Seals" in regard to Ur-nigingar), with more than one type of imagery, for use at the same time—possibly representing the distinction between one's various offices and/or personal seal.
71. See Buchanan, *Early Seals*, nos. 642, 644, 649 and Legrain, *UE* 10, nos. 422, 433, 436.
72. For example, Legrain, *UE* 10, nos. 403, 404.

In this way, the legend was bracketed by figures; but, since the rollings were made especially carefully to give the complete figure of the king, not just enough to get past the inscription, we might further suggest that the royal figure was purposely impressed, as the most important element in the image—the visual signal of the authority that lay behind the seal-holder in his transactions.

Nevertheless it is clear that primary emphasis was placed on the inscription, especially on bullae where the space was limited. This verbal emphasis is best understood in the light of the expanded bureaucracy of the Ur III period. The earliest seals and sealings preserved, those of the Uruk period, contained no inscriptions. Legends were first systematically added to figural representations on seals in the Early Dynastic III period, ca. 2500 B.C. In the subsequent Akkadian period, ca. 2350 B.C., the organization of the inscription became a significant part of the balance of the composition,[73] yet, even then, the percentage of inscribed seals was relatively small.[74] By the Ur III period, it would seem that the information contained in the legend had come to take precedence over the imagery—particularly within the official circles in which royal appointees functioned. It is important to note in this regard that those to whom seal impressions were directed were, after all, literate fellow bureaucrats. In earlier times (and perhaps also in later periods, for transactions outside the official state machinery), seals of individuals must have been recognized by associating identifiable variants in the imagery with particular owners. But by the Ur III period, with the increased standardization of the imagery, and a concomitant increase in the number of individuals active in administrative affairs, seal owners had to be identified by a reading of name, patronym, and titles. In addition, it may have become increasingly more important to verify that the individual held the appropriate office for the authority he was assuming. The visual imagery was not entirely abandoned on official seals, as it was on later Islamic and Chinese seals; but it came to provide a more general category of information, the generic of official position and sanction, while the verbal text provided the specifics.

In this view, the seals represent a special charter from the king—a validation of position and function, in which the king's image and name in the legend serve as the state approval for the legitimacy of the official and his right to function in office. This can be argued not only for the in-na-ba seals explicitly given by the king to highly placed individuals, but also for the arad-zu seals, as shown by the way in which the various ensis and šaginas possessing them functioned.

Such a reconstruction makes sense, given the historical context of the Ur III period as a whole. We have evidence of an expanding and increasingly complex administrative bureaucracy throughout the period,[75] coupled with large-scale economic expansion, reflected in the growth of an extensive overseas trade network.[76] Yet it must be remembered that the presentation scenes we have been discussing are not used on seals belonging to the relatively independent merchants of the period, but rather on seals of functionaries within the royal bureaucracy. The large number of royal presentation scenes, especially those with full RN-formula in the legend, thus correlates directly with the expansion of the royal bureaucracy—just as the standardization of the scenes correlates with the standardization of certain types of administrative texts.[77]

73. See Frankfort, *Cylinder Seals*, pp. 55 and 84.
74. See R. M. Boehmer, *Die Entwicklung der Glyptik während der Akkad-Zeit* (Berlin, 1965) passim.
75. See Hallo in Hallo and Simpson, *The Ancient Near East*, pp. 81 and 86; T. B. Jones, "Sumerian Administrative Documents: an Essay," *Sumerological Studies Jacobsen*, p. 59; R. McC. Adams, "Strategies of Maximization, Stability, and Resilience in Mesopotamian Society, Settlement, and Agriculture," *Proceedings of the American Philosophical Society*, vol. 122, no. 5 (1978) 329–35.
76. Oppenheim, "The Seafaring Merchants of Ur," and J. B. Curtis and W. W. Hallo, "Money and Merchants in Ur III," *HUCA* 30 (1959) 103–39.
77. See M. Lambert, "Les Archives de Urabba fils de Bazig," *RA* 54 (1960) 115.

Weber, in his *Theory of Social and Economic Organization*, as quoted by Goody,[78] noted that a "primary characteristic of bureaucratic organization is the conduct of business on the basis of written documents." Obvious in light of modern economic history, it is necessary to underscore this observation in relation to the importance of scribes and the steady increase of scribal seals from the Akkadian period onwards. It would be tempting to see all of the royal presentation-scene seals, including those without inscription, and those with only the three-line citation, as equally reflecting individuals at work in the extended bureaucratic network of the state; but this cannot be documented at present.

The more completely inscribed arad-zu and arad-da-ni-ir / in-na-ba seals, however, consistently represent very highly-placed scribes connected to royal and state offices. These scribes are often described as government officers at the same time, or else pass on to higher government service later.[79] As for the fully-established government officials—ensis, šaginas, sukkal-mahs, šadubas—there is at present no way to reconstruct the rationale by which certain individuals had seals which showed them in audience with the seated king, and others did not.[80] But if we are correct that there is a rational system behind the imagery on seals of some temple officials and women, then there is likely to be a code governing those variant in-na-ba and arad-zu seals noted by Franke and cited above as well; we simply have not cracked it yet.

It does make a certain amount of sense that officials connected to Drehem and Nippur, with which cities the kings of Ur maintained especially close relationships of patronage, consistently had such seals; and similarly, that officials connected to places which either disputed the hegemony of Ur (such as Uruk early on), or were prone to instability (such as the states and provinces on the eastern and northeastern frontiers), had such seals as well.

Hence, even without determining the absolute rules by which Ur III seals of a certain type were distributed to, or were in the possession of, certain individuals, I feel we can understand something of their purpose. For the officials concerned, the seals marked the legitimacy of their authority and of the status conferred by the king within the bureaucratic and administrative network that was the very fabric of the political and economic system constituting the Third Dynasty of Ur.[81] In exchange for this, they paid the necessary dues of subservience, if not hommage (viz., the ensis of Ešnunna up to Ibbi-Suʾen year 2).

I would therefore see the 1950s view of "hommage to a deified king" in a purely cultic sense[82] as too limited for the larger, systemic perspective in which we now see the ancient world, and particularly the Ur III period. But it would not do to reject the divine overtones entirely and to concentrate only on the economic aspects of state officialdom. The fact that our seals were used in civil transactions, even seals belonging to temple functionaries, led Barrelet, in celebrating the "precious index" which seal legends offer us in seeing the direct relationship between the sovereign and his dedicatee, to suggest that we

78. J. Goody, *The Domestication of the Savage Mind* (Cambridge, 1977) 15f.
79. See above and *Appendix 3* below; also Jones, "Sumerian Administrative Documents," p. 53.
80. See Franke, "Presentation Seals."
81. While it has not been my purpose to discuss the patronymics as employed in the legends of these seals, it should be noted that they, too, vary in consistency of inclusion and/or addition of father's profession. Where included, these patronymics can serve multiple functions. First, and most obvious, the patronym provides a more specific identification of the seal owner, as some personal names recur rather frequently in the period. Second, as with the ensis of Lagaš patronyms identify family, and hence the social position of the owner. And third, they can signal prestige beyond the seal-holder's own office when the father is a particularly high official. A good illustration of the likelihood that patronymics carried associations of family prestige or power is provided on the two known seals of the scribe Gududu: just "son of Dada(ga)" under Šu-Suʾen, but "son of Dadaga, ensi of Umma" under Ibbi-Suʾen, once his father had risen to that position (McGuiness, "Family of giri$_x$-zal," seals H and I).
82. Van Buren, "Hommage to a Deified King."

should view the king in a "civil" guise vis-à-vis his functionary.[83] But I wonder if this does not err equally at the opposite extreme. As Kramer implied in his study of the "ideal king,"[84] essential qualities of the ruler include a balance between divine election (and often claims to divine parentage) and earthly skills (administrative, judicial, and military).[85]

The very appearance of the seated king on seals in a position formerly reserved for gods at the same time historically that the kings received the divine determinative before their names, suggests a non-random correlation. Yet here again, social and political evidence suggests that the effects of this elevation were not limited to the religious sector. As was the case in Hellenistic Greece, where the "deification" of Alexander was at least in part a political measure to gain authority over old Greek cities which otherwise had their own rulers and hierarchies,[86] I would argue that for Ur as well, the phenomenon is best seen in the context of contemporary political structure, as Ur expanded to establish effective hegemony over the other city-states of Mesopotamia. For, whatever else the deification of kings accomplished, it was certainly an effective means of raising the ruler of one polity (here, the city-state of Ur) from a lateral position with respect to the rulers of other such polities, to a dominant position a significant level above them.[87]

It has been amply demonstrated that from the Uruk period on, minimal requirements for the urban organization of the city-state consisted of a three-tiered social and political hierarchy, including ruling authority at the top, implementing and managerial cadres (officials) in the middle, and general populace at the bottom. The elevation of the king of Ur to "divine" status should be seen, I feel, as inextricably linked to the elevation of his city-state to hegemony over formerly autonomous units—in effect, the creation of a nation-state—now organized into a four-tiered hierarchy, with a central ruling authority overriding local authorities and their dependent strata.

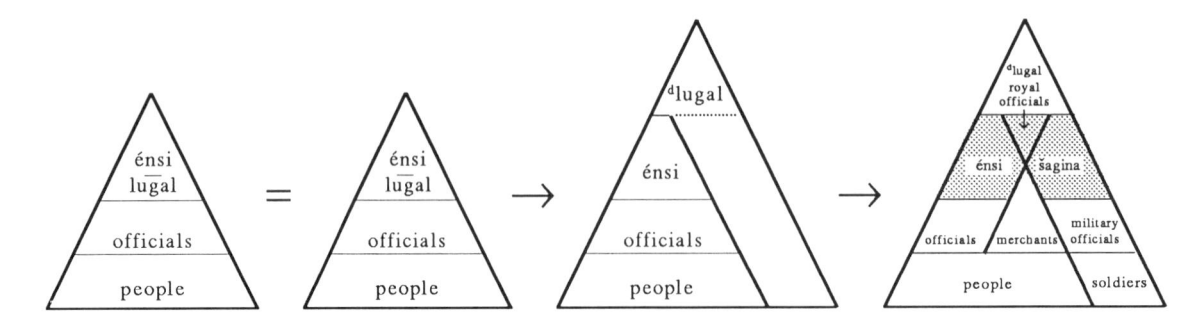

Figure 1. Schematic Model of Administrative Reorganization under Šulgi

Figure 1 suggests a schematic model for the way in which the new system incorporated formerly independent units. The king was above, but dislocated in place from, and not limited to, the local unit.

83. Barrelet, "La 'Figure du roi'," pp. 53, 39, and n. 26.
84. S. N. Kramer, "Kingship in Sumer and Akkad: The Ideal King," in Garelli, ed., *Le Palais et la royauté*, pp. 163–76.
85. For a fuller discussion of this, see Winter, "The King and the Cup," which began as a part of the current study, and was subsequently divided due to restrictions of space in the intended volume. If we are correct there in our analogy between the king and the sun-god, Utu/Šamaš he would be shown as the authority par excellence—dispenser of judgments and decisions.
86. See W. W. Tarn, *Hellenistic Civilization*, 3d ed. (New York, 1951) 49.
87. B. Kienast, "Der Weg zur Einheit Babyloniens unter staatsrechtlichen Aspekten," *Or.* n.s. 42 (1973) 499.

That unit retained its ensi (but not a lugal) at the top, which now constituted the second tier, but note that some of the power associated with this office has been truncated. In the model, with the positioning of the king over the formerly three-tiered pyramidal hierarchy, a new column is created at the right. Into this void was inserted the office of šagina, or military governor—more or less equal in status to the ensi, but responsible predominantly for the provinces—and his attendant constituency of military officers and soldiers.[88] Such was the administrative genius of Šulgi,[89] however, that the šagina, as appointee of the central government, served not only as the administrator of the province under his command, but also on occasion as check on the local ensis (for example, Apilaša in the Aradmu correspondence). The existence of these two parallel and comparable offices leaves, in the diagram as well as in the administrative hierarchy, an inverted triangular space in the second tier, which constitutes the space occupied by royal officials outside local units, often based at Ur itself, and responsible directly to the king—from personal officers, such as the cup-bearer and majordomo of the royal household to accountants, archivists, and the chancellor of the realm.

What is now in the third tier are those officials and military officers responsible to the ensi or šagina (many of whom employ the ensi- rather than RN-formula on their cylinder seal legends). It would also include the common rank of ugula, or "overseer"—i.e., a managerial, rather than administrative class— and a variety of individuals called "scribes," but who are in fact engaged in commercial enterprises.[90] Also in this tier, with very little point of contact with the royal network, is the category of individuals called "merchant"—more mobile than the officials tied to either the ensi or the šagina, able to operate in and around the system, occasionally employed on official "state" business, but relatively independent nonetheless. And finally, in the fourth tier is the general class of "worker"—civil and military, including

---

88. This model is also helpful in clarifying what went wrong in the Akkadian period, when Naram-Sin and Šar-kali-šarri had similarly adopted the divine determinative and attempted to elevate Akkad to hegemony over the rest of the region (see the discussion by Kienast, "Der Weg zur Einheit Babyloniens"). For, in so doing, Naram-Sin designated himself "god of Agade"—i.e., kept himself associated with his own city, whereas the Ur III kings did not take the title "god of Ur," but rather "god of the land" (dingir kalam-ma-na, "god of his land"); I would suggest this to be a significant distinction in integration or lack thereof of the power structure into a coherent whole. One could perhaps diagram the Akkadian system as illustrated in figure 2. The resulting model is clearly less tightly interlocked, hence much less stable structurally, and in the end, less successful. (This observation is the result of stimulating conversations with Piotr Steinkeller, who raised the question of the different titles employed in the Akkadian period. I have only applied it to the present model; the distinction is his.) It further leads one to wonder whether the Ur III emphasis upon Enlil of Nippur, not Nanna of Ur, as chief god of the Sumerian pantheon (Kienast, Or. n.s. 42, 499) was not a similar attempt to avoid the pitfalls of the Akkadian elevation of Ištar—that is, an attempt to establish an appropriate and more universally acceptable state god, rather than impose a former city god.

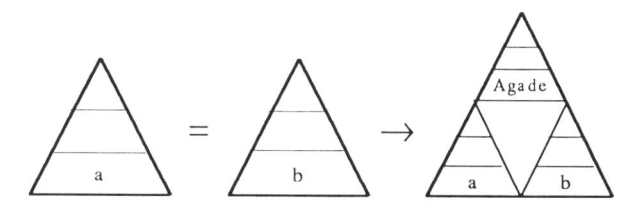

Figure 2. Schematic Model of Administrative Organization in the Akkadian Period

89. See Goetze, "Šakkanakkus of the Ur III Empire," JCS 17 (1963) 1–31.
90. For example, at Umma, overseers of the forest sector who report to the fiscal office, Ur-tarluh and Ur-emaš both of the erín-class (Steinkeller, "The Foresters of Umma," p. 89); and at Tello, Ur-Abba, who deals directly with the sukkal-mah under Šulgi but is himself outside the official royal bureaucracy (M. Lambert, "Les Archives de Urabba," p. 123).

those laborers known as erín, partly subject to corvée service (with the exception of the erín-managers with ugula status, who fall into the third tier).[91]

It should be stated here that, while this model is a modern construct useful in the visualization of social structure in the Ur III period, its organization has emerged from evidence preserved in Ur III texts. The model therefore reflects a level of actual praxis, and hence is a model *for*, rather than a model *of* the Ur III state. Evidence for the three tiers below that of king may be found embedded in records of the tax structure applied to military personnel on the periphery (see Steinkeller in this volume), in which the amounts paid signal clear differentiations between the šagina (top level), his senior officers equivalent to "majors" and "captains" (middle level), and the general soldier/workers with their immediate supervisors (bottom level). Similar evidence can also be extracted from economic texts of Umma, where a bureaucratic structure is apparent that ranks the ensi along with chief comptrollers of the "national" fiscal office based in that city in an upper stratum; managerial personnel running individual sectors subordinate to the fiscal office in the middle stratum; and erín-class workers in the lower stratum.[92] What the model adds is the relationship of the king to this hierarchy, but this, too, is readily demonstrable from texts—including the seal legends we have been discussing.

It will be noted that all of the RN-formula legends and royal presentation scenes on seals are associated with offices found in the second tier, just below the king: ensis, šaginas, and officials of the royal bureaucracy. Individuals in the third tier have their seals either with simple three-line legends, or with legends that indicate ties to their immediate superiors in the second tier, rather than to the king (see, for example, officials of ensis cited above; or Ur-emaš, overseer of foresters in Umma;[93] or Ur-Abba of Lagaš, purveyor to the royal bureaucracy, but not himself a part of it).[94] It is thus the second tier that maintains the densest set of official relations: both up to the ruler, and down to bureaucratic subordinates. And it is this same second tier that would thus have need to demonstrate publicly its direct authority from the king—hence the use of visual "badges" such as the royal presentation scene seals.

The model provided in figure 1, then, illustrates the complex, tightly interlocked political and administrative system of the Ur III period. If we may metaphorically extend the analogy of geometry-to-social-structure, the seal impressions we have been discussing not only occur within, but actually correspond to, one horizontal band in the model. Just as they are rolled as a band on clay, they also give the individual's place in that band of society into which he fits and in which he functions.

One may therefore argue that our seals constitute a far richer source of information than has previously been suspected. But one must further argue that they are not, in this case, effective isomorphs for the state as a whole. Only certain categories of artworks in any given period can address the full range of contemporary social and political issues; and here one would wish that the single major

---

91. See Steinkeller, "The Foresters of Umma," p. 97.
92. Ibid., passim.
93. Ibid., pp. 88ff.; for the seal see Buchanan, *Early Seals*, no. 624.
94. M. Lambert, "Archives de Urabba," p. 123, and the seals in L. Delaporte, *Catalogue des cylindres, Musée du Louvre* (Paris, 1920) nos. T. 132 and T. 136. It would be useful to determine from both extant seals and preserved sealings just what the proportions are of presentation-scene seals with seated king vs. those with seated god; and those with no legend vs. simple three-line legend vs. extended RN-formula. From an initial survey, it would seem that seals showing a seated god plus three-line legend are the most frequent. Since we have noted above the seal of a merchant containing a presentation scene before a seated god (Porada, *Corpus*, no. 277), it is likely that these seals were not limited to individuals within the temple administrative system, but rather, in the lower ranks, constituted the standard representation-type. In that case, seals with seated king could indicate higher rank than those with seated god, or at least indicate participation within the official state bureaucracy, especially when found with the full RN-formula; while the highest ranking functionaries within the temple bureaucracies may well have had seals with non-standardized cultic scenes, such as that of Lugal-engardu of Nippur, cited above.

monument preserved, the Stele of Ur-Nammu, were not so fragmentary, particularly on the reverse. The seals, by contrast, represent a limited—albeit meaningful—spectrum of concerns, and employ a limited vocabulary: by a combination of text and image, they situate the individual within the bureaucratic and administrative hierarchy of the Ur III state.

Possession of a royal presentation-scene seal that included an extended RN-formula as legend thus bound official to king and king to official, in a reciprocal, mutually-affirming system. The seal owner is identified in the legend, along with his office and usually his patronym (status and attributes), under the guise of acknowledging his service to the king. The complementary image also presents him in relation to the king, such that, as with the legend, they are not only "introduced," but linked in that mutuality of recognition upon which the entire political system is based. The nature of the visual representation is clear no matter where (or whether) an interceding deity is represented; the orientation of standing official to seated king is the constant, creating a balance—if not a tension—between the two as prime actors in the scene, even on those occasions in which the interceding goddess seems to be leading the individual into the royal presence.[95]

In the resulting balance, one is led to perceive that the king sanctions the position of the individual within the state hierarchy on the one hand, while, on the other, the king's higher position is acknowledged by the individual. (It is in this light that we must view the distress of Aradmu as Apilaša remained seated in his presence, as well as the change of seals at Ešnunna, once independent of the hegemony of Ur.)

As a functioning "artifact" used within the system to witness or validate actions on the part of the owner, the seal itself becomes an "ideal" witness also to the fact that the individual named on the seal has a specific relationship to the king. It has been observed that the shift to complex administrative organization, accompanied by the need for documentation on a large scale, is generally also associated with a corresponding diminution of importance given to "face-to-face" encounters,[96] whether in the form of interview, audience, or personal service. Yet, in the context of the burgeoning bureaucracy of the Ur III period, the face-to-face presentation scene is just what is emphasized on cylinder seals. Perhaps one might suggest that such a visual formula is especially important precisely in periods of extended bureaucracy, when in fact the distance between the individual and the highest authority becomes greater—as a rhetorical compensation for the loss of actual interaction.

On the "ideal" plane, then, the image (king + attributes: individual) and the legend (king + titles: individual) bind the two principal figures into their proper positions in the social and administrative order, affirming the political order, and acceding to the divine order. But it is equally important to look at the "real" plane on which these seals were employed, and hence, to give as much attention to sealings as to seals; for here we catch a glimpse of the period not just as it would present itself ideally, but also as it functioned in practice. With impressed sealings, we see that the legend oftentimes dominated over the image in limited space; and there is a certain measure of flexibility in the use of any individual's seal, or in strict correlation to the ruler named on the seal and the actual reign noted on the dated tablet. Yet, despite the looseness of actual practice, there are clearly-perceivable operational rules. What we see is evidence for a tightly controlled network of relations within the organization of the state—in which seals

---

95. The Ur III period is far from unique in devising a standard vocabulary of representation for the royal figure: visual formulas that include conventional poses and gestures which amplify or complement the accompanying text. In an analysis of Aztec codices, for example, Galarza ("Lire l'image aztèque," *Communications* 29 [1978] 13–42), discusses the process by which one "reads" the royal image. He suggests that lack of movement becomes a significant device to indicate that the text which accompanies the image concentrates on the "personage" himself, his status and attributes (ibid., p. 26).

96. See Goody, *Domestication of the Savage Mind*, p. 16 and R. Redfield, *The Primitive World and Its Transformation* (Chicago, 1953), passim.

are used to legitimize actual transactions on the one hand, and the power of the individual to engage in such transactions on the other. Finally, the very use of the seal is based upon the power of the king to hold the system together, to rule effectively, and to delegate responsibility.

The present study is far from conclusive. The need for closer analysis of seal inscriptions in conjunction with representations is apparent, as is a more precise tabulation of the status of individuals cited in legends in relation to the organization of the imagery. More comprehensive studies of the nature of transactions on tablets in conjunction with the seals used are likewise much to be desired, toward a better understanding of the functions of both administrative officials and their personal markers.

All of the above afford promising avenues of research for decoding the cultural information contained in the glyptic arts. For the present, on the basis of the current survey of presentation scenes with seated king and RN-formulas of the Ur III period, we are a bit closer to an understanding of the role, not only of this specific motif, but also of the socio-political order in the period and the place of seals within that order. The unprecedented standardization of seals in the Ur III period corresponds to an equally unprecedented concentration and distribution of resources within a highly centralized bureaucracy. As noted at the very beginning of this study, the seals are rather like a combination of coinage and identity cards. With their restricted vocabulary, they serve at once as markers of the unity of the system and of an individual's place within the system.

The standardization of these seals as indicators of rank and status may well be a unique and short-lived phenomenon in Mesopotamian history, correlated with the unusual degree of control initiated by Šulgi and exercised by subsequent kings of Ur over developments in the entire administrative system. For this period, at least, then, we have argued that the legitimacy of the official before the king is proclaimed by the public statement of his title(s) in the seal legend, and by his representation in direct juxtaposition to the ruler in the image. We have also argued that the legitimacy of the king is equally asserted on these seals, verbally by his titles and strings of epithets, visually as he is seated on his throne accompanied by recognized attributes associated with his right to rule.

From the perspective of praxis—how these seals were used in the context of the administrative hierarchy of the state—it becomes clear that, with the relative uniformity of the royal presentation scene plus the standardized formulas of royal dedication, the seals functioned as very powerful and effective documents in the centralized bureaucracy, signaling the highest administrative levels just below the king. As such, the seals not only reflect, but actually provide evidence for, the organization of the state bureaucracy.

The king with his distinctive attributes and epithets—strong king, king of Ur, king of the four quarters, god of the land—emerges as a most potent figure. Authorized to rule by divine sanction, he in turn authorizes others to act in official capacity in his name. The seals must then be viewed, not merely as chronological or typological phenomena, but, especially when image and legend are taken together, as functional signifiers: emblematic artifacts of bureaucratic authority, fully integrated into both the symbolic and the practical polity that was the Third Dynasty of Ur.

# APPENDIX 1

## LIST OF OFFICIALS BY REIGN OF KING CITED IN SEAL INSCRIPTIONS

To save space in this tabulation, references are abbreviated as much as possible. The special abbreviations used in this section are given below. Since most references are to seal numbers or text numbers, "no." has usually been omitted. In the case of names followed by an asterisk, the seal in question is an in-na-ba seal.

| | |
|---|---|
| *arad-zu* | N. Schneider, "Die *arad-zu-*, *dumu-ni-* und *in-na-ba-* Siegel von Ur III," *Or.* n.s. 5 (1936) 109–20, cited according to his numbering system |
| *Ashmolean* | B. Buchanan, *Catalogue of Ancient Near-Eastern Seals in the Ashmolean Museum*, vol. 1, *Cylinder Seals* (Oxford, 1966) |
| *AUCT* 3 | M. Sigrist, *Neo-Sumerian Account Texts in the Horn Archaeological Museum*, Andrews University Cuneiform Texts, vol. 3 (Berrien Springs, 1988) (cited by number) |
| *BM* 2 | D. Collon, *Catalogue of the Western Asiatic Seals in the British Museum, Cylinder Seals*, vol. 2, *Akkadian-Post Akkadian Ur III Periods* (London, 1982) |
| *Brett* | H. H. von der Osten, *Ancient Oriental Seals in the Collection of Mrs. Agnes Baldwin Brett*, OIP 37 (Chicago, 1936) |
| *Early Seals* | B. Buchanan, *Early Near Eastern Seals in the Yale Babylonian Collection* (New Haven and London, 1981) |
| *Louvre* | L. Delaporte, *Catalogue des cylindres, cachets et pierres gravées de style orientale, Musée du Louvre*, vol. 1, *Fouilles et missions* (Paris, 1920), vol. 2, *Acquisitions* (Paris, 1923) |
| *NATN* | D. I. Owen, *Neo-Sumerian Archival Texts Primarily from Nippur* (Winona Lake, Indiana, 1982) |
| *SACT* | S. T. Kang, *Sumerian and Akkadian Cuneiform Texts in the Collection of the World Heritage Museum of the University of Illinois*, vol. 1, *Sumerian Economic Texts from the Drehem Archive* (Urbana, Chicago, and London, 1972), vol. 2, *Sumerian Economic Texts from the Umma Archive* (Urbana, Chicago, and London, 1973) |

List of Officials by Reign of King Cited in Seal Inscriptions

| *King and Official* | *Title of Official* | *Reference* |
|---|---|---|
| I. Ur-Nammu | | |
| a. Hašhamer | ensi of Iškun-Su'en | Wiseman, *Seals* 40; *BM* 2, 469 |
| II. Šulgi | | |
| a. En-igi-nibzu | title not preserved | *ITT* 4 7218, 7475; *MVN* 6 234, 451 |
| b. Lišanum | ensi of Marada dumu Šuili | Goetze, *JCS* 16 26; *PBS* 13 28 = 14 286; Hallo, *HUCA* 33 p. 34 |
| c. Lu-Bau | rá-gaba | *Early Seals* 639 |
| d. Lu-dingira (dumu?) nu-banda | dub-sar | *SACT* 1 105 |
| e. Lu-Nanna | dub-sar, later šagina of Simudar | *UE* 10 422 |

Appendix 1: List of Officials by Reign of King Cited in Seal Inscriptions (*cont.*)

| King and Official | Title of Official | Reference |
|---|---|---|
| II. Šulgi (*cont.*) | | |
| f. Naram-ili-1 | sukkal, ì-du$_8$ | *Early Seals* 648; *BRM* 3 24, 39, 43, 74 |
| g. Naram-ili-2 | dumu Naša | Sauren, *NY Public Library* 353 |
| h. Naša | kurušda | *Early Seals* 643 |
| i. Šu-Su'en dumu lugal | šagina of Uruk | Goetze, *JCS* 17 15; *BRM* 3 52 |
| j. Ur-bagara(?) | šabra of Šulgi | *Ashmolean* 411; *UE* 10 221 |
| k. Ur-Dumuzida | di-kud | CBS 5136; *arad-zu* 2d5; *BE* 3 pl. 8 no. 14 |
| l. Ur-Hendursag | ensi of Šulgi-Utu | *Louvre* 1 pl. 12 T.185 |
| m. Ur-Lama | dub-sar, later ensi of Lagaš | *Louvre* 1 pl. 12 T.215; *MVN* 6 213, 235; Limet, *RAI* 17 68 |
| n. Ur-Lisi | ensi of Umma | Parr, *JCS* 24 135; *SACT* 2 Seal no. 91; Hallo, *HUCA* 33 34 |
| o. Ur-Nanibgal | ensi of Nippur | *NATN* 213; *NRVN* 249; CBS 9540; Zettler, *AfO* 31 3 n. 11 |
| p. Ur-nigingar | title not preserved | *BRM* 3 42; *arad-zu* 2b9 |
| q. Ur-Šulpae | sukkal-mah dumu Lani | *Louvre* 1 pl. 12 T.186; *NATN* 388 |
| r. Utu-[GÍR-gal] | dub-sar, šà-tam | *Early Seals* 642 |
| III. Amar-Su'en | | |
| a. A'akalla | ensi of Umma | *BRM* 3 47; *MVN* 1 1; Hallo, *HUCA* 33 37 |
| b. Babati-1* | šagina of Maškan-šarrum ensi of Awal (also šaduba, šà-tam lugal, uncle of king) | *MVN* 6 386; Goetze, *JCS* 17 22; Whiting, *JCS* 28 178 f.; Franke, *Seals and Sealing* C3; *BRM* 3 37, 38 |
| c. Babati-2 | dub-sar | Sauren, *NY Public Library* 354 |
| d. Lugal-$^d$[ ] | title not preserved | Meltzer, *Annual Review of RIM*, vol. 1, p. 21 |
| e. Lugal-ituda | dub-sar dumu Ur-dumuzida | *arad-zu* 3a3 |
| f. Namhani | sukkal | *Louvre* 1 pl. 12 T.216 |
| g. Ur-Lisi | ensi of umma | Parr, *JCS* 24 135; *SACT* 2 Seal no. 90; *BRM* 3 16 |
| h. Ur-kugnuna-1 | sukkal dumu Aradani, di-kud | *UE* 10 428 |
| i. Ur-sagamu | dub-sar lugal dumu Lugal-kagina | *Louvre* 1 pl. 11 T.188 |
| j. Ur-Šulpae | dub-sar dumu Ur-Haya | *AUCT* 3 82–86; Legrain, *TRU* 3, 9; Oppenheim, *Eames* H37 |

Appendix 1: List of Officials by Reign of King Cited in Seal Inscriptions (*cont.*)

| King and Official | Title of Official | Reference |
|---|---|---|
| III. Amar-Su'en (*cont.*) | | |
|    k. [PN] | ensi of [ ... ] | *SACT* 1 117 |
|    l. Lu-Enlil | dub-sar<br>dumu Lugal-ezen | Moortgat, *Rollsiegel* 255 |
| IV. Šu-Su'en | | |
|    a. A'akalla | ensi of Umma | *Early Seals* 651, 652 |
|    b. Aba-Enlilgin | dumu Ada, dam-gàr<br>(perhaps title of father) | *NATN* 765, 689 |
|    c. Abi-abih* | sagi | Franke, *Seals and Sealing* 62; Hallo, *HUCA* 33 39; *Louvre* 2 A.258 = *TCL* 2 5552 |
|    d. Aham-waqar | dub-sar | *AUCT* 3 306 |
|    e. Ahuni | sagi | Brett 48; *UE* 10 432 |
|    f. Apilaša | šagina of Kazallu | Kutscher, *JCS* 22 63–65; *Early Seals* 648x; Wilcke, in Garelli, *Le Palais et la royauté* 182 |
|    g. Arad-Nanna | sukkal-mah<br>dumu Ur-Šulpae | *Louvre* 1 pl. 12 T.217, 218 |
|    h. Babati-1* | see III b above | *Early Seals* 654 |
|    i. Babati-2 | dub-sar | *Early Seals* 637 |
|    j. Gududu | dub-sar<br>dumu Dadaga<br>(ensi of Umma) | *BRM* 3 114, Morgan Library, *Ancient Mesopotamian Art* pl. 12 a, b |
|    k. Igi-anakezu | sukkal<br>dumu Aradani, di-kud | *UE* 10 433 |
|    l. Ku(g)-Nanna | AB (profession?)<br>dumu Lu-Nanna | Nies, *UDT* 160 |
|    m. Lugal-ituda | dub-sar<br>dumu Ur-Dumuzida | *Louvre* 2 pl. 112 8; arad-zu 4b17 |
|    n. Lugal-melam | dub-sar<br>dumu Enlil-la | *BRM* 3 156 |
|    o. Lu-melam | dub-sar<br>dumu Ur-Lama(?) | *Early Seals* 647 |
|    p. Lu-Nanna-1 | šagina of Simudar | *NATN* 776 |
|    q. Lu-Nanna-2 | šà-tam<br>dumu Ur-Gilgameš | *AUCT* 3 489 |
|    r. Lu-Ningir[su] | dub-sar<br>dumu Lu-Bau, rá-gaba | *Louvre* 1 pl. 12 T.219; probably Grégoire, *AAS* 196 |
|    s. Lu-Utu | ensi of Adab<br>dumu Ur-Ašgi | *BE* 3 pl. III no. 10 |

Appendix 1: List of Officials by Reign of King Cited in Seal Inscriptions (*cont.*)

| King and Official | Title of Official | Reference |
|---|---|---|
| IV. Šu-Su'en (*cont.*) | | |
| t. Namzitarra | ensi of Nippur<br>dumu Ur-Nanibgal | Owen, *AOAT* 22 132 |
| u. Nur-Su'en | dub-sar<br>dumu Itirra | *AUCT* 3 203–209 |
| v. Šu-Irra | dub-sar<br>dumu I-din-[ ... ] | *AUCT* 3 508 |
| w. Ur-kugnuna-1 | sukkal<br>dumu Aradani, di-kud | *UE* 10 430 |
| x. Ur-kugnuna-2 | dub-sar<br>dumu Lu-Ningirsu | *Early Seals* 646; *AUCT* 3 1–34 |
| y. Ur-Nanše | dub-sar<br>dumu Na-mu | *AUCT* 3 454 |
| z. Ur-Nungal | dub-sar<br>dumu Ur-Šara | *Ashmolean* 439 |
| aa. Ur-Šulpae | dub-sar<br>dumu Ur-Haya | *Early Seals* 650; *AUCT* 3 95–102 |
| bb. Inim-Šara | dub-sar<br>dumu Bašaga | Moortgat, *Rollsiegel* 253 |
| cc. A-da-[ ] | dumu [ ] | *AUCT* 3 379, 482 |
| V. Ibbi-Su'en | | |
| a. Aham-arši | dub-sar<br>dumu Babati<br>šagina of Maškan-šarrum | *BM* 2 446 |
| b. Arad-Nanna* | sukkal-mah<br>dumu Ur-Šulpae | Franke, *Seals and Sealing* C-4a;<br>*ITT* 2 937; Scheil, *RA* 23 147 |
| c. Dada | ensi of Nippur<br>dumu Ur-Nanibgal<br>ensi of Nippur | *UET* 1 89; *UE* 10 418, 419; Hallo,<br>*HUCA* 33 40; Zettler, *AfO* 31 5 |
| d. Dadaga | ensi of Umma | Oppenheim, *Eames* F19 |
| e. En-temenie | sukkal<br>árad Nam-dumu-kani | *UET* 1 92 |
| f. Gududu | dub-sar<br>dumu Dadaga<br>ensi of Umma | *BRM* 3 32 |
| g. Lugal-azida* | šà-tam lugal<br>sanga of Enlil,<br>(son[?] of Ur-meme,<br>ugula of Inanna at Nippur) | Franke, *Seals and Sealing* C-4b;<br>Zettler, *AfO* 31 3 |
| h. Lu-ni-[ša$_6$(?)] | dub-sar<br>dumu Babati, šaduba | Oppenheim, *Eames* S4 |

Appendix 1: List of Officials by Reign of King Cited in Seal Inscriptions (*cont.*)

| King and Official | Title of Official | Reference |
|---|---|---|
| V. Ibbi-Suʾen (*cont.*) | | |
|   i. Lu-Šara | sukkal | *Louvre* 1 pl. 12 T.221 |
|   j. Nanna-ludug | dub-sar<br>dumu Lu-dingira | *UE* 10 435 |
|   k. Nanna-kiag | dub-sar<br>dumu-Lu-Nanna | *UE* 10 416 |
|   l. Ninlil-[amamu?] | sukkal-[mah(?)] | Hallo, *HUCA* 33 40; Sollberger, *JCS* 19 29; *UET* 1 97; *UE* 10 418; *Early Seals* 653, see Hallo p. 453 |
|   m. Sag-Enlil | ugula of Inanna<br>dumu Lugal-Engardu | Zettler, *AfO* 31 8f. |
|   n. Sag-Nannazu* | sanga of Enlil | Franke, *Seals and Sealing* C-7; *PBS* 13 5 and pl. 1; Hallo, *HUCA* 33 40; *PBS* 14 pl. 18 284 |
|   o. Suʾen-bani | muhaldim<br>dumu I-ti-ia | *AUCT* 3 323 |
|   p. Šu-ilia | dumu Ituria<br>ensi of Ešnunna | Frankfort, *Cylinder Seals* 5 |
|   q. Umani | dub-sar | *Early Seals* 636 |
|   r. Ur-kugnuna-2 | dub-sar<br>dumu Aradani, di-kud | Scheil, *RA* 23 35 |
|   s. Ur-nigingar* | šaduba | Franke, *Seals and Sealing* 3–6; *UE* 10 436, 437, 439; Hallo, *HUCA* 33 40 |
|   t. Ur-sag-kud(?) | ù-kul(?) | Porada, *Corpus* 292 |
|   u. Ur-Šumah | dub-sar<br>dumu Ur-nigingar | *Early Seals* 649 |

## APPENDIX 2
### LIST OF TITLES OR OFFICES BY REIGN OF CITED KING[†]

| King and Title or Office | Correspondence with Appendix 1 |
|---|---|
| I. Ur-Nammu | |
|   ensi of Iškun-Suʾen | Ia |
| II. Šulgi | |
|   ensi of Marada | IIb |
|   ensi of Šulgi-Utu | III |
|   ensi of Umma | IIn |

[†] An asterisk after a title or office indicates arad-da-ni-ir in-na-ba seals, presented by the king to the official.

Appendix 2: List of Titles or Offices by Reign of Cited King (*cont.*)

| King and Title or Office | Correspondence with Appendix 1 |
|---|---|
| II. Šulgi (*cont.*) | |
|     ensi of Nippur | IIo (father of IVt and Vc) |
|     šagina of Uruk, son of the king | IIi |
|     sukkal-mah | IIq (father of IVg = Vb) |
|     sukkal, ì-du$_8$ | IIf |
|     šabra of Šulgi | IIj |
|     kurušda | IIh (father of IIg) |
|     son of the kurušda | IIg (son of IIh) |
|     rá-gaba | IIc (father of IVq; grandfather of IVx) |
|     di-kud | IIk (father of IIIe = IVm) |
|     dub-sar (later ensi of Lagaš) | IIm (father of IVo) |
|     dub-sar (later šagina of Simudar) | IIe (= IVp; father of Vk) |
|     dub-sar, also nu-banda(?) | IId (father of Vj) |
|     dub-sar, also šà-tam | IIr |
| III. Amar-Su'en | |
|     ensi of Umma | IIIa (= IVa) |
|     ensi of Umma | IIIg |
|     ensi of [ … ] | IIIk |
|     šagina of Maškan-šarrum<br>    ensi of Awal (also šaduba, šà-tam lugal)* | IIIb (= IVh; father of Va) |
|     sukkal | IIIf |
|     sukkal | IIIh (= IVw; brother of IVk) |
|     dub-sar lugal | IIIi |
|     dub-sar | IIIc |
|     dub-sar | IIIe (= IVi; son of IIk) |
|     dub-sar | IIIj (= IVaa) |
|     dub-sar | IIIl |
| IV. Šu-Su'en | |
|     ensi of Umma | IVa (= IIIa) |
|     ensi of Adab | IVr |
|     ensi of Nippur | IVt (son of IIo; brother of Vc) |
|     šagina of Maškan-šarrum,<br>    ensi of Awal (also šaduba, šà-tam lugal)* | IVh (= IIIb; father of Va) |
|     šagina of Kazallu | IVf |
|     šagina of Simudar | IVp (= IIe; father of Vj) |
|     sukkal-mah | IVg (= Vb; son of IIq = IVaa) |
|     sukkal | IVk (brother of IVw = IIIh) |

Appendix 2: List of Titles or Offices by Reign of Cited King (*cont.*)

| King and Title or Office | Correspondence with Appendix 1 |
|---|---|
| IV. Šu-Su'en (*cont.*) | |
| sukkal | IVw (= IIIh; brother of IVk) |
| šà-tam | IVq |
| sagi* | IVc |
| sagi | IVe |
| dub-sar | IVd |
| dub-sar | IVi |
| dub-sar (son of ensi) | IVj (= Vf; son of Vd) |
| dub-sar (son of judge) | IVm (son of IIk) |
| dub-sar | IVn |
| dub-sar | IVo |
| dub-sar (son of rá-gaba) | IVr (son of IIc; father of IVx) |
| dub-sar | IVu |
| dub-sar | IVv |
| dub-sar | IVx (= Vr; son of IVq; grandson of IIc) |
| dub-sar | IVy |
| dub-sar | IVz |
| dub-sar | IVaa (= IIIj) |
| dub-sar | IVbb |
| dam-gàr (?) | IVb |
| V. Ibbi-Su'en | |
| ensi of Nippur | Vc (son of IIo; brother of IVt) |
| ensi of Umma | Vd (father of IVj = Vf) |
| son of ensi of Ešnunna | Vp |
| sukkal-mah* | Vb (j = IVg; son of IIq) |
| sukkal-mah (?) | Vl |
| sukkal | Ve |
| sukkal | Vi |
| šaduba* | Vs (= IIp?; father of Vu?) |
| šà-tam lugal, also sanga of Enlil* | Vg |
| sanga of Enlil* | Vn |
| ugula of Inanna | Vm |
| ù-kul(?) | Vt |
| dub-sar | Va (son of IIIb = IVh) |
| dub-sar | Vf (= IVj; son of Vd) |
| dub-sar | Vh |
| dub-sar | Vj (son of IId) |

Appendix 2: List of Titles or Offices by Reign of Cited King (*cont.*)

| King and Title or Office | Correspondence with Appendix 1 |
|---|---|
| V.  Ibbi-Su'en (*cont.*) | |
|     dub-sar | Vk (son of IVp = IIe) |
|     dub-sar | Vq |
|     dub-sar | Vr (= IVx) |
|     dub-sar | Vu (son of Vs or IIp?) |

## APPENDIX 3

### RELATIONSHIPS AMONG SEAL-HOLDERS

I. Tabulation: 81 seals of 69 individuals.

II. Twelve individuals appear with seal change in two different reigns (either new seal cut, or new royal name added to old seal—the latter particularly true of seals in the change from Amar-Su'en to Šu-Su'en):

>       Lu-Nanna (IIe = IVp)
>       Ur-Lisi (IIn = IIIg)
>       Ur-Šulpae (IIq = IIIj)
>       A'akalla (IIIa = IVa)
>       Babati-1 (IIIb = IVh)
>       Babati-2 (IIIc = IVi)
>       Lugal-ituda (IIIe = IVm)
>       Ur-kugnuna-1 (IIIh = IVw)
>       Ur-kugnuna-2 (IVx = Vr)
>       Aham-arši (IVd = Va)
>       Arad-Nanna (IVg = Vb)
>       Gududu (IVj = Vf)

III. Six in-na-ba seals, presented by the king to official (one individual twice):

>       Babati-1 (IIIb and IVh)
>       Abi-abih (IVc)
>       Arad-Nanna (Vb)
>       Lugal-azida (Vg)
>       Sag-Nannazu (Vn)
>       Ur-nigingar (Vs)

Appendix 3: Relationships Among Seal-Holders (*cont.*)

IV. Ten individuals are sons of officials who also have this seal-type, including one linkage of father-to-son-to-grandson:

|  |  |  |
|---|---|---|
| Lugal-ituda (IIIe = IVm) | = | son of Ur-Dumuzida (IIk) |
| Arad-Nanna (IVg = Vb) | = | son of Ur-Šulpae (IIIj = IVaa) |
| Lu-Ningirsu (IVr) | = | son of Lu-Bau (IIc) |
| Ur-kugnuna-2 (IVx = Vr) | = | son of Lu-Ningirsu (IVq) |
| Aham-arši (IVd = Va) | = | son of Babati-1 (IIIb = IVh) |
| Gududu (IVj = Vf) | = | son of Dadaga (Vd) |
| Namzitarra (IVt) | = | son of Ur-Nanibgal (IIo) |
| Dada (Vc) | = | son of Ur-Nanibgal (IIo) |
| Nanna-ludug (Vj) | = | son of Lu-dingira (IId) |
| Nanna-kiag (Vk) | = | son of Lu-Nanna (IIe = IVp) |

V. There are two sets of brothers:

Igi-anakezu (IVk) and Ur-kugnuna-1 (IIIh = IVw), both sukkals, sons of Aradani, di-kud;

and

Namzitarra (IVt) and Dada (Vc), both ensis of Nippur, succeeding their father, Ur-Nanibgal (IIo).

VI. Of the various scribes:

one is subsequently ensi of Lagaš: Ur-Lama (IIm)
one is subsequently šagina of Simudar: Lu-Nanna (IIe = IVp)
one is dub-sar lugal, royal scribe: Ur-sagamu (IIIi)
one is also a šà-tam, comptroller: Utu-[GÍR-gal] (IIr)
one is the son of the ensi of Umma: Gududu (IVj = Vf)
one is the son of the rá-gaba: Lu-Ningirsu (IVr); and his son, likewise a scribe, also bears this seal-type: Ur-kugnuna-2 (IVx = Vr)
one is the son of a šaduba under Ibbi-Suʾen and/or an official under Šulgi: Ur-Šumah (Vu)

---

ACKNOWLEDGMENTS

I am grateful to several institutions for supplying the photographs which appear on plates 1–10 and for permission to reproduce them: the Trustees of the British Museum, London (pl. 1a); the University Museum, Philadelphia (pls. 1b, 2a, 3a, 3b, 4a, 8a, 9a, and 10b); the Yale Babylonian Collection, New Haven (pls. 1c, 5a, 5b, 5c, 8b, and 9b); the Pierpont Morgan Library, New York (pls. 2b and 6); The Oriental Institute, Chicago (pls. 4b, 9c, and 10c); the Hilprecht Sammlung, Friedrich-Schiller-Universität, Jena (DDR) (pl. 7a and 7b). I thank Richard L. Zettler for permission to republish his drawing on pl. 10a.

PLATE 1

a. Seal of Hašhamer, Ensi of Iškun-Suʾen, Citing Ur-Nammu(?). Modern Impression. British Museum, BM 59126; Collon, *British Museum* 2 469

b. Seal of Lišanum, Ensi of Marada, Citing Šulgi. Envelope Fragment, Ur; University Museum, CBS 14193; *PBS* 13 28, Photo *PBS* 14 286

c. Seal of Naram-ili, Sukkal, Citing Šulgi. Bulla, Drehem; Yale Babylonian Collection, YBC 3648; Buchanan, *Early Seals* 648

PLATE 2

a. Seal of Ur-Dumuzida, Di-kud, Citing Šulgi. Tablet, Ur;
University Museum, CBS 5136; *BE* 3 14 and pl. IV

b. Seal of Ur-Lisi, Ensi of Umma, Citing Amar-Su'en.
Bulla; Morgan Library 2302; *BRM* 3 16

PLATE 3

a. Seal of Ur-kugnuna-l, Sukkal, Citing Amar-Su'en. Envelope,
Ur; University Museum, U 6748a; *UE* 10 429

b. Seal of Ur-kugnuna-l, Sukkal, Citing Šu-Su'en. Envelope,
Ur; University Museum, U 6748b; *UE* 10 430

PLATE 4

a. Seal of Igi-annakezu, Sukkal, Citing Šu-Su'en. Envelope,
Ur; University Museum, U 6960; *UE* 10 433

b. Seal of Babati, Šagina of Maškan-šarrum, Ensi of Awal, Uncle of the King,
Presented by Either Amar-Su'en or Šu-Su'en. Tablet, Tell Asmar;
Oriental Institute, As 31.T615; Whiting, *JCS* 28 173–82

PLATE 5

a. Seal of Apilaša, Šagina of Kazallu, Citing Šu-Suʾen. Bulla, Nippur; Yale Babylonian Collection, NBCT 2307; Buchanan, *Early Seals* 648x

b. Seal of Lu-melam, Dub-sar, Citing Šu-Suʾen. Envelope, Drehem; Yale Babylonian Collection, YBC 3918; Buchanan, *Early Seals* 647

c. Seal of Lu-melam, as in pl. 5b, Side View of Envelope

PLATE 6

Seal of Lugal-melam, Dub-sar, Citing Šu-Suʾen. Bulla; Morgan Library 2354; *BRM* 3 156

PLATE 7

a

b

Seal of Dada, Ensi of Nippur, Citing Ibbi-Su'en. Envelope Edge (a)
and Envelope Obverse (b); Hilprecht Sammlung 1351,
Friedrich-Schiller-Universität, Jena (DDR)

PLATE 8

a. Seal of Ur-nigingar, Šaduba, Presented by Ibbi-Su'en. Envelope Verso, Ur; University Museum, U 6342 ; *UE* 10 436

b. Seal of Ur-Šumah, Dub-sar, Son of Ur-nigingar, Citing Ibbi-Su'en. Envelope, Nippur; Yale Babylonian Collection, NBC 6645; Buchanan, *Early Seals* 649

PLATE 9

a. Seal of Gìr-né-ì-ša₆, Dub-sar, Citing Šulgi as Ennirzianna, Priest of Nanna. Bulla, Dated Šulgi year 35; Ur, University Museum, U 7024; *UE* 10 403

b. Seal of Lugal-engardu, Ugula of the Temple of Inanna, Priest of Enlil, Citing Amar-Su'en, Beloved of Inanna. Tablet, Nippur; Yale Babylonian Collection, NBC 10539; Buchanan, *Early Seals* 681

c. Clay Sealing as in pl. 9b above. Oriental Institute, A. 30769 (= 5 NT 603)

PLATE 10

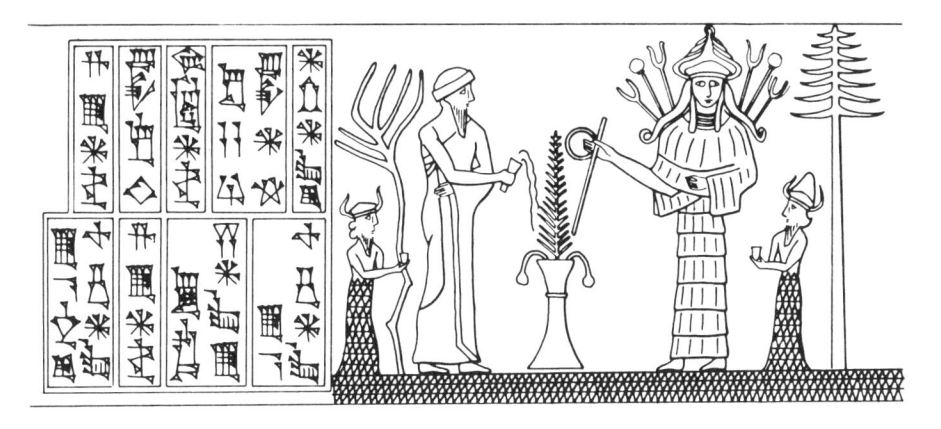

a. Reconstructed Drawing of the Seal of Lugal-engardu
(from Richard L. Zettler's Review of Buchanan, *Early Seals*, in *JNES* 46 [1987] 60)

b. Seal of Nin-addana, Wife of Zilim, Daughter of Lala,
Detail of Tablet. Ur; University Museum,
U 10130; *UE* 10 423

c. Seal of Bilalama, Presented by His Father, Kirikiri, Ensi of Ešnunna, Citing the God
Tišpak. Modern Impression, Tell Asmar; Oriental Institute, A. 7468;
Frankfort, *Stratified Cylinder Seals* 709

# CHAPTER 6

## ADMINISTRATION OF THE TEMPLE OF INANNA AT NIPPUR UNDER THE THIRD DYNASTY OF UR: ARCHAEOLOGICAL AND DOCUMENTARY EVIDENCE*

RICHARD L. ZETTLER

*The University Museum, The University of Pennsylvania*

In excavations carried out over the years 1951 to 1963 the Joint Expedition to Nippur in southern Iraq uncovered a sequence of twenty-three buildings and re-buildings of the temple of Inanna/Ištar, goddess of love and war.[1] Here I intend to focus on a single building in that sequence, the building of Level IV. The Level IV temple can be securely dated to the period of the Third Dynasty of Ur, ca. 2112–2004 B.C. Inscriptions on door sockets and on baked bricks indicate that it was built by Šulgi, second king of the dynasty.[2] Not only was a good portion of the plan of the building recovered, but also hundreds of

---

*Abbreviations where used are those of the *Chicago Assyrian Dictionary*. For purposes of this article, royal names, place names, etc., whether in Sumerian or Akkadian, have been normalized. Personal names other than royal names have been given in transliteration. In translations Sumerian units of measure have been retained. One sìla is approximately a liter, one iku about 3600 square meters, and a gín roughly 8⅓ grams.

1. On the excavations in the area of the Inanna temple at Nippur, see Vaughn E. Crawford, "Nippur, the Holy City," *Archaeology* 12 (1959) 74–83; Richard C. Haines, "Where a Goddess of Love and War Was Worshipped 4000 Years Ago," *The Illustrated London News*, August 18, 1956, pp. 266–69, "Further Excavations at the Temple of Inanna," *The Illustrated London News*, September 6, 1958, pp. 386–89, and "The Temple of Inanna at Nippur," *The Illustrated London News*, September 9, 1961, pp. 408–11; Donald P. Hansen and George F. Dales, "The Temple of Inanna, Queen of Heaven at Nippur," *Archaeology* 15 (1962) 75–84; Donald E. McCown, "A Discovery Which Has Immensely Enriched the World's Oldest Literature: Excavations at Nippur, the 4400 Year Old City of Sumeria and Babylonia," *The Illustrated London News*, June 28, 1952, pp. 1084–87, and "Recent Finds at Nippur," *Archaeology* 5 (1952) 70–75. No final report on the excavations has yet appeared, but Donald P. Hansen, Karen Wilson, and I are currently preparing one.

2. Six door sockets, each with the same inscription recording Šulgi's construction of the temple for Inanna, were found in situ in the Level IV building in the third (1951–52), fifth (1955–56) and sixth (1957–58) seasons of work. They were registered as 3 N 407 (Locus 2), 5 NT 678 (Locus 13), 5 NT 679 (Locus 16), 5 NT 680 (Locus 21), 6 NT 1146 (Locus 120) and 6 NT 1147 (Locus 141). The door socket found in the third season is pictured in McCown, "Recent Finds at Nippur," p. 74. A door socket with the same inscription as those found in situ in the building was found at Nippur by the University of Pennsylvania excavators in the nineteenth century. See L. Legrain, *Royal Inscriptions and Fragments from Nippur and Babylon*, PBS 15 (Philadelphia, 1926), No. 42 (pictured in L. Legrain, "Two Door Sockets of the Kings of Ur," *The Museum Journal* 15 [1924] 77–79).

small finds and, perhaps more important, the remains of its administrative archive. By considering the remains of the building, the small finds, and its administrative archive I can, I think, present a reasonable reconstruction of the temple as a social institution and make a contribution to the consideration of bureaucratic administration in the ancient Near East.

Figure 1 is a reconstructed plan of the Level IV temple. Leveling operations undertaken in conjunction with the construction of a foundation platform for a temple of the Parthian period left only the northwesternmost rank or two of rooms well preserved.[3] Still, enough remained of the rest of the building—frequently only an isolated corner, a patch of flooring or a door socket alongside the foundation—to reconstruct the layout and pattern of circulation through all but the southeasternmost third of it. Where only the foundations remained to outline the rooms of the building it has been possible, at least in certain instances, to reconstruct something of the circulation based on room arrangement patterns well known in Mesopotamian architectural tradition.

The temple was a large, rectangular structure, measuring more than a hundred meters northwest to southeast and over sixty meters northeast to southwest. The main entrance was in the northwestern wall; two subsidiary entrances were located in the southwestern wall, presumably fronting on the canal which ran through the center of Nippur. The building was, in effect, a fusion of two parts, a southwestern and a northeastern sector. Access into the northeastern sector was tightly restricted and apparently no doorways led from the outside into that part of the building. Access from the southwestern sector was only through a narrow corridor (Locus 16) which led from the western courtyard (Locus 28) into the northern courtyard (Locus 3) or through two connecting rooms (Loci 126 and 135) from the southern courtyard (Locus 118) into a corridor (Locus 125) running northwest to southeast. Doors inside the two connecting rooms, Loci 16 and 135, could control or prevent all communication between the two sectors of the temple.

The southwestern sector of the temple was the more public part, the part connected with the functioning of the cult. The dominating features of the sector were two large courtyards, Loci 28 and 118. In the southwestern wall of each of the courtyards was a recessed doorway decorated by double-stepped niches and flanked by projecting towers. Those doorways duplicated the main entry into the temple and directed circulation from it to the southeast. Below the brickwork on each side of the main entrance and on each side of the doorways in the southeastern walls of the courtyards were foundation deposits. Those deposits emphasize the importance of the line represented by the doorways, which led to the cella or cellae of the temple. The cella or cellae, as is evident from figure 1, were not preserved. Few objects or texts were found in the southwestern sector of the building and, so, no specifics of its functioning can be determined.

What was preserved of the less public northeastern part of the building consisted of two main complexes of rooms, one in the northwest centered on the courtyard, Locus 3, and the other associated

---

The inscription on the door sockets reads ᵈInanna, nin-a-ni, Šul-gi, nita kalag-ga, lugal Úri$^{ki}$-ma, lugal ki-en-gi ki-uri-ke₄, é Dur-an-ki-ka-ni, mu-na-dù, ki-bi mu-na-gi₄, nam-ti-la-ni-šè, a mu-na-ru, "(For) Inanna, his lady, Šulgi, powerful man, king of Ur, king of Sumer and Akkad, her house in Duranki, built; he restored its place, (and) for his life he dedicated it." On the translation "her house in Duranki" for the Sumerian é Dur-an-ki-ka-ni, see E. Bergmann, "Untersuchungen zu syllabisch geschriebene sumerischen Texten" *ZA* 56 (1964) 8–9.

Of the baked bricks found in the course of the excavations only seven were registered and all of them had been used in constructing the "boxes" in which the foundation deposits were held. The seven were registered as 5 NT 685–87 (Level IV, Loci 55–57), 5 NT 688 (Level IV, Locus 86), 6 NT 1128–29 (Level IV, Locus 127) and 6 NT 1130 (Level IV, Locus 128). The inscription stamped on the bricks duplicates the first eight lines of that on the door sockets.

3. On the platform of the Parthian period, see Crawford, "Nippur, the Holy City," pp. 77–79.

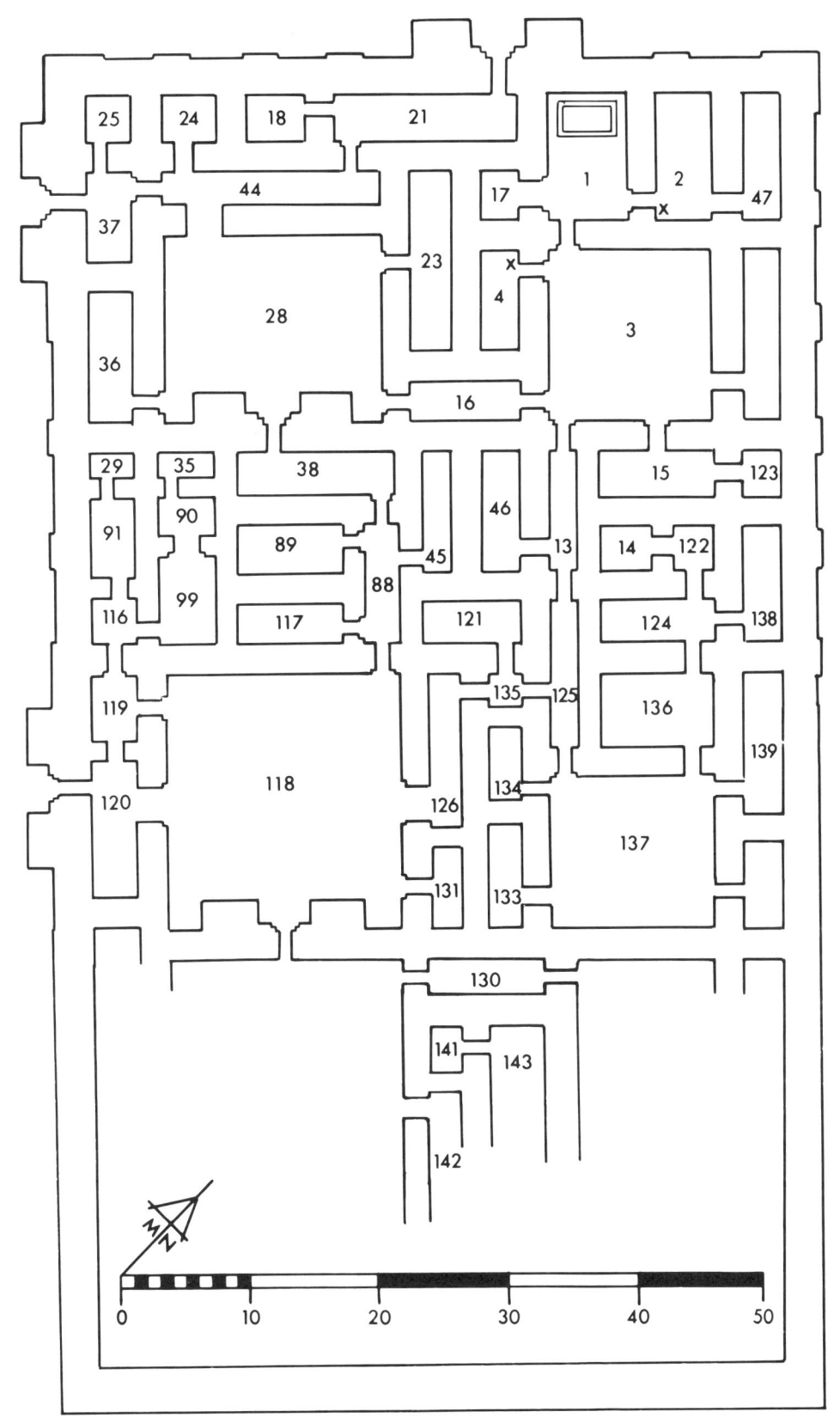

Figure 1. Reconstructed Plan of the Inanna Temple, Level IV

with a courtyard in the southeast, Locus 137. The two complexes were linked by a corridor chain (Loci 13 and 125).

The nine rooms around Locus 3 functioned as the administrative center of the temple: Loci 1, 17, 2 and possibly 47 as the chancery with its associated magazines and storage spaces; Loci 15 and 123 as the principal reception suite. Loci 1, 17 and 2 were well-preserved rooms. Excluding the major courtyards, Locus 1 was the largest room in the building. It measured six meters by nine meters, both distances too great to span effectively with locally available roofing beams.[4] It was probably open to the sky, and was thus a subsidiary courtyard off the larger and busier courtyard, Locus 3. Such a courtyard would have been a suitable space for drawing up administrative records and other texts, and twenty or so tablets were, in fact, found on various floors in Locus 1. At the northwestern end of Locus 1, below floor level, but accessible from the floor, was a rectangular structure of mud brick. The insides of the walls of the structure were coated with bitumen and the structure had been partially roofed. The fill inside the bin was loose, apparently unstratified, and contained broken and mangled tablets, a number recognizable as school exercises, as well as fragmentary clay sealings. More than half of the clay sealings had been broken off knobs and, so, had secured doors.[5] The bin was, I would suggest, used for storage of clean clay or clay which could be recycled for making tablets. Alternatively, the bin might have been used for levigating that clay. When the bin went out of use at a late floor level, it was replaced by a large storage jar coated inside with bitumen, which doubtless served the same purpose.

Locus 2, which opened off Locus 1, could be closed off by a door. Certain of the sealings found in the bin in Locus 1 had perhaps originally secured that door. Numerous clay tablets, many of them large, summary accounts, the sort of records presumably held for some time, were found on the floor in Locus 2 and, perhaps, indicate that it was the archive room of the temple.

The two rooms, Loci 15 and 123, which lay southeast of Locus 3, were preserved only at foundation level. The layout of those two rooms, however, is characteristic of reception suites.[6] A single foundation deposit lay below the preserved brickwork of the wall between Locus 3 and Locus 15. No trace remained of a second deposit, but the foundation of most of the wall between Locus 3 and Locus 15 had been cut away by a large pit of the Parthian period. I assume that a second deposit had originally existed northeast of the one excavated, but had been cut away. The two deposits would probably have flanked a doorway centered in the wall and I have therefore restored such a doorway in the plan, figure 1.[7] The foundation deposits were doubtless intended to emphasize the importance of the reception suite.

4. Split palm logs are commonly used, although not preferred, as roofing beams in southern Iraq today and doubtless were in ancient times. Palm logs can span little more than 3.50 meters. See Donald E. McCown and Richard C. Haines, *Nippur I: Temple of Enlil, Scribal Quarter, and Soundings*, OIP 78 (Chicago, 1967) 36–37.

5. On knobs, their function in "locking" doors, and the appearance of the backs of sealings broken off them, see Enrica Fiandra, "Ancora a proposito delle cretule de Festòs: connessione tra i systemi amministrativi centralizzati e l'uso delle cretule nell'età del bronzo," *Bollettino d'Arte*, ser. 5 60 (1975) 1–25, "Attività a Kish di un mercante di Lagash in epoca presargonica," *Oriens Antiquus* 20 (1981) 165–74, "Porte e chiusure di sicurezza nell'antico oriente," *Bollettino d'Arte*, ser. 6 67 (1982) 1–18; P. Ferioli, E. Fiandra, and S. Tusa, "Stamp Seals and the Functional Analysis of Their Sealings at Shahr-i Sokhta II–III," in J. E. Van Lohuizen-De Leeuw, ed., *South Asian Archaeology 1975* (Leiden, 1979) 7–26. For a full discussion of the clay sealings found in the temple, see Richard L. Zettler, "Sealings as Artifacts of Institutional Administration in Ancient Mesopotamia," *JCS* 39 (1987) 197–240.

6. On the character of the principal reception suite, at least as it relates to palaces of the late Assyrian period, see Geoffrey Turner, "The State Apartments of Late Assyrian Palaces," *Iraq* 32 (1970) 181–94.

7. Richard C. Haines, field director and architect at Nippur during the Inanna temple excavations, apparently assumed that only a single foundation deposit existed under the brickwork of the wall between Loci 3 and 15 and in a plan published at the end of the fifth season he reconstructed a doorway in the east corner of the courtyard, Locus 3, into Locus 15 (Haines, "Where a Goddess," fig. 1). There is no evidence to support his

The courtyard in the east corner of the temple, Locus 137, occupied roughly the same area as Locus 3. In that courtyard were an oven, apparently used for cooking, a fireplace, and a trash pit, from which were recovered several clay figurines, a clay plaque with an erotic scene incised on it, several pottery jars, some fifty tablets, including many school exercises, and more than a hundred fragmentary clay sealings. More than half of the sealings found in the trash pit had been broken off knobs.

The domestic features in Locus 137 were, I would suggest, associated with the rooms (Loci 136, 124, 14, and 122) which lay northwest of the courtyard. Although enough was preserved of the foundations to outline those rooms, very little remained of the walls and floors and no indications as to the entry into or circulation through those rooms existed. The arrangement of the rooms, however, is striking in its similarity to apartment suites in late Assyrian palaces, in fact identical to the so-called master private apartment in Residence K on the citadel at Khorsabad.[8] Such apartment suites were not restricted to late Assyrian palaces. In an unpublished thesis on room arrangement and circulation variables in Mesopotamian architecture, John Sanders, architect of the Oriental Institute's Nippur excavations, argued that prototypes of such apartment suites of late Assyrian palaces existed in southern Mesopotamia as early as the Early Dynastic period.[9] I would argue that Loci 136, 124, 14, and 122 constituted a residential unit—Locus 136 a courtyard; Locus 124 a reception room; and Loci 14 and 122 retiring rooms—off the courtyard, Locus 137, and I have restored circulation through those rooms accordingly in the plan, figure 1.

That the temple of Inanna at Nippur had a residential unit within it should not be surprising. In southern Mesopotamia already in the Early Dynastic period there were houses inside the compounds at least of major temples, for example, House D in the Temple Oval at Khafajah. Closer in date to level IV of the temple of Inanna at Nippur, the temple of Ningal and the residence of the *entu*-priestess at Ur were within one building. The question of who occupied the apartment suite cannot be answered with absolute certainty, but I would suggest, for reasons that I hope will be evident later, that it was the chief administrator of the temple of Inanna and his family who resided there.

Up to this point I have focused almost exclusively on the temple building and said little about the texts which make up the remains of the administrative archive of the temple. That is due largely to the fact that only ten percent of those texts were found in situ in the building and most of those in contexts, for example, the bin in Locus 1 or the trash pit in Locus 137, which shed little light of the functioning of specific rooms in the building. The bulk of the 1,160 or so texts which make up the remains of the archive of the temple were found in secondary contexts. They had, apparently, been dug out of the building in the Parthian period in the course of the leveling operations which I mentioned above and redeposited as fill in the foundation platform. In effect, when Oriental Institute archaeologists found them in 1953–58, they were excavating them for the second time. The earlier Parthian excavators, I might add, took nowhere near the time and care in digging the tablets up and redepositing them that the later archaeologists did

---

reconstruction of a doorway in the east corner of Locus 3 into Locus 15. On the contrary, given the regular and planned placement of the other foundation deposits uncovered in the course of the excavation of the Level IV building, a single deposit not near a doorway would seem to make little sense. For these reasons, I have assumed a second deposit not preserved.

8. On the apartment suites of late Assyrian palaces, see Gordon Loud, "An Architectural Formula for Assyrian Planning Based on the Results of Excavations at Khorsabad," *Revue d'assyriologie* 33 (1936) 153–60; Turner, "The State Apartments," pp. 177–213.

9. Specifically, Sanders pointed to the southern residential complex in the Šara temple at Tell Agrab. According to him, rooms M 14: 7–8 and M 15: 2–4 in that complex constituted an apartment suite off the courtyard M 15: 1 and exhibited practically all of the room arrangement and circulation patterns characteristic of the typical late Assyrian suite. See John C. Sanders, "Aspects of Mesopotamian Settlement Geography: An Empirical and Computer-aided Analysis of Building Forms, Room Arrangements and Circulation," (M.A. diss., University of Wisconsin–Milwaukee, 1981) 88–91.

and most were fragmentary when found. Despite the secondary context and their fragmentary state, however, the texts can be identified unmistakably as part of the administrative archive of the temple. A few carry the notation é ᵈInanna, "temple of Inanna"; others can be identified as part of the archive because personal names which occur in them match the names in texts and on sealings found in the building. The remarks on the economy and administrative structure of the temple which follow are based on my study of all of the texts which make up the remains of the administrative archive, both those found in the building and those from the fill of the Parthian platform, as well as on the hundreds of fragmentary clay sealings found in the excavations. Full documentation for the conclusions which I will present here will have to await the publication of the excavation report, the texts, and my interpretative study of the temple.[10]

Three fragmentary balanced accounts, 4 NT 191, 4 NT 218, and 5 NT 464, record probably the total capital available to and the expenditures of the temple of Inanna in three separate years. Of the three only 4 NT 191 can be dated and that to late in the reign of Amar-Suen.[11] The capital listed in the three texts derives in part from the temple's real property and animals and in part from commodities and goods delivered from outside. In this last category, the texts 4 NT 191 and 5 NT 464 list, for example, grain and beer from the "sanctuary" or temple of Enlil;[12] 4 NT 218 lists substantial quantities of grain from the chief administrators of other temples. In addition, whatever the mechanics of the so-called bala-system,[13] it is a well-established fact that at least a portion of the animals, commodities, and goods delivered to Puzriš-Dagan (Drehem), Du-sabara[14] and other royal depots was redirected to the support of the cult of various of the temples at Nippur. I would suggest that at least a part of the commodities and goods delivered to the temple from outside and listed as capital in balanced accounts such as 4 NT 190, 4 NT 218, and 5 NT 464 derived from bala contributions. The rubric níg-diri zi-ga mu énsi bal-a é la-ba-an-sum-ma-šè, roughly translated "extra distribution (made) because the governor of (responsible for) the bala (contributions) did not provide it for the temple," which characterizes certain expenditures in monthly summaries of distributions of the chief administrator of the temple in Ibbi-Suen year 6 suggests that provisions for the cult were routinely provided to the temple from the bala-account. The sections of 4 NT 191, 4 NT 218, and 5 NT 464 which detail the expenditures are badly broken and not more than a

---

10. Preliminarily, see Richard L. Zettler, "The Ur III Inanna Temple at Nippur" (Ph.D. diss., The University of Chicago, 1984).

11. The date of 4 NT 191 is not preserved, but the first entry (obv. iii 7′–9′) in the expenditure section of that text reads 4 duh gur, itu bár-zag-gar, mu hu-úh-nu-ri^ki, ba-hul, that is, "1,200 sìla of bran (expenses for) the first month of the year in which Huhnuri was raided." The year formula is that for Amar-Suen year 7, and its occurrence in the text suggests that it should be dated to late in the reign of Amar-Suen or perhaps early in the reign of Šu-Suen.

12. At least a part of the capital listed in 4 NT 191 is described in obv. ii 4′–5′ by the rubric [ ] sá-dug₄ kaš zi-ga-dil-dil ù kaš še èš-ta DU-a, "... (part of) the fixed issues, beer (part of) miscellaneous distributions and beer (and) grain which have come from the sanctuary (temple of Enlil)." The same rubric occurs in 5 NT 464 obv. i 11′.

   The Sumerian èš, "sanctuary," is the term regularly used in the texts of the Inanna temple archive in referring to the temple of Enlil. Note that the temple of Enlil is, at times, referred to as èš Nibru^ki (Jacob Klein, Three Šulgi Hymns [Ramat Gan, 1981] 86, Šulgi D, line 375; Åke W. Sjöberg and E. Bergmann, The Collection of the Sumerian Temple Hymns, TCS 3 [Locust Valley, New York, 1970] 18, TH no. 2, line 36). On èš as referring to the temple of Enlil within the Ekur complex, see Aage Westenholz, Early Cuneiform Texts in Jena (Copenhagen, 1975) 27.

13. On the bala, see W. W. Hallo, "A Sumerian Amphictyony," JCS 14 (1960) 88–114. Also now Piotr Steinkeller, "The Administrative and Economic Organization of the Ur III State: The Core and the Periphery," in this volume.

14. On Du-sabara as a royal grain depot, see Robert M. Whiting, "Some Observations on the Drehem Calendar," ZA 69 (1979) 16, n. 19.

few of the rubrics describing the distributions listed there are preserved. The expenditures include those for festivals, rations and seed, fodder, and wages.

Text 4 NT 197, according to its colophon, is a balanced account of the temple of Inanna for a period of twelve months. It is dated Amar-Suen year 9. If it does not date to the same fiscal period as 4 NT 191, one of the texts just mentioned, it must be close in date to that text. The available capital and expenditures which it records make up only a fraction of those listed in balanced accounts such as 4 NT 191, 4 NT 218, and 5 NT 464 for the comparable fiscal period. The capital listed derives wholly from the temple's real property and animals. The total capital in barley is given as 294,944 sìla. The figure is roughly 60 percent of the total capital in barley and wheat available to the temple.[15]

The categories of expenditures recorded in 4 NT 197 parallel only certain of those listed in 4 NT 191, 4 NT 218, and 5 NT 464 and those under the rubrics rations and seed, fodder and wages for hired men are at roughly the same level as in those texts. What that implies is, presumably, that the issues listed under those rubrics were covered wholly from the yield of real property and animals in the possession of the temple.

The balanced accounts 4 NT 191, 4 NT 418, and 5 NT 464 and the balanced account 4 NT 197, then, indicate that the total capital available to the temple in any given year consisted of commodities and goods contributed from outside the institution and the yield from the real property (farm lands and gardens) and animals held by the temple.

The texts of the archive provide little information on the handling of that part of the annual operating capital of the temple derived from sources outside it. Perhaps the mechanics directing the handling of that part of the capital were set up outside the temple. The texts of the archive do, however, provide information on the management of the real property and animals held by the temple, and the expenditures from the capital which those sources generated, that is, the larger part of the annual operating capital. What the texts suggest is that the management of the temple's real property and animals was highly centralized in the hands of a single official, titled in Sumerian ugula é (šabra) ᵈInanna, a title perhaps best translated "chief administrator."[16] Although I cannot go into all of the arguments here, I will note that a high degree of centralization is suggested by the fact that the balanced account 4 NT 197, which I said above records capital derived from the temple's real property and animals and expenditures from that capital, can plausibly be interpreted as recording capital available to the chief administrator and his expenditures.

Presumably because of his central role in the administration of the temple, the transactions of the chief administrator make up the largest discrete group of texts within the temple archive. The texts constitute de facto an archive and the few preserved tablet basket labels (pisan dub-ba) suggest that those texts were filed together, at least prior to being sorted into larger, summary accounts.[17]

---

15. The total for the amount of barley and wheat available for expenditure in 4 NT 191 (obv. ii 6′) is 495,193 sìla, far in excess of the amount of grain listed in 4 NT 197.

16. For a discussion of the terms ugula é ᵈInanna and šabra ᵈInanna, see Richard L. Zettler, "The Genealogy of the House of Ur-Me-me: A Second Look," AfO 31 (1984) 1–9.

17. Three tablet basket labels were found in the fill of the platform constructed for the original version of the Parthian temple. These three are 5 NT 671, 6 NT 564, and 6 NT 712. The tag 5 NT 671 is rectangular in shape, but with rounded corners. A string hole runs through the tag. The text reads pisan šu ugula é, mu Ki-maš^ki ba-hul. I have not seen the tag 6 NT 564, which is in the Iraq Museum, Baghdad. The text on the tag reads pisan šu ugu[la é], mu ús-[sa], Ki-maš^ki ba-h[ul], mu íb-ús-sa. The tag 6 NT 712 is roughly square in shape. Two string holes are visible on the left edge, but none on the right. This suggests that the tag held the two ends of a single cord in a loop. The text is identical to those on the two just discussed; the year formula is that for Šu-Suen year 9.

Foster has translated the term pisan šu "basket: at hand (?)." He suggested that the basket would have held records which were current or pending (Benjamin R. Foster, "Archive and Record-keeping in Sargonic

The texts which make up the archive of the chief administrator are consistent in showing him to be the "public face" of the temple of Inanna. He was responsible for the receipt of commodities or goods into the temple. In addition, he acted on behalf of the temple in concluding purchase and sale contracts and in other legal proceedings such as claims raised against the temple. For example, the text 6 NT 28, dated in the fifth month of Šu-Suen year 1, records that Lugal-ùsar, a merchant (dam-gàr) with whom the temple of Inanna had frequent business dealings, appeared in court and under oath demanded that the chief administrator of the temple of Inanna pay what was due him, namely, eleven gín of silver, the purchase price of a slave named Ip-pa-pa, five gín of silver, the purchase price of an ox, and one garment intended for a man named Ur-dEn-líl-lá.

Perhaps the most interesting of the texts in the archive of the chief administrator are two sets of monthly summaries which record his expenditures. The two sets of texts are dated some thirty years apart, the earlier in the later part of the reign of Šulgi and the latter from year 6 of Ibbi-Suen.[18] The texts indicate that the distributions of the chief administrator of the temple fell into a number of broad categories; for example, rations, issues related to agricultural production, e.g., seed and fodder, and provisions for cultic activities. Perhaps more important, however, the two sets of texts suggest a change in the administrative responsibilities of the chief administrator, perhaps a loosening of his control, over the period of thirty years.

From a number of isolated references in the texts of the archive, I would suggest that the chief administrator, in addition to managing the temple's resources, had cultic and judicial functions.[19] Perhaps

---

Mesopotamia," *ZA* 72 [1982] 16–17). Piotr Steinkeller, however, has indicated to me (letter dated January 15, 1985) that šu ugula é is better translated "authority of or under the charge of the chief administrator."

18. The earlier set of monthly summaries consists of four texts, 4 NT 212, 6 NT 226, 6 NT 250, and 6 NT 567. The four texts are poorly preserved. The colophons, where intact, are identical, reading ki ugula é dInanna-ta, ba-zi, "from the chief administrator of the temple of Inanna, given out." Text 4 NT 212 is dated to the fourth month (year name not preserved), 6 NT 226 to the eighth month of Šulgi year 39, and 6 NT 250 to the seventh month of Šulgi year 48. The date of 6 NT 567 is not preserved, but one of the entries in the text suggests that it dates to the sixth month of the year.

    The later series of monthly accounts of expenditures of the chief administrator consists of sixteen registered texts (fourteen or fifteen different texts altogether). The colophons of the texts, where intact, are usually given as sá-dug$_4$ é u$_4$-7 níg-ezen-ma níg-diri zi-ga ù še-ba géme dumu é dInanna, ki šabra dInanna-ta, ba-zi, "(for) fixed offerings, é u$_4$-7, provisions for festivals, extra distributions and rations for the women and children of the temple of Inanna, from the chief administrator of (the temple of) Inanna, were given out." A few of the texts have the colophon ki Sag-dEn-líl-lá šabra dInanna-ta, ba-zi. The texts are apparently all dated to Ibbi-Suen year 6. Within that year the texts are distributed as follows: Month I, 6 NT 453 and 6 NT 462; Month II, 6 NT 366, 6 NT 430, 6 NT 479, and 6 NT 495; Months III–IV, none; Month V, 6 NT 431; Month VI, 6 NT 452; Month VII, none; Month VIII, 6 NT 444 + 521; Month IX, none; Month X, 5 NT 436 and 6 NT 361; Month XI, none; and, Month XII, 6 NT 367 (?). The dates of 6 NT 438, 6 NT 445, and 6 NT 464 are not preserved. As is apparent, there exist multiple copies of what is basically the same text for each month.

    I have discussed the monthly accounts of the chief administrator in detail in "The Ur III Inanna Temple at Nippur," pp. 370–92.

19. Several texts in the temple archive include references, I assume, to formal or legal, ceremonial or cultic activities of the chief administrator of the temple. Three texts (6 NT 229, 6 NT 629, and 6 NT 635), for example, list distributions under the rubric ér sù-a ugula é (šabra), "the long lament of the chief administrator." The exact meaning of the phrase is uncertain; it would seem to imply that the chief administrator had cultic functions. On texts mentioning ér sù-a, see A. Goetze, "Šakkanakkus of the Ur III Empire," *JCS* 17 (1963) 8–9.

    One text (5 NT 435) lists a distribution of flour under the rubric šabra gu-za-a tuš-a, literally, "(on the occasion) when the chief administrator was seated on the chair." The precise implications of the phrase are uncertain. Barrelet has suggested that the act of sitting is synonymous with rendering justice (Marie-Thérèse Barrelet, "La 'figure du roi' dans l'iconographie et dans les textes depuis Ur-nanše jusqu'à la fin de la 1$^{re}$ dynastie de Babylone," in Paul Garelli, ed., *Le Palais et la royauté* [Paris, 1974] 51). Irene Winter elaborates on the suggestion in her article "The King and the Cup: Iconography of the Royal Presentation Scene on Ur III Seals," in M. Kelly-Buccellati, ed., *Insight through Images: Studies in Honor of Edith*

by way of recompense, the chief administrator received land. The text 6 NT 777 indicates that he held at least forty-nine iku (17.29 hectares) of prebend land in a-šà gibil, for example. In addition, he leased land from the temple in return for a share of the produce. The text 6 NT 643 records that he leased three parcels, totaling ten iku (3.5 hectares) in a-šà ezen SAR.

In a study published some ten years ago, to which I have now made a number of additions and corrections, William W. Hallo pointed out that the post of chief administrator of the temple of Inanna was heritable and passed from father to son through four generations during the period of the Third Dynasty of Ur.[20] Prior to Šulgi year 35 the post was held by Ur-Me-me and his putative son $^d$En-líl-á-mah; from Šulgi year 35 perhaps to Ibbi-Suen year 5 by Lugal-engar-du$_{10}$, the son of $^d$En-líl-á-mah; and from Ibbi-Suen year 5 perhaps well into the reign of Išbi-Erra, first king of the Dynasty of Isin, by Lugal-engar-du$_{10}$'s son, Sag-$^d$En-líl-lá.[21]

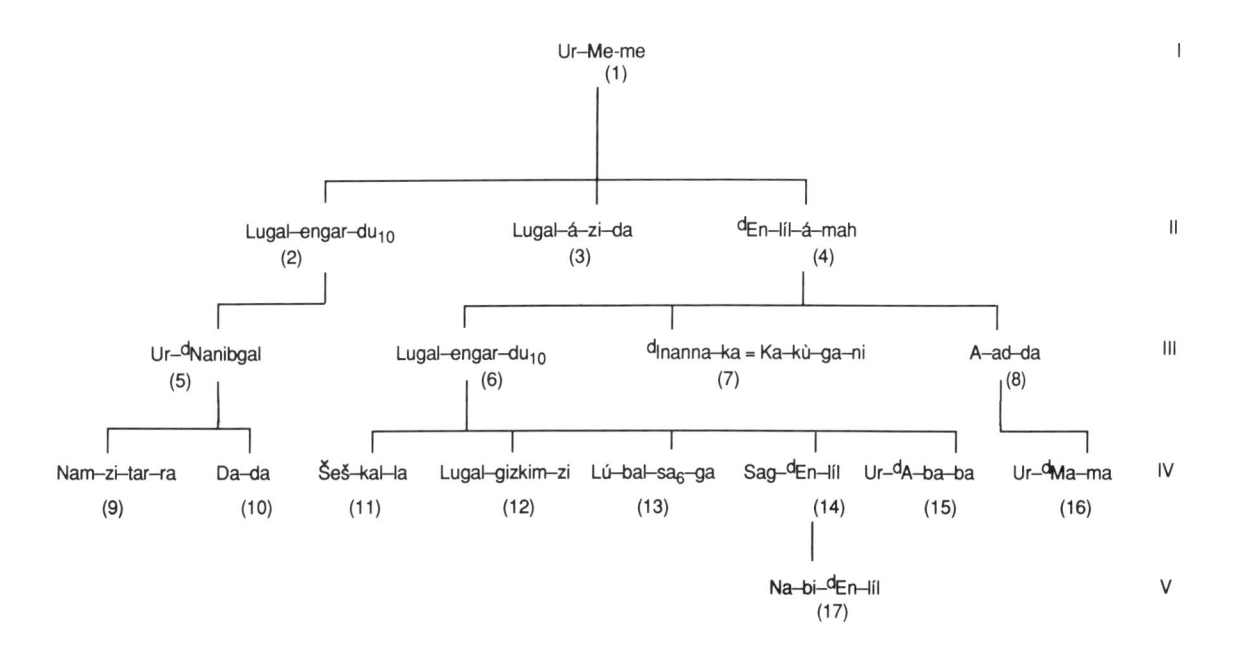

Figure 2. Genealogy of Ur-Me-me's Family

My analysis of the texts of the temple archive and the clay sealings found in the temple indicates not only that the post of chief administrator was hereditary, but also that a good portion of the extended kin group to which the successive chief administrators belonged was tied into the temple. A revised and extended genealogy of that kin group is given in figure 2.[22] The genealogy covers five generations. Those generations are numbered in roman numerals along the right side of the figure. Detailed information is available only on the individuals in generations III and IV, reflecting the chronological

---

*Porada*, Bibliotheca Mesopotamica, vol. 21 (Malibu, 1986) 253–68. Perhaps the phrase gu-za-a tuš-a indicated that the chief administrator had certain judicial functions.

20. William W. Hallo, "The House of Ur-Meme," *JNES* 31 (1972) 87–95. For additions and corrections, see Zettler, "The Genealogy of the House of Ur-Me-me."
21. Ibid.
22. Ibid., fig. 2.

distribution of texts in the archive.[23] Ur-Me-me was the earliest known member of the family and he was, as I indicated above, chief administrator of the temple. He does not appear active in the texts of the archive, but is known from inscriptions on the seals of his two sons, Lugal-engar-du$_{10}$ (No. 2) and Lugal-á-zi-da (No. 3). One branch of Ur-Me-me's family, that given on the left and headed by Lugal-engar-du$_{10}$ (No. 2), monopolized the post of énsi or governor of Nippur under the kings of the Third Dynasty of Ur. A second branch followed Ur-Me-me in control of the post of chief administrator of the temple. I do not have the space here to discuss the details of the genealogy or to discuss each of those listed in it. I do, however, want to focus on some of them and say what can plausibly be said of the contexts in which they occur in the texts of the archive. In that way I think I can make clear the nature of the family's involvement with the temple.

$^d$En-líl-á-mah (No. 4) apparently succeeded his father Ur-Me-me as chief administrator of the temple of Inanna. Although one text (6 NT 647) in the temple archive may have been drawn up during his tenure of office, $^d$En-líl-á-mah is known only from the inscriptions on the seals of his son and successor, Lugal-engar-du$_{10}$ (No. 6).[24] On the other hand, $^d$En-líl-á-mah's two brothers, Lugal-engar-du$_{10}$ (No. 2) and Lugal-á-zi-da (No. 3) are better known. Neither occurs in the texts of the temple archive, but numerous clay sealings with impressions of their seals were found in the temple. For example, sealings with impressions of a seal of Lugal-engar-du$_{10}$, son of Ur-Me-me, were found, along with fragmentary sealings with impressions of the official seal of Lugal-engar-du$_{10}$ (No. 6), the chief administrator, in the bin in the chancery courtyard;[25] other sealings were found in the trash pit in the back courtyard, Locus 137.[26] The sealings had apparently been discarded after having been broken off what they had sealed. A few sealings with impressions of one or the other of the two known seals of Lugal-engar-du$_{10}$, son of Ur-Me-me, which originally had been in the temple, were recovered from the fill of the Parthian platform.[27]

23. Isolated texts occur from early in the reign of Šulgi, but the bulk of texts in the archive is distributed over a period of time from Šulgi, years 39–40 through Ibbi-Suen, year 7, with a fairly heavy concentration in the years of Šu-Suen and Ibbi-Suen. Two texts are dated in the early years of Išbi-Erra.

24. Two seals of Lugal-engar-du$_{10}$ (No. 6) are known. The chronologically earlier of the two seals, presumably Lugal-engar-du$_{10}$'s personal seal, is known from impressions on six fragmentary sealings (4 NT 271–72, 5 NT 521–22, and 6 N 301–02) found in the excavations. It occurs as well on a text recording the redistribution of the inheritance of Lugal-engar-du$_{10}$'s sons (Jean-Marie Durand, "Une Condemnation à mort à l'époque d'Ur III," RA 71 [1977] 125–36; Martha Roth, "A Reassessment of RA 71 [1977] 125ff.," AfO 31 [1984]: 9–14). The seal shows a presentation scene. For the inscription on the seal, see Hallo, "The House of Ur-Meme," p. 90. The later, presumably official, seal of Lugal-engar-du$_{10}$, is that published by Briggs Buchanan (Briggs Buchanan, "An Extraordinary Seal Impression of the Third Dynasty of Ur," JNES 31 [1972]: 96–101). It is known from twenty-nine impressions on both clay sealings (5 NT 14, 5 NT 35, 5 NT 593–610, 5 NT 622–23, 5 NT 629, 6 N 440, and 6 NT 149) and tablets (4 NT 132–33, 4 NT 148a, and 6 NT 27). The inscription on the seal is that published by Hallo, "The House of Ur-Meme," p. 87.

The inscriptions on both seals name $^d$En-líl-á-mah as Lugal-engar-du$_{10}$'s father and give his titles as chief administrator of the temple of Inanna and nu-èš of Enlil.

25. Two sealings (6 NT 653–54) have impressions of one of the two known seals of Lugal-engar-du$_{10}$, the son of Ur-Me-me, specifically the one showing an Akkadian animal combat scene. On that seal, see Hallo, "The House of Ur-Meme," pp. 88 and 95; Zettler, "The Genealogy of the House of Ur-Me-me," 3, n. 8. Twenty-one of the sealings (5 NT 593–610, 5 NT 622–23, and 5 NT 629) have impressions of the official seal of Lugal-engar-du$_{10}$, son of $^d$En-líl-á-mah and chief administrator of the temple.

26. Twenty-eight fragmentary sealings have impressions of the Akkadian animal combat seal of Lugal-engar-du$_{10}$, son of Ur-Me-me. Four of the eight (6 N 436a–d) were registered. Fifty-nine sealings have impressions of the seal of Lugal-á-zi-da, son of Ur-Me-me. On those nine, 6 N 430a–d and 6 N 435a–e were listed in the field register. On Lugal-á-zi-da's seal, see Zettler, "The Genealogy of the House of Ur-Me-me"; for the inscription on the seal, see Hallo, "The House of Ur-Meme," p. 87.

27. A single sealing (6 N 261) has impressions of the Akkadian animal combat seal of Lugal-engar-du$_{10}$ (No. 2). Two sealings (6 N 311 and 6 N 439) have impressions of a seal of Lugal-engar-du$_{10}$ which shows a presentation scene. On this seal, see Zettler, "The Genealogy of the House of Ur-me-me."

Most of the sealings, both those from the building and those from the fill of the platform, had been broken off knobs and, so, had secured doors. What all this implies, I would argue, is that certainly Lugal-engar-du₁₀ (No. 2) and probably Lugal-á-zi-da (No. 3), even if neither was acting in any official capacity, had authority in the temple at the time their brother's son was chief administrator.

Lugal-engar-du₁₀ (No. 6), as I noted earlier, followed his father, ᵈEn-líl-á-mah, as chief administrator of the temple, and it is as chief administrator that he occurs most frequently in the texts of the archive. He does not occur exclusively in that context, however. Lugal-engar-du₁₀ occurs in one text that must be dated prior to the time he became chief administrator. The text 6 NT 647 is fragmentary, but apparently records the sale of a slave by Lugal-engar-du₁₀, the son of the chief administrator of the temple of Inanna. Lugal-engar-du₁₀ may also occur in several texts which date from the time after his son had succeeded him as chief administrator. It is possibly he, for example, who is party to two loans and a legal declaration concerning a male slave recorded in the texts 5 NT 561, 5 NT 566, and 5 NT 463, respectively.[28] Neither in the text dated prior to the time he became chief administrator nor in the three texts dating to his retirement is there any indication that Lugal-engar-du₁₀ had any official capacity in the temple administration at the time of the transaction.

Of Lugal-engar-du₁₀'s two known siblings only ᵈInanna-ka (No. 7) occurs in any meaningful context in the temple archive.[29] Text 6 NT 894 is a fragmentary list of expenditures. The issue recorded in obv. iii 24–26 of that text reads 10 sìla še <é>-mu-ta, ᵈInanna-ka, é ugula é, "ten sìla of barley from the kitchen, (for) ᵈInanna-ka, (in) the house of the chief administrator." The date of 6 NT 894 is not preserved, but it is reasonably certain, given the general distribution of texts in the archive, that it is either from the time of Lugal-engar-du₁₀ or Sag-ᵈEn-líl-lá (No. 14). At that time ᵈInanna-ka may have been a dependent living in the household of her brother or her brother's son.

The names of five of Lugal-engar-du₁₀'s sons are known. Four of those sons occur in the texts of the temple archive. One, Lugal-gizkim-zi (No. 12), does not. Why he does not is perhaps made clear by a recently published text recording a redistribution of the inheritance to be received by Lugal-engar-du₁₀'s sons.[30] According to that text, at some point in the reign of Amar-Suen, Lugal-gizkim-zi, his father's principal heir, brought charges under the jurisdiction of the king against his father. He was apparently able to substantiate the charges and his father was condemned to death. The sentence was never carried out. The text notes that Lugal-engar-du₁₀ managed to reconcile himself with the king.

Some ten years later, in the second year of Ibbi-Suen, Lugal-gizkim-zi again brought charges against his father. The text details the charges in the case. They included "infringing a cultic taboo, ... intercepting (and diverting) the sheep, the butter, and flour for the royal offering, ... intercepting the butter for the regular offerings amounting to three sìla per month, and ... diluting the butter of the regular

---

28. The texts 5 NT 461 and 5 NT 466 both record interest-bearing loans of silver. Text 5 NT 461 records that Ur-ᵈŠer-ri-da₅ received from Lugal-engar one shekel of silver as a loan. The interest is given as one gín of silver for each five gín borrowed. The text is dated to the first day, ninth month of Ibbi-Suen, year 5. Text 5 NT 466 records that Ur-abul received from Lugal-engar an amount of silver. The interest is given as in 5 NT 461. The text is dated to the twelfth month of Ibbi-Suen, year 5.

    Text 5 NT 463, apparently, records a legal declaration concerning a male slave. It notes that Ur-abul swore an oath to Lugal-engar that he would raise no claim concerning the slave. The text preserves the names of four witnesses to the declaration. It is dated Ibbi-Suen, year 5.

    Because the transactions which the three texts record are similar in character to transactions to which the chief administrator is known to have been party, for example, loans, and because the name Lugal-engar occurs otherwise only in lists of rations distributed to the women and children of the temple, I think it must be reckoned a possibility that the name Lugal-engar is an abbreviated writing of Lugal-engar-du₁₀ and that all three texts record affairs of the former chief administrator of the temple.

29. On ᵈInanna-ka, see Hallo, "The House of Ur-Meme," pp. 91–92; Zettler, "The Genealogy of the House of Ur-Me-me."

30. Durand, "Une Condemnation à mort," pp. 125–36.

offering."[31] He brought the charges against his father before a high-ranking panel, including Arad-mu, the sukkal-mah, Da-da (No. 10), governor of Nippur (and a relative of Lugal-engar-du$_{10}$ and his son) and perhaps Sag-$^d$Nanna-zu, sanga of Enlil.[32] Apparently Lugal-gizkim-zi was unable to substantiate the charges and he was himself condemned to death.

The strain which existed between Lugal-engar-du$_{10}$ and his son at least from the time of Amar-Suen is amply attested by the inheritance text just discussed. That strain would probably have kept Lugal-gizkim-zi from playing any sort of active role in the affairs of the temple from the time he first brought charges against his father, even if he were not formally disinherited.

When Lugal-gizkim-zi was condemned to death, Lugal-engar-du$_{10}$ made a younger son, Lú-bal-sa$_6$-ga (No. 13), his principal heir, intended to succeed to his post as chief administrator of the temple.[33] Although the name Lú-bal-sa$_6$-ga occurs in twenty texts in the temple archive, in only seven of those texts can Lú-bal-sa$_6$-ga be identified with certainty or at least plausibly as the son of the chief administrator. Those seven texts suggest that during the reign of Šu-Suen, Lú-bal-sa$_6$-ga acted for his father in receiving commodities and items into the temple, in giving out commodities for specific purposes, and in concluding loan agreements. The text 6 NT 274, for example, records that the chief administrator of the temple received wool from Dug$_4$-ga-zi-da. The text is not sealed by the seal of the chief administrator, however, but by that of Lú-bal-sa$_6$-ga, indicating that he received the wool on behalf of his father. The text 6 NT 887 records Lú-bal-sa$_6$-ga's distributions in connection with trips of (the statue of) Inanna to the temples of Enlil and Suen. The two texts 6 NT 2 and 6 NT 627 record loans made by Lú-bal-sa$_6$-ga. In addition to showing him acting on behalf of his father, texts (6 NT 777 and 6 NT 643) record that Lú-bal-sa$_6$-ga held nine iku (3.18 hectares) of prebend land with his father and brother in a-šà gibil and held a small amount of land on lease from the temple in a-šà mah.

Although Lú-bal-sa$_6$-ga was intended to succeed to his father's post and his activities in the texts of the archive suggest that he was trained for that eventuality, he apparently never became chief administrator of the temple. Instead, his brother, Sag-$^d$En-líl-lá (No. 14), succeeded Lugal-engar-du$_{10}$ as chief administrator of the temple no later than the sixth month of Ibbi-Suen, year 5.[34] Sag-$^d$En-líl-lá, however, did not just walk onto the scene. He had been active in the affairs of the temple for about twenty years since the end of the reign of Šulgi. In a text (6 NT 635) recording distributions of various types and grades of flour during the eleventh, twelfth and intercalary months of Šulgi, year 47, and the first month of Šulgi, year 48, Sag-$^d$En-líl-lá is listed as receiving small quantities of flour and as acting as maškim for the distribution of ten sìla of coarsely ground flour.[35]

Two other texts evidence Sag-$^d$En-líl-lá's involvement in the temple prior to the time he became chief administrator. A text found in the course of the University of Pennsylvania's excavations at Nippur in the nineteenth century indicates that in Amar-Suen, year 6, he contracted a loan of barley for the temple. The barley is described as še ur$_5$-ra $^d$Inanna, "a loan for Inanna." The tablet is sealed not by Sag-$^d$En-líl-lá's seal, but by that of Gìr-ni, perhaps Gìr-ni the nu-èš of Inanna, indicating that he took the grain

---

31. Roth, "A Reassessment," pp. 9–10.
32. Piotr Michalowski has suggested restoring the name broken in the text as Sag-$^d$Nanna-[zu]. Sag-$^d$Nanna-zu was sanga of Enlil. See Goetze, "Šakkanakkus of the Ur III Empire," p. 21.
33. Durand, "Une Condemnation à mort," p. 128. See also Roth, "A Reassessment." On Lú-bal-sa$_6$-ga, see Zettler, "The Genealogy of the House of Ur-Me-me."
34. On Sag-$^d$En-líl-lá, see Hallo, "The House of Ur-Meme," pp. 92–93. See also Zettler, "The Genealogy of the House of Ur-Me-me."
35. On maškim as deputy with authority to authorize transactions, see Setsuko Oh'e, "On the Function of the Maškim, I," *ASJ* 5 (1983) 113–26.

in hand.³⁶ A text (6 NT 399) from the temple archive shows Sag-ᵈEn-líl-lá involved in the purchase of a slave in Ibbi-Suen, year 4.

A land record (6 NT 777) which I have mentioned above indicates that Sag-ᵈEn-líl-lá held prebend land of the temple with his father, the chief administrator of the temple, and his brother, Lú-bal-sa₆-ga in a-šà gibil. The plot marked on the text as Sag-ᵈEn-líl-lá's is 14¼ iku or roughly five hectares.

The other two sons of Lugal-engar-du₁₀ who occur in the temple archive appear in only one or two texts. Šeš-kal-la (No. 11) occurs in 6 NT 842 as witness to a loan made by his father, the chief administrator of the temple, in the eleventh month of Šulgi, year 47. Whether he occurs in other texts as well cannot be determined with certainty since the name Šeš-kal-la is a very common one in the temple archive. Ur-ᵈA-ba-ba (No. 15) occurs with certainty only in 5 NT 500, a text dated to the fifth month of Ibbi-Suen, year 1. That text, a memo, records simply that eight gín of bronze, described as íb-tak₄, "remainder," is with Ur-ᵈA-ba-ba. The tablet is sealed by his seal.³⁷

In addition to his own sons, Lugal-engar-du₁₀'s brother's son, Ur-ᵈMa-ma (No. 16), occurs in the temple archive, for example, in 6 NT 538 and 6 NT 552. Text 6 NT 538 is fragmentary, but records that Ur-ᵈMa-ma, the son of A-ad-da (No. 8), brother of the chief administrator of the temple of Inanna, received a loan from Maš-da₅-gu-la. It is dated to the twelfth month of Šulgi, year 36. It would seem from the memo 6 NT 552 that Ur-ᵈMa-ma had been unable to repay the loan. That text gives the specifics of the loan, namely, that in Šulgi, year 36, Ur-ᵈMa-ma received 1,440 sìla of grain as a loan from Maš-da₅-gu-la, cupbearer of the king, and adds that in Amar-Suen, year 1, the chief administrator of the temple of Inanna repaid the loan for him. Neither 6 NT 552 nor any other text in the temple archive gives any indication of the conditions under which Lugal-engar-du₁₀ repaid the loan for his brother's son.

Ur-ᵈMa-ma, the son of A-ad-da, occurs also in a list of witnesses in the broken text 6 NT 593.

I have now reviewed, albeit briefly, the contexts in which the various members of the lineage of the successive chief administrators occur in the texts of the temple archive. I would argue that the level of the family's involvement in the affairs of the temple went well beyond what might reasonably be expected by the fact that the post of chief administrator of the temple was hereditary and passed from father to son. Members of the family, without apparently having any official capacity in the temple administration, but presumably because they were members of the family, had sufficient authority to secure doors within the temple building, even within the chancery complex. They could conclude contracts for the temple and at least on occasion act on behalf of the chief administrator. Members of the family received commodities from the temple and, if the two texts (6 NT 538 and 6 NT 552) involving the chief administrator's brother's son are read in one way, had a legitimate claim on the resources of the temple. Alternatively, those two texts might simply indicate that the chief administrator could use resources at his discretion for family or private purposes. In addition, family members held prebend land of the temple and had access to temple lands leased for a share of the produce.

The question of how exactly the family of the successive chief administrators of the temple of Inanna at Nippur came to dominate that institution is one which I am unable to answer. The precise time at which the earliest known member of that family, Ur-Me-me, lived and held office cannot at present be established with certainty and, therefore, it is not possible to determine whether he was part of a prominent and powerful family at Nippur before the Third Dynasty of Ur or a "new man" appointed to his post by Ur-Nammu or Šulgi, first kings of that dynasty.³⁸ The likelihood that Ur-Me-me's third

---

36. Owen, *NATN* 650. Gìr-ni, nu-èš occurs in the fragmentary text 6 NT 476.
37. On Šeš-kal-la and Ur-ᵈA-ba-ba, see Zettler, "The Genealogy of the house of Ur-Me-me."
38. The chronological positioning of Ur-Me-me is in large part a function of the dates assigned his two sons, Lugal-á-zi-da and Lugal-engar-du₁₀, on the basis of the styles of their known seals. For a general discussion of their dating, see Zettler, "The Genealogy of the House of Ur-Me-me."

successor, Sag-ᵈEn-líl-lá, survived the transition between Ibbi-Suen, last king of the Third Dynasty of Ur, and Išbi-Erra, founder of the Dynasty of Isin, suggests, however, that the family was one with entrenched interests in the Nippur area going well back in time, a family which found it easier and more profitable to cooperate with the rulers of successive dynasties than to incite their hostility.

Whatever the source of their control, the Ur-Me-me family evidently manipulated the resources of the temple of Inanna at Nippur in a sense to guarantee its continued prosperity and prominence. That being the case, I think the term bureaucratic is hardly an apt description for the administrative organization of that institution. It is rather what Weber called patrimonial administration.[39]

The extent to which extended families dominated or manipulated ostensibly religious institutions throughout Mesopotamian history is not known. The few studies of temple archives published to date have shed little light on the question, although Ellis' forthcoming work on the archive of the Inanna Kititum temple at Ishchali will perhaps do so.[40] Situations similar to that seen in the case of the Inanna temple at Nippur, that is, ones in which control of the institution is in the hands of an administrator whose extended family shares in the proceeds, do, however, exist in the Islamic period, specifically within the legal framework of *waqf ahli*.[41] I might suggest in closing that it is worth asking to what extent that institution had its roots in pre-Islamic traditions or developments.

---

39. Max Weber, *Economy and Society*, Guenther Roth and Calus Wittich, eds. (Berkeley, 1978), vol. 2, pp. 1010–69, esp. 1028–31.
40. See, for example, Maria DeJong Ellis, "Correlation of Archaeological and Written Evidence for the Study of Mesopotamian Institutions and Chronology," *AJA* 87 (1983) 504–07.
41. On *waqf*, see *The Encyclopaedia of Islam* (Leiden, 1934), vol. 4, pp. 1096–1102.

# CHAPTER 7

# THE ORGANIZATION AND FUNCTIONING OF THE ROYAL MORTUARY CULTS OF THE OLD KINGDOM IN EGYPT *

ANN MACY ROTH**

### 1. INTRODUCTION AND SOURCES

The institution of the royal mortuary cult flourished throughout the history of Pharaonic Egypt. Theoretically, a new cult was set up for every succeeding king. Each cult was intended to function forever, financed by the income from land set aside as a mortuary endowment by the founding king. (This mechanism is often compared to the later Islamic *waqf*.) In most periods, a temple was built to perpetuate the memory of the king and to house his cult after his death, when he had become fully divine. Although the basic purpose of these cults was constant, the nature of their organizational structure varied widely over the course of Egyptian history. In the Old Kingdom (Third through Sixth Dynasties, about 2700 to 2200 B.C.), this institution was particularly strong, and the manner in which it functioned exerted a subtle influence over the political and economic history of the period.

Three principal types of evidence can be applied to the investigation of royal mortuary cults during the Old Kingdom: administrative records, monumental records of special privileges granted, and the titles of temple functionaries.

Administrative records preserved on papyri from two Fifth Dynasty royal mortuary temples at Abu Sir are the primary source for the day-to-day functioning of the cult. Those from the temple of Neferirkare, a king of the middle Fifth Dynasty, date to the late Fifth and early Sixth Dynasties and include duty rosters, inventories, and payrolls.[1] They are incomplete and necessarily somewhat enigmatic; and although a thorough translation and analysis has been published,[2] many questions still remain. In the spring of 1982, the Czech expedition to Abu Sir began to uncover another archive in a storeroom of the neighboring temple of Neferefre, one of the kings who ruled briefly after Neferirkare.

---

*I am very grateful to Klaus Baer for his suggestions and advice, both regarding this paper and the talk from which it is derived. Edward Brovarski and Del Nord also suggested a number of useful improvements, which I very much appreciate.

**Address: 405 South Croskey Street, Philadelphia, PA 19164.

1. Paule Posener-Kriéger and Jean Louis de Cenival, *The Abu Sir Papyri*, Hieratic Papyri in the British Museum, Fifth Series (London, 1968).

2. Paule Posener-Kriéger, *Les Archives du temple funéraire de Néferirkarê-Kakaï (Les papyrus d'Abousir)*, Bibliothèque d'Etude 65, 2 vols. (Cairo, 1976).

115

Only a preliminary account of this archive has been published,[3] but the documents in it have been dated to approximately the same period. When the new archive is fully published, comparisons with the system known from the Neferirkare papyri should reveal the extent of variation in organization from one cult to another.

The monumental records of special privileges granted to cult functionaries by later kings are less informative.[4] They generally contain exemptions from specified kinds of taxes or forced labor for certain classes of the temple staff, and thus suggest the kind of impositions to which those not exempted might have been subject; but they do not give much information about the internal organization of the cult. Like the Abu Sir archives, these texts date to the Fifth and Sixth Dynasties, though some deal with cults established in the Fourth Dynasty.

Finally, the governmental titles of officials who also have titles relating to royal mortuary cults can suggest the social and economic level of the personnel of these cults.[5] Such titularies are a favorite source for all aspects of the history of the Old Kingdom, since they are one of the few kinds of evidence covering the period before the Fifth Dynasty.

The weight of the documentation necessitates a focus on the Fifth and Sixth Dynasties; the situation in earlier periods of the Old Kingdom can usually be extrapolated only from the better-known periods. Even for the latter it is dangerous to generalize: the newly discovered Neferefre papyri include many texts of a type not known in the Neferirkare papyri,[6] demonstrating how limited our evidence is.

## 2. THE FUNCTIONING OF ROYAL CULTS

The royal mortuary temples of the Old Kingdom were not scattered throughout Egypt, but were concentrated along the desert edge on the west bank of the Nile for a distance of about 55 kilometers; most were within 20 kilometers of the capital of Egypt at Memphis. The funerary-endowment lands, however, were distributed throughout the country.[7] The functionaries of a cult would have been given portions of these lands in exchange for their services in the temple; all offerings and other materials necessary for the carrying on of the cult would have been supplied out of the produce of this land. These allotments were then treated almost as private property by the temple functionaries, who divided the property among their heirs or used it to set up their own mortuary cults.[8] As a result, most royal mortuary

---

3. Idem, "Les Nouveaux papyrus d'Abousir," *SSEA Journal* 13 (1983) 51–57.
4. Hans Goedicke, *Königliche Dokumente aus dem Alten Reich*, Ägyptologische Abhandlung 14 (Wiesbaden, 1967), translates and discusses all the examples that are not meaningless fragments: the edict of Shepseskaf for Menkaure (pp. 16–21); that of Pepi I for Snefru (pp. 55–77); that of Pepi II for Menkaure (pp. 148–54); and two edicts of unknown authorship for Menkaure (pp. 78–80) and Sahure (p. 226).
5. A sampling of such titularies can be found in the "Order of Titles" section of Margaret Murray, *Index of Names and Titles of the Old Kingdom* (London, 1908), pls. 47–58. This sampling is, of course, very incomplete and skewed in favor of higher officials with long titularies; nonetheless, it makes a useful corpus.
6. Posener-Kriéger, "Les Nouveaux papyrus," pp. 55f.
7. Helen K. Jacquet-Gordon, *Les Noms de domains funéraires sous l'ancien empire égyptien*, Bibliothèque d'Etude 34 (Cairo, 1962) 5f.
8. There is no direct evidence for the adoption of royal mortuary endowment lands for private use; however the concern that these lands might fall into the wrong hands is frequently expressed in the royal edicts concerning them (see n. 4 above). This suggests that such transfers could, and did, take place where they were not specifically prohibited, and perhaps even where they were prohibited. The common occurrence of estates with names built on the names of kings in lists of private mortuary endowment lands (Jacquet-Gordon, *Les Noms de domains*, pp. 202–455) is also extremely suggestive.

cults were supported by a complex web of transfers of goods involving other royal cults, cults of the gods, cults of private officials, and the household of the reigning king.[9]

The rituals required by the cult were not unlike those required for the maintenance of a living person. Every day, at least one of the five statues of the dead king was dressed and undressed, anointed with perfume, adorned with eye-paint, and offered food. Twice daily a rite was performed that involved a procession around the pyramid. Festivals and journeys to visit other cults doubtless required special additional rites. In addition the temple staff was employed in guarding various parts of the temple and transporting temple revenues and property.[10]

## 3. THE SYSTEM OF PHYLES

These temple personnel were organized in a system of periodic, part-time service. This system was of great importance to the history of the Old Kingdom. By tying together the central government of Egypt and the numerous mortuary temples, it served as a counterbalance to the fragmentation of state resources caused by the setting aside of royal land for the endowment of multiple mortuary cults. As will be shown below, it contributed to the concentration of status and resources in the hands of the officials of the state bureaucracy, and may have been partly responsible for the stability of the state during the Old Kingdom.[11]

Most classes of functionaries in royal mortuary cults were divided into five groups, called phyles (Greek φυλή : Egyptian z̉).[12] Egyptian phyles were primarily groups of people who worked together rather than "tribes" in the Greek sense; they may have originated in some sort of system of clans, however, as they existed already in the early First Dynasty.[13] Each of the phyles used in the Old Kingdom had a distinctive adjectival name (for example, "great," "green," and "little"), which was used in all contexts where the system is attested: royal mortuary cults, royal work crews, perhaps the royal palace, and, with some modification, private mortuary cults. It is not clear whether the population as a whole was divided into phyles; but it seems unlikely since the system is rarely mentioned outside the Memphite area.

In royal mortuary temples, each phyle was further divided into two divisions.[14] Divisions also had special names, but these names rarely occur in more than one cult, and probably then only by chance. Each division served in the temple to which its members were attached for one calendar month out of every ten in rotation with the other nine divisions. The members of these divisions spent the remainder of their time doing other jobs. In some cases, this may have meant farming the land of the funerary domain

9. Posener-Kriéger, *Les Archives*, vol. 2, pp. 611–34, describes and discusses such a web. The information from the temple of Neferefre seems to be equally complicated; see idem, "Les Nouveaux papyrus," p. 56.
10. Posener-Kriéger, *Les Archives*, vol. 2, pp. 536–43, is the source for the preceding summary.
11. The Old Kingdom lasted for approximately five hundred years. Although there were three changes of dynasty during that time, the transitions appear to have been orderly, and may simply have been transfers of power to collateral lines of the same family. There is no textual or archaeological indication of any popular unrest during the entire period; there were no large or sudden changes in governmental organization or personnel. Famine is sometimes depicted, but seems not to have brought about significant social upheaval.
12. This system has been discussed recently in Posener-Kriéger, *Les Archives*, vol. 2, pp. 565–74, and by Wolfgang Helck, "Die Handwerker- und Priesterphylen des Alten Reiches in Ägypten," *Welt des Orients* 7 (1973) 1–8.
13. See, for example, W. M. F. Petrie, *The Royal Tombs of the First Dynasty*, 2 vols. (London, 1900), vol. 1, pl. 9, nos. 2, 4, and 5; Pierre Lacau and Jean-Phillipe Lauer, *La Pyramid à degrés IV: Inscriptions gravées sur les vases* (Cairo, 1959), pl. 4, nos. 19 and 20, pl. 8, no. 40.
14. Elmar Edel, "Die Kalksteintäfelchen," in *Das Sonnenheiligtum des Königs Userkaf*, Beiträge zur ägyptischen Bauforschung 8, ed. Herbert Ricke (Wiesbaden, 1969) 11–15.

for which they were responsible. Many of the functionaries, however, seem to have made other arrangements for the cultivation of this land, and returned from their cult duties to positions in the government bureaucracy. This is clear from the titularies of various cult functionaries who have government titles such as vizier, overseer of all the king's works, chiefs of various provinces, inspector of scribes of the treasury, director of the palace, overseer of messengers, or royal hairdresser.[15] The entire range of officials attached to the court and the government seems to have been represented in the royal mortuary cults. Indeed most of the people in the Old Kingdom who could afford to have funerary monuments held positions in one or more royal cults, a situation made possible by the rotation of the phyles which allowed them to fill positions in the bureaucracy as well. Positions in the mortuary cult of a king were thus presumably awarded to people who had served him well during his lifetime. Beginning in the late Fifth Dynasty, an office in the kings' cult outranked even the highest governmental title;[16] thus the temple office conferred status as well as a measure of financial compensation.

It used to be thought that the system of phyles was brought into the mortuary cults by the phyles of work crews who built the temples, later settled in the nearby pyramid towns, and finally took up positions in the royal cult when time and successive kings had diminished the income and prestige attached to the service.[17] Recent archaeological and textual research has shown, however, that the settlements of cult personnel around the pyramids can be distinguished from workers' settlements,[18] and that the organization of phyles in work crews may have differed from that used in mortuary cults.[19] When this evidence is added to the fact that phyle affiliations are sometimes given with royal cult titles in the tombs of high officials (albeit rarely),[20] it seems clear that the system of rotation by phyles and divisions was established in these cults at the outset, and that the official class took part in this rotation. Without some sort of system for temporary service, it would have been impossible for officials to perform their double roles.

## 4. CLASSES OF CULT PERSONNEL

There are four cult titles attested in the Abu Sir papyri whose holders seem to have served in the rotation of phyles.[21] The title ḥm-nṯr, literally "god's servant" but usually translated "prophet" (from the Greek προφήτης), was applied to the most prestigious level of the phyle organization. These functionaries carried out the rituals described above, and served as guards, but were apparently exempted from transport duty. Each division's ḥmw-nṯr were supervised by an inspector and an assistant inspector (sḥḏ and jmj-ḫt) of ḥmw-nṯr. The other large category of functionaries attested at Abu Sir are

---

15. Examples of all these titles are to be found associated with offices in royal mortuary cults in Murray, *Index of Names and Titles*, pls. 47–58.
16. Klaus Baer, *Rank and Title in the Old Kingdom* (Chicago, 1960) 257.
17. Wolfgang Helck, "Pyramiden," in *Paulys Realencyclopädie der Classischen Altertumswissenschaft*, ed. Georg Wissowa, Wilhelm Kroll, and Karl Mittlehaus, vol. 23/2 (46. Halbband), (Stuttgart, 1959), cols. 2257–58.
18. Rainer Stadelmann, "La Ville de pyramide à l'ancien empire," *Revue d'Egyptologie* 33 (1981) 67f.
19. Ann Roth, "A Preliminary Report on a Study of the System of Phyles in the Old Kingdom," *American Research Center in Egypt Newsletter* 124 (Winter 1983) 34.
20. Examples of such phyle identifications, always specifying the wr phyle, are cited in Edel, "Kalksteintäfelchen," p. 18. Only his nos. 2, 3, 4, and 5 support this point; the other examples are all men of unknown position and wealth depicted in tomb chapels in which they served and not in their own tombs.
21. The following summary is largely taken from the discussion in Posener-Kriéger, *Les Archives*, pp. 574–81.

those who bore the title ẖntj–š. This title is usually translated "tenant landholder,"[22] which is not completely appropriate in the case of royal mortuary cults since their duties there were almost identical with those of the ḥmw-nṯr (they differed only in that the ẖnt jw-s could be assigned transport duty). Counterparts of the mortuary ẖntjw-š were attached to the palace of the reigning king, but even less is known about their duties. Each division of ẖntjw-š had its own inspector and assistant inspector, parallel to the hierarchy of the ḥmw-nṯr. Most of the people mentioned in the Abu Sir papyri who function in the cult were either ḥmw-nṯr or ẖntjw-š.

The other two titles held by phyle members were much less common. The ḥrjw-nst, literally "who are on the seat," appear to have been young men who did much of the heavier work. They may have been apprentices, destined to inherit their fathers' positions in the cult.[23] Finally, the zšw, or "scribes," were sometimes, and perhaps always, attached to phyles, as the title zš n zȝ, "scribe of a phyle," indicates. These scribes may simply have been chosen from among the other phyle members, however, as many of them also bore the title ḥmw-nṯr or ẖntj-š.

The only important temple functionary not clearly connected with the system of phyles was the ḥrj-ḥȝbjt, the "lector priest" (literally "he who carries the festival text"). He was responsible for reading the ritual text and supervising the performance of the ritual by the ḥmw-nṯr and ẖntjw-š. His title is distinguished from these other cult functionaries by the lack of any particular cult affiliation when listed in his titulary, and by a different internal hierarchy: rather than the prefixes sḥḏ- and jmj-ḫt-, used by the higher ranking ḥmw-nṯr and ẖntjw-š, the supervisors of ḥrjw-ḥȝbjt were qualified by the phrase ḥrj-tp, "chief." It is thus unlikely that ḥrjw-ḥȝ bjt participated in phyle rotation.[24] Since this title is common in the titularies of government officials, however, it presumably also denoted a periodic or temporary service. One possible kind of rotation is suggested by a reference to a "lector priest who is in his year,"[25] which may refer to a year-long period of service; phyle members were occasionally called "he who is in his month."[26]

Whatever the mechanism for replacing or rotating the service of ḥrjw-ḥȝbjt, they were clearly not professional priests, permanently associated with a single cult to which they devoted all their time and energies. Instead, like the functionaries who served in the system of rotating phyles, they were people with other responsibilities who had been rewarded with cult offices that brought them additional status and income.

## 5. THE CONSEQUENCES OF THIS SYSTEM

The system of part-time temple service had an important influence on the structure of power in the Old Kingdom. If the revenues and status of positions in royal mortuary cults had been given to full-time professionals, the result would have been to create autonomous institutions with religious and historical

22. Henry Fischer, *Dendera in the Third Millennium B.C.* (Locust Valley, New York, 1968) 171. This discussion, of course, predates the publication of the Abu Sir papyri.
23. Posener-Kriéger, *Les Archives*, p. 584. This suggestion is supported by the use of the phrase ḥrj-nst in the tomb of Nj-kȝ-ʿnḫ in conjunction with the phrase "heir of all my property." Ḥrj-nst probably refers to the inheritance of offices, since the two phrases seem to specify the inheritance of the heir, who does indeed seem to have inherited his father's offices.
24. Posener-Kriéger, *Les Archives*, 565–74, does not include ḥrjw-ḥȝbjt among the classes she discusses along with phyles; however, the Abu Sir documents do not entirely rule out the possibility.
25. Cecil M. Firth and Battiscomb Gunn, *Teti Pyramid Cemeteries*, vol. 1 (Cairo, 1926) 284.
26. I know of only two texts that so explicitly join monthly service and the system of phyles: Henry Frederick Lutz, *Egyptian Tomb Steles and Offering Stones* (Leipzig, 1927), pl. 32, no. 63; and an unpublished text in the Giza mastaba of ʿnḫ-m-ʿ-Rʿ (G7837 and 7843). I am grateful to the Egyptian Department of the Museum of Fine Arts, Boston, for allowing me access to its photographs and tracings of the latter.

authority as well as great wealth. Initially, a system of full-time functionaries would have been cheaper, as it would have required only one-tenth the personnel that the phyle system did. However, the individual shares of the endowment would have been somewhat greater (though probably not ten times greater), and the prestige attached to the offices would have been much greater, since only a few officials could be selected to hold them. The holders of such offices would have had a greater incentive to protect the endowment, and the resources and independence to do so. Eventually these full-time personnel would have acquired a great deal of power, as well as economic and political interests that must frequently have come into conflict with those of the king and the central government. This is, in fact, very like what actually did happen in the New Kingdom, partly as a result of the large core of independent professional priests in the cult of Amon-Reʿ at Karnak.

In the Old Kingdom, however, the temple functionaries were given smaller shares and temporary duties, allowing the king to reward ten times as many people with jobs. One suspects from the distribution of these jobs that they may have been used in a patronage system, to reward the higher-ranking civil servants and the lower-ranking members of their entourages. The limitations of the income from these part-time positions kept cult functionaries dependent on their positions in the central government, which were in turn dependent either directly upon the king or indirectly upon him through a patron. As a result, temple revenues were quite vulnerable to efforts of subsequent kings to re-appropriate them: such encroachments would not have met an independent opposition from wealthy cult functionaries with a great pecuniary interest in maintaining the endowment intact; instead, if there was any opposition at all, it would come from individuals who had as great an interest in maintaining good relations with the king as in maintaining temple revenues. The interests of government bureaucrats could not come into conflict with the interests of cult functionaries because the same people filled both roles.

The effects of this system can be seen in the history of the period. No single mortuary cult became especially important; rather, they all tended to decline in importance with time, enrolling fewer and fewer people who were able to afford mortuary monuments.[27] The kings remained secure enough in their power to grant special exemptions to some mortuary cults, perhaps those of past kings with whom they wanted to be identified or allied for political reasons.[28] When the power of the Old Kingdom monarchs finally began to wane, it was the provincial officials rather than the personnel of the royal mortuary cults who took over their authority.

## 6. THE ORGANIZATION OF OTHER CULTS

The phyle system employed by royal mortuary cults was not used in all Old Kingdom temples. One of the few examples of a non-royal cult about which anything is known offers a marked contrast to the system described above.

In the tomb of the overseer of *ḥmw-nṯr* of the goddess Hathor in the Upper Egyptian town of *R-Jnt*, *Nj-kȝ-ʿnḫ*,[29] there is a text in which the tomb owner explains his reorganization of this local cult for the

---

27. The decline in the number of high officials in service at a cult over time can be seen in the chart of multiple priesthoods plotted against time in Wolfgang Helck, "Bemerkungen zu den Pyramidenstädten im Alten Reich," *MDAIK* 15 (1957) 91–111.
28. It is interesting that Snefru and Menkaure, two of the kings whose cults are known to have been granted such exemptions, were both considered in later generations to have been good and benevolent kings. The later reputation of Snefru is thoroughly discussed by George Posener, *Littérature et politique dans l'Egypt de la XII<sup>e</sup> dynastie* (Paris, 1956) 31–33; Menkaure (= Mycerinus) was still honored as a great and benevolent king in the Greek period; see Herodotus ii, 131ff.
29. This name has been read *Nj-ʿnḫ-kȝ(j)* by Fischer, *Dendera*, pp. 19 and 21, and also by Elmar Edel, *Hieroglyphischen Inschriften des Alten Reiches*, Abhandlung der Rheinisch-Westfälischen Akademie der Wissenschaften 67 (Opladen, 1981) 38ff.

benefit of his family after his death.[30] This cult had been founded by Menkaure in the late Fourth Dynasty with a donation of two auroras of land, and *Nj-kȝ-ʿnḫ* was appointed to serve in the cult by Userkaf, in the early Fifth Dynasty.[31] The cult was a very modest enterprise, honoring a provincial incarnation of the goddess whose sphere was probably limited to the village of *R-Jnt* and its immediate environs. Despite his title of "overseer," it seems certain that during his lifetime *Nj-kȝ-ʿnḫ* was the cult's sole employee: Edel has noted that in an earlier tomb, he bore only the title *ḥm-nṯr*; and only after he had appointed his family to succeed him did he attain the dignity of overseer.[32] Even more conclusively, the land he distributed to his family was divided into twelve parcels of five *tȝ* each: the recipient of each share was responsible for two months of service, one in the cult of Hathor and another in the mortuary cult of a certain *Ḫnw-kȝ* and his family. The total amount of land distributed was thus 60 *tȝ*, which in this period was equal to two aurora[33] or the entire amount of the temple endowment. It seems likely that *Ḫnw-kȝ* was either a previous holder of the endowment revenues or someone with a special relationship to *Nj-kȝ-ʿnḫ*, since his cult has been grafted on to that of Hathor without any corresponding addition to the endowment.

## 7. CONCLUSIONS

The provisions of *Nj-kȝ-ʿnḫ*'s reorganization of the Hathor cult at *R-Jnt* reveal a situation very different from that known from the royal mortuary cults of roughly the same period. A family is left in control of what was originally a state cult, and the patriarch is shown to exercise considerable autonomy in the appointment of his successors, the distribution of the endowment, and the addition of new conditions and responsibilities to those originally attached to the receipt of endowment revenues.

On the one hand, then, the royal mortuary cults were organized in a peculiarly Egyptian fashion, staffed by a complex system of periodic service which drew cult functionaries from the civil bureaucracy and contributed to a stable integration of the religious and political establishments of the state. On the other hand, in a small provincial cult, relatively distant from the Egyptian capital at Memphis and controlling a much smaller amount of endowment land, a system of administration existed that was much more comparable to the patrimonial, family-centered temple organization described in Mesopotamia.

---

30. The following summary of this text is based on the hand-copy of the text in Hans Goedicke, *Die privaten Rechtsinschriften aus dem Alten Reich*, Beihefte zur Wiener Zeitschrift für die Kunde des Morgenlandes 5 (Vienna, 1970), pl. 14, and in part on the discussion in ibid., pp. 131–43.

31. Goedicke has pointed out that certain grammatical forms and titles used in this tomb are not known before the reign of Unis, and hence that the reference to Userkaf concerns confirmation of the endowment rather than the date of *Nj-kȝ-ʿnḫ*'s appointment to the priesthood, ibid., pp. 134–37. However it seems strange that this would be noted in a different part of the text than the record of the original endowment, directly preceding *Nj-kȝ-ʿnḫ*'s claim to have exercised the office. The reading "It was the majesty of Userkaf who appointed me ..." seems much more probable and appropriate. Although it is hardly possible that *Nj-kȝ-ʿnḫ* lived until the reign of Unis, some hundred years after the death of Userkaf, his tomb could easily have been built considerably after his patron's death.

32. Edel, *Hieroglyphische Inschriften*, p. 38.

33. Klaus Baer, "A Note on Egyptian Area Units in the Old Kingdom," *JNES* 15 (1956) 115.

# CHAPTER 8

# PTOLEMAIC BUREAUCRACY FROM AN EGYPTIAN POINT OF VIEW

JANET H. JOHNSON
*University of Chicago*

Bureaucracy is a chronic problem throughout the world, but perhaps nowhere is it more frustrating than here in Egypt. The Egyptian government's overstaffed, inefficient agencies produce waste and corruption that drain the scarce resources of the Egyptian economy. The problem is so pervasive, says one Western diplomat, that objecting to it is "like complaining about the dust." ...

Many analysts argue that the bureaucratic mentality here dates back over 4,000 years, to the centralized administration developed by the Pharaohs ...

One theory holds that such a culture was a result of the "hydropolitics" of the Nile: that in a river society, rigid rules were necessary to harness the annual flooding. Other historians blame foreign invaders—the French and the British—for creating the modern bureaucracy.[1]

This same question, the origin of the bureaucracy, is the first basic question asked about Ptolemaic bureaucracy: Was it inherited from Pharaonic times or introduced by the Greeks? Directly opposite opinions have been expressed by two of the most famous historians of Ptolemaic Egypt.[2] Préaux argued that the the Ptolemaic system of administration was based on the Pharaonic one, " ... les formes et les techniques grecques imposées à l'administration égyptienne n'ont modifié ni les problèmes fondamentaux ni l'antique mouvement de la vie égyptienne."[3] Such an opinion is in very sharp contrast with that of Rostovtzeff,

No doubt the bureaucratic machinery of the Ptolemies ... was in part inherited from the past. To a certain extent, but to a certain extent only, it was a continuation and hellenization of Oriental bureaucracy.... how much more refined, more logical and coherent the latter [i.e., the

---

1. David Ignatius, *Wall Street Journal*, vol. 63, no. 114 [March 24, 1983] 1.
2. See also the summary of early discussions in C. Bradford Welles, "The Ptolemaic Administration in Egypt," *Journal of Juristic Papyrology* 3 (1949) 21–47.
3. Claire Préaux, *L'Économie royale des Lagides* (Brussels, 1939) 570.

bureaucratic machinery of the Ptolemies] was, and how many new Greek features it contained. This new Greek element was not confined to the Greek names of the offices, to the elaborate Greek administrative and financial terminology ... ; nor to the use of the Greek language in administration and taxation; nor to the Greek accounting system; it consisted above all in the general design of the administration and the spirit that permeated it.[4]

A cautionary note was sounded by Thomas, who noted that,

The nature of our source material also crucially affects one major problem which must be faced in studying the Ptolemaic administration, namely the extent to which this administration was based on Pharaonic models ... The student of Hellenistic Egypt seeking to find out about the immediate antecedents of his period finds it impossible to discover more than a handful of facts. Furthermore ..., there is virtually no evidence for the administration during the first fifty years of Ptolemaic rule. Therefore often the best one can hope to do is to compare the situation under the New Kingdom with that prevailing at about 250 B.C. [ca. 1000 years later]. Many changes will be observed, but we usually have very little idea whether these changes are due to the Saite dynasty, the Persians, or the Ptolemies.[5]

These discussions and conclusions are generally based on information collected from Greek papyri and it is well to note the comments of Clarysse,[6]

With Alexander the Great and the Ptolemies the rise of a Greek administration and colonisation marks for us a break in the history of Egypt. This is, I think, mainly due to the sudden appearance of a mass of Greek papyri and inscriptions, which have attracted the attention of classical scholars to this period.

From the Egyptian point of view, however, the break is not really all that important. The Egyptians were used to foreign domination since several generations and the replacement of the Persian ruler by a Macedonian king did not necessitate a change in their attitude. Under the Ptolemies ... the life of the common people hardly changed except for a few regions such as Alexandria and the Fayum.

Especially on the life of the temples and on all that was connected with them, that is to say, most of native cultural life, the "changes of dynasties, the wars and invasions had remarkably little effect."[7]

If we look at documents written in Egyptian, we can find a few specific cases by which we can begin to answer the question. For instance, there are pre-conquest examples of people bearing the title *sḫ n pr-ꜥꜣ* "king's scribe" or *sḫ n pꜣ tš* "scribe of the nome," which in the Ptolemaic period is the demotic equivalent of the Greek title βασιλικός γραμματεύς "king's scribe." There is even an Egyptian family

---

4. M. Rostovtzeff, *The Social and Economic History of the Hellenistic World* (Oxford, 1941) 1079.
5. J. David Thomas, "Aspects of the Ptolemaic Civil Service: The Dioiketes and the Nomarch," in Herwig Maehler and Volker Michael Strocka, eds., *Das ptolemäische Ägypten: Akten des Internationalen Symposions 27.–29. September 1976 in Berlin* (Mainz am Rhein, 1978) 188.
6. Willy Clarysse, "Prosopography and the Dating of Egyptian Monuments of the Ptolemaic Period," ibid., p. 239.
7. Quoting from B. V. Bothmer, "Introduction," to The Brooklyn Museum, *Egyptian Sculpture of the Late Period 700 B.C. to A.D. 100* (New York, 1960) xxxii.

from Thebes with members holding this title both pre-conquest and post-conquest,[8] suggesting that some Ptolemaic positions were direct continuations of pre-Ptolemaic ones.

A second basic question about Ptolemaic bureaucracy is: After it had been set up, whatever its origin, what was the relationship between Egyptians and Greeks in the bureaucracy and what was the relationship of the average Egyptian to the bureaucracy? The first thing which must be borne in mind in trying to answer this question is that the Ptolemaic bureaucracy, as most bureaucracies, was differentiated and, at least in part, a hierarchical structure.

> It is an oversimplification, but not, I think, one that is seriously misleading, to regard the Ptolemaic administration as composed of three layers: at the top, we have officials who controlled the whole of Egypt, usually in fact the whole of the Ptolemaic domain; in the middle we have officials who operated at the level of a nome; while at the bottom we have officials who controlled a village.[9]

Although in all periods in Ptolemaic Egypt the majority of people in the top layer had Greek names, by far the majority of bureaucrats, and the majority of people with whom the average Egyptian had to deal in the course of his life, were the people in the middle and lower levels of the bureaucracy. Here there are many people with Egyptian names (in some jobs the majority or all known holders of the position have Egyptian names). We shall return later to the question whether a name in Egyptian or Greek papyri is a reliable indication of ethnic background of the individual named. Here it should only be noted that, especially on the local level and in jobs dealing directly with the Egyptian populace, bureaucrats tended to have Egyptian names; for example, king's scribes (mentioned above), scribes of the district, scribes of the village, village heads, etc., consistently had Egyptian names throughout the Ptolemaic period.[10] In an important study of a large number of Greek papyri from el-Hibeh, Samuel was able to show that

> Once the non-Greeks had learned Greek and were prepared to operate in that language, they suffered no impediment from their ethnic origin, or indeed, from the ethnic nature of their names.
>
> ... They had more or less equal opportunity, at least at the local level, to join the ranks of officials.
>
> Indeed, not only does the opportunity to join seem to have been equal, but the opportunity to rise seems to have been there as well. I see no differentiation in the types of jobs held. Non-Greeks became nomarchs, basilikoi grammateis, and filled a variety of important offices. The ranks of the local bureaucracy seem to have been filled indifferently by Greeks or non-Greeks ...
>
> What does all this mean? In the first place, it seems clear that it was not difficult for a non-Greek to enter the bureaucracy, and that there was neither necessity, pressure, nor even a tendency for non-Greeks to change their names to Greek ... There does not seem to be any indication of a policy here, unless one calls complete indifference to ethnic origin a policy. The evidence shows an openness of the bureaucracy to non-Greeks, and we seem to have a situation

---

8. See P. W. Pestman, "A Family of Egyptian Scribes," *Bulletin of the American Society of Papyrologists* 5 (1968) 61.
9. Thomas, "Aspects," p. 188.
10. W. Peremans, "Egyptiens et étrangers dans l'administration civile et financière de l'Egypte ptolémaïque," *Ancient Society* 2 (1971) 33–45. W. Clarysse, "Greeks and Egyptians in the Ptolemaic Army and Administration," *Aegyptus* 65 (1985) 57–66, has shown that some jobs seem to have been "felt to be Egyptian in character" while others were "felt to be Greek" and that people in government service with both Greek and Egyptian names used the name appropriate to the job.

in which the only requirement for full participation in the life of the country is knowledge of the dominant language.[11]

El-Hibeh, with which Samuel was dealing, was an old town with a fairly large number of both Greeks and Egyptians. Bingen has studied documents from the Fayum, where there were a large number of new settlements by the Ptolemies. He has shown that the Greeks tended to live in the nome capitals, leaving the villages to develop (or perpetuate) a class of little notables, largely Egyptians, who entered the Ptolemaic system as bureaucrats, entrepreneurs, or (in the second half of the Ptolemaic period especially) soldiers. He would characterize the Egyptians in the urban population as largely priests and long-established bureaucrats.[12]

One clear example of how knowledge of Greek, even imperfect Greek, could open the door to the Ptolemaic bureaucracy for people whose native language was Egyptian is seen in a study of the office of *agoranomos* at Gebelein. In the early Ptolemaic period, both Greek and Egyptian legal documents recorded a transaction which was signed by a scribe and accompanied by a list of witnesses, who could be called in case of a dispute about the transaction. In the course of the Ptolemaic period, the Ptolemies introduced the office of *agoranomos*, who was not merely a scribe but a notary, authenticating what he recorded in the document so that there was no need for witnesses. This has been called one of the most typically "Greek" jobs in the Ptolemaic administration. The *agoranomos* always wrote Greek and had a Greek name; it has even been suggested the the Ptolemies created the position of *agoranomos* "to combat the prestige of the native scribes." But at Gebelein (which is a double city, the residents of Pathyris being mainly Egyptian, those of Crocodilopolis being mainly Greek) the earliest *agoranomos* had a father with an Egyptian name and all the rest of the *agoranomai* to the end of the second century in Gebelein were members of one family—two brothers, each with a son who succeeded him in the office. They were all Egyptians who had learned Greek to become *agoranomai*. All took Greek names based on their Egyptian names for use in their professional duties; their personal archives included both Greek and demotic documents, but some of them wrote horrible Greek (although good demotic). "S'il est vrai que la création de l'agoranomie était dirigée, fût-ce en partie, contre les scribes égyptiens, les Egyptiens n'en ont pas moins habilement réussi à s'emparer de cet instrument qui aurait été dirigé contre les scribes égyptiens."[13]

Crawford, in an interesting study of the recruitment and training of Ptolemaic bureaucrats, found that, in selection, moral qualities received the greatest emphasis; basically, the bureaucrat learned through on-the-job training. She concluded,

Some intellectual ability ($\dot{\alpha}\kappa\rho\iota\beta\varepsilon\iota\alpha$ and $\pi\rho\acute{o}\nu o\iota\alpha$) but no prior specialist knowledge was necessary for an official ...

There is only one area in which specific skills were required of the Ptolemaic official. This of course was the question of language and arises directly from the fact of conquest. At the top level of the administration appointments were made by the king or by his representative the

---

11. Alan E. Samuel, "The Greek Element in the Ptolemaic Bureaucracy," in *Proceedings of the XII International Congress of Papyrology*, American Studies in Papyrology, vol. 7 (1970) 450–52. For a short study of bilingualism in the Ptolemaic administration, see also Willy Peremans, "Le Bilinguisme dans les relations gréco-égyptiennes sous les Lagides," in E. Van't Dack, P. Van Dessel, and W. Van Gucht, eds., *Egypt and the Hellenistic World*, Studia Hellenistica, vol. 27 (Leuven, 1983) 268–73.
12. Jean Bingen, "Le Milieu urbain dans la Chôra égyptienne à l'époque ptolémaïque," in *Proceedings of the XIV International Congress of Papyrology*, Graeco-Roman Memoirs, vol. 61 (1975) 367–73.
13. P. W. Pestman, "L'Agoranomie: Un avant-poste de l'administration grecque enlevé par les égyptiens?," in Herwig Maehler and Volker Michael Strocka, eds., *Das ptolemäische Ägypten, Akten des Internationalen Symposions 27.–29. September 1976 in Berlin* (Mainz am Rhein, 1978) 210.

διοικητής who was expected to vet all lower appointments also. Whereas it was to be expected that Greeks would fill the senior appointments, in any post where contact with Egyptians was necessary, and this was true of nearly all local appointments, an Egyptian was the obvious choice. It is not, I think, so much a policy of positive non-discrimination which leads to the equal opportunities for Egyptians at a local level, as the practical need for a sufficient number of men with knowledge of local conditions and the means of communication with the peasants whose function in life was to serve the interests of the king.[14]

But all of this is still based on Greek documents. From the Old Kingdom on, Egyptian inscriptions show two conflicting ideals: a man should be able to rise in accordance with his ability but at the same time he wants to be able to pass on to his son everything which he has gained. There is a corollary to the second ideal: extended families often controlled a wide range of jobs. Examples of both types of recruitment abound throughout the Pharaonic period; when one looks at Egyptian documents from the Ptolemaic period, one still sees both ideals. The example of the *agoranomai* from Gebelein discussed above illustrates one family's monopoly of a specific job. Further examples are found throughout Ptolemaic Egyptian documents. Prime examples of important families collecting a large number of titles, at least some of which reflected considerable influence, and passing on their positions to their children are found in the religious sphere which, although in the Ptolemaic period a separate bureaucratic system from the secular system so far discussed, reflects the same organizational scheme. As an example one may mention the family controlling the position of High Priest of Ptah in Memphis, the highest religious position in Ptolemaic Egypt derived from the older, Pharaonic period. A large number of funerary stele, funerary papyri, sarcophagi, and statues inscribed in hieroglyphs and/or demotic belonging to members of this family show that there were thirteen High Priests of Ptah from Ptolemy I through Augustus (a period of nearly 300 years). Eleven of these were members of one family, ten generations from father to son and one pair of brothers. The twelfth was the brother-in-law of the preceding and the thirteenth was his son.[15] Each of these men amassed a large number of titles (e.g., in the Alexander inscription of Psenptais, Psenptais already had 24 titles and he had not yet become the High Priest);[16] in addition, the siblings, in-laws, wives, and daughters of the High Priests also amassed a large number of titles, largely religious. One can easily see how this family had accrued a great amount of religious and even secular power and how anyone wishing to deal with the temple of Ptah in Memphis had to go through a member of this family. This same pattern was identified by Crawford in her description of the "way in which Egyptian society worked,"

> Besides being a highly centralised country with an administration organised for the maximisation of the royal revenues Egypt was, and remained, a traditional peasant society in which primary social relations, those of family and friend, of patron and client, remained of supreme importance. The focus of loyalty was the village and within the village community there were traditional groupings and ties, obligations and expectations. ... The traditional ties of family were equally strong in Egyptian rural society and the administration could not avoid this influence among its officials. Attempts might be made to control such an influence but they probably had little effect. ... The realisation that family connections within the ranks of

---

14. Dorothy J. Crawford, "The Good Official of Ptolemaic Egypt," ibid., pp. 196 and 198.
15. See the chart in Jan Quaegebeur, "The Genealogy of the Memphite High Priest Family in the Hellenistic Period," in Dorothy J. Crawford, Jan Quaegebeur, and Willy Clarysse, *Studies on Ptolemaic Memphis*, Studia Hellenistica, vol. 24 (1980) 52.
16. Ibid., pp. 55–56.

officialdom and the inheritance of posts might not be desirable was not sufficient to check the practice.[17]

Rather than continuing with generalities, I would like to turn, finally, to the question of the bureaucrats with whom the "average" "middle class" Egyptian had to deal. To do this, we shall look at the channels followed in the legal suit recorded in the so-called Family Archive from Siut.[18] In this case, a woman named Khertiankh sued her brother-in-law for property which this younger half-brother of her husband had inherited from his father but which she thought should have been inherited by her husband. Here we are not concerned with the legal questions, although the documents and the law around which the decision turns are interesting. We shall look, rather, at the channels followed by the principals and the roles of people with Egyptian and Greek names.

Before we begin, we must deal with a question mentioned above: whether or not names accurately reflect ethnic origin. When Greek papyrologists assume that large numbers of Egyptians were taking Greek names in order to acquire jobs in the bureaucracy and advance within it, they have to question whether a man with a Greek name was "really" Greek. But we have seen that the assumption of mass "conversion" for the sake of bureaucratic jobs is unsupported. In addition, studies based on Greek papyri of both ethnics (which give the part of the Greek world from which the family of an individual derived) and patronymics (whether parents of people with Greek names had Greek or Egyptian names) show that we can, for the most part, take the names seriously. Indeed, statistically there are more examples of people with Greek names giving their children Egyptian names than there are examples of people with Egyptian names giving their children Greek names, although examples of either are quite rare;[19] the number of people with both Greek and Egyptian names is also small.

If one looks at the patronymics in the Family Archive from Siut, one finds 156 people with Egyptian names whose father (and occasionally the mother's name is given) had Egyptian names and eleven people with Greek names whose fathers had Greek names. There is only one clear case of a person with a Greek name whose parents had Egyptian names, this being a man who is said to have worked as herdsman for a high official with a Greek name. There is also one man with an Egyptian name whose father's name is very unusual and may perhaps be Greek. These two possible cases, out of 170 in the archive, allow us to conclude that, in the Family Archive from Siut, names accurately reflected ethnic origin.

All documents in the case (at least all the preserved documents) were written in demotic by a scribe with an Egyptian name. The deeds, etc., were signed by the person initiating the transfer and, when appropriate, by any members of the family having a vested interest in the property concerned. In addition to the people mentioned in the following outline of the action in the case, it should be noted that there are numerous Egyptians and some Greeks mentioned as owners of land adjacent to land owned by members of the disputing family. In addition, the plot of land most consistently disputed by the half-brothers was leased by the two Egyptians to three Greeks to be farmed. These leases were written in demotic, not Greek.

---

17. Crawford, "The Good Official," pp. 199–201.
18. Sir Herbert Thompson, *A Family Archive from Siut from Papyri in the British Museum* (Oxford, 1934).
19. W. Peremans, "Sur l'identification des égyptiens et des étrangers dans l'Egypte des Lagides," *Ancient Society* 1 (1970) 30.

## SUMMARY OF THE CASE

Year 8 of Ptolemy VI Philometor (173 B.C.)

The young half-brother Tefhapy sued to gain his inheritance from his father. Although the property was in Siut, he petitioned the Greek Theomnestos, the Strategos (originally a military title but by now that of the senior civil official) of the Nome of Thebes, with whom Tefhapy had an "in" since his uncles worked for Theomnestos. Theomnestos sent to another Greek with the title Strategos of the District of Siut to hear the case. Thus, the personal contact to Theomnestos was passed through channels to the person in whose jurisdiction the contested property lay. Khertiankh's husband Tot wrote a deed to the property to Tefhapy without going to court since he was "unable to go to the Registry Office" with his younger half-brother. Presumably it was at this time that the two half-brothers submitted to the "*hp* (law, jurisdiction) of the Elders and Chief Overseers ... of the Temple of Wepwawet (the god of Siut)" to which reference is made later in the text.

Year 11 of Ptolemy VI Philometor (170 B.C.)

Tefhapy petitioned to an Egyptian with the Egyptian titles Overseer of Pharaoh and Prophet of Thoth to get his inherited land which his half-brother was still holding. He sent another copy of the petition to an Egyptian with the Egyptian title Scribe of the Town. The Greek Theomnestos, Strategos of the Nome of Thebes, who by implication was partial to Tefhapy, had by year 11 "gone north" and the Strategos of the District of Siut "reported concerning the matters," evidently as a result of another petition from Tefhapy. The woman Khertiankh petitioned the Greek Numenios, the new Strategos of the Nome of Thebes, and had him send to the judges of Siut (in whose jurisdiction the property lay) to hear the case. We have the preserved transcript of this case, in which the judges were the three Egyptian priests of Wepwawet, the god of Siut. Tefhapy noted in his reply to Khertiankh that the fact that the Strategos requested the judges to hear the case proved nothing about the legitimacy of her claim since it was simply the job of the Strategos, when anyone complained to him, to refer the question to the appropriate office.

The procedure of the court case involved written statements by the plaintiff and defendant; both parties then appeared before the judges and verified their statements as read aloud by the scribe of the judges. Any further comments were added and they were asked to produce the actual documents and contracts cited in their statements. These were read into the court record. Following a summary of the arguments, the decree was made, in this case in favor of the defendant Tefhapy. The judges gave an order to an Egyptian with the Egyptian title translated Bailiff, who worked for or in concert with a Greek with the Greek title Eisagogeus, which means literally "introducer," he being the one who introduced cases in court. The Bailiff was ordered to put Tefhapy in possession of the disputed property and to have Tot, the husband of Khertiankh, make a quit claim deed to the property. The document ends with the signature and title of the scribe who made the record, an Egyptian with the title Scribe of the Judges and Priests of Wepwawet, and with the signatures and titles of the three judges, all Egyptian, as noted above.

Khertiankh was not satisfied. She sent another petition to the judges "in the place where Theomnestos, the Strategos, was" and sent a copy to the Strategos requesting that Tefhapy be brought to Ptolemais (north of Thebes; Ptolemais was the administrative center of Upper Egypt during the Ptolemaic period). The judges turned the petition over to a Greek with the Greek title Epistates (a high financial and administrative position often associated with a temple but appointed from outside) of the District of Siut. Khertiankh claimed that an Egyptian Bailiff and the Greek Andromachos (probably the Eisagogeus with or for whom this Bailiff was said above to work) went to the prison with an Egyptian called the Scribe of the Records with an order to write a quit claim deed. Eventually the judges found against Khertiankh but relieved her husband Tot of any responsibility. The decree was pronounced by another Greek who also had the Greek title Eisagogeus "introducer." In the meantime, Tefhapy sent another petition to an Egyptian with the Egyptian titles Overseer of Pharaoh and Prophet of Thoth and to an Egyptian Scribe of the Town of the West of the District of Siut. In it, he complained that, although the judgment of the court was in his favor, his half-brother was still holding on to the property. This is the end of the archive, although presumably not the end of the fight.

On the verso of the papyrus recording this court case is a copy of a petition and supporting documentation concerning a dispute between the priests of Isis at Aswan and two private individuals with the non-Egyptian (and non-Greek) names *Hty₃* and *Wrgy(r)*. While the case was being adjudicated, a Greek called the Strategos of the the Places around Aswan ordered the relevant documents to be held by a Greek with the Greek titles of Strategos of the Nome of Thebes and Archisomatophylax (Chief of the Bodyguard). He was to keep the documents in the name of the king. The said documents were submitted to this individual together with a petition to him from the priests of Isis asking judgment in their favor. After a favorable decision, the priests sent another petition asking for their documents back. In this same petition, the priests ask this high Greek official to write to a fellow Greek who bears an Egyptian title translated Chief of Police by the editor of the text although it is not the normal title for Chief of Police. This man also had the Greek title Epistates. The priests were asking that he be requested to "satisfy the banks" (i.e., "the royal granaries where [the tax] payments in kind were delivered")[20] with regard to the wine from the vineyard under dispute but to "hold up" the rest of the wine until the priests come up with a "fixed plan." The petition notes that it was written in the presence of an Egyptian named Tot (a different Tot from the one in the first case since they had different fathers). This Tot may have had a vested interest in the wine but he also wrote to the priests of Onuris (the god of the ancient capital of This, 12 miles south of Ptolemais which, being a Greek foundation, had no local Egyptian temple) in their capacity as judges, recounting the petition of the priests about having the wine "held up," and indicating that he, Tot, should be consulted about legal aspects of the case.

Thompson points out that, although Egyptian, Tot must have been in a position to act as intermediary and advocate of the priests of Aswan with the court. If he were the Chief Prophet and Lesonis (the highest administrative positions in the temple), the text would have said so. Therefore Thompson suggested that he might have been an official of the Ptolemaic Court sent from Ptolemais to Aswan to find out the facts of the case and put them into correct form as a petition for the priests.[21]

Whatever the explanation, and whatever the relationship between the two different suits which led them to be copied onto the same papyrus, one can reach certain general conclusions: The highest officials, functioning on a district level, were generally Greek, with titles written in demotic texts in transliteration from the Greek—e.g., the Strategos and Epistates. But these people had no direct influence on the court case: When they received a request, either through personal lines of communication or formal written petition, they simply referred it to the appropriate local officials for action.

Similarly, the other position mentioned in these texts regularly held by a Greek, with a title transliterated from Greek, was the Eisagogeus, who merely "introduced" cases. He had no judicial or investigative powers. The only Greek in the documents with "executionary" powers was the man who has one Greek title (Epistates) and one Egyptian title (here translated Chief of Police).

The officials who actually are seen taking part in the investigations, making decisions, recording decisions, and implementing decisions were Egyptians. Thus the judges were the priests of Wepwawet;

20. Thompson, *Family Archive*, p. 51, n. 27.
21. Ibid., p. 49.

the Bailiff who was to put Tefhape in possession of the property and who was to secure a quit claim deed from Khertiankh and Tot was an Egyptian; the Overseer (perhaps Overseer of Farmlands) of Pharaoh was an Egyptian, as were all the scribes met in the documents. All the titles these men bear are old Egyptian titles.

This is just one case and it can certainly not be concluded that Greeks never had any contact with, or influence over, Egyptians. Clearly that was not the case. But from an Egyptian point of view things may not have changed as much in Ptolemaic Egypt as a study of only the Greek records would suggest. Egypt remained, as Crawford pointed out, a traditional peasant society where immediate loyalty went to one's family and friends and to one's village, and personal contacts based on these ties were used whenever possible.[22] Thus one almost must agree with Préaux that the Ptolemies brought with them no fundamental changes in the structure of Egyptian society, including bureaucracy.

---

22. "The Good Official," p. 199.

# CHAPTER 9

# SOME PERSPECTIVES ON BYZANTINE BUREAUCRACY

WALTER EMIL KAEGI, JR.
*University of Chicago*

The Byzantine Empire was bureaucratic throughout its existence, although the degree of bureaucratic efficiency varied greatly between the fourth and the fifteenth centuries. Its bureaucracy did not appear *ex nihilo*, but was itself a continuation and elaboration of Hellenistic and earlier Roman bureaucratic practices, especially those of Hellenistic Egypt and other Greek-speaking eastern provinces of the Roman Empire. Its structure and terminology were the products of long evolution and not the creation of any one emperor or adviser. The nerve center of Byzantine bureaucracy was Constantinople, except for its temporary removal to Nicaea during the thirteenth-century occupation of Constantinople by Latin Crusaders. In addition to imperial and local bureaucracies, there was a complex ecclesiastical bureaucracy which is important but outside of the scope of this discussion.

It is inappropriate to summarize details of Byzantine bureaucratic offices and hierarchy here, because they receive, insofar as they are understood, specialized inquiry in numerous publications by many scholars. Instead, these are some observations on the nature of Byzantine bureaucracy and problems that deserve more investigation.

Byzantine bureaucracy had some constant characteristics throughout its lengthy history. Although education was not a public responsibility, candidates for higher bureaucratic positions were expected to have acquired a sound literary education. Although some excellent scholarly studies have appeared on problems of advanced teaching and learning in Byzantium, many gaps remain in understanding of the earliest elementary education of Byzantine bureaucrats. Byzantium did have that important prerequisite for an effective functioning of a bureaucracy, a pool of literate men. The Byzantine Empire was extremely rank-conscious, as its ceremonial protocol lists and notitiae demonstrate. The concept of *taxis* (order) is critical for understanding the mentality, formation, and functioning of Byzantine bureaucracy. The bureaucracy's positions, honors, ranks, and monetary compensation were the objects of intensive and bitter personal competition. Envy and rivalry permeated Byzantine bureaucracy. Nominal salaries were often inadequate and still worse, candidates for offices were often expected to purchase (or offer gifts for) their positions. The quality of Byzantine bureaucratic administration depended on many variables, but among the most important was the reigning emperor's ability to win confidence and wield effective authority. There was no hereditary possession of bureaucratic offices, but emperors and their immediate subordinates often filled positions for personal or factional reasons, rather than on the basis of merit alone. The term of office for the most important positions depended on the pleasure of the emperor.

Byzantine bureaucracy changed, however slowly—it was not static, even though the survival of obsolete ranks and titles in some protocol lists may suggest the illusion of changelessness. Some bureaucratic changes took place because of changing needs and conditions, but many of them resulted from specific rivalries and real or perceived threats by or to specific personalities.

Byzantine bureaucracy was the object of hatred and envy within and from outside the empire. Yet it contributed to the endurance of the empire. Its formalized procedures helped to make the empire itself more important than any particular political or intellectual or military leader. The empire did not depend exclusively on finding exceptional personal leaders. It had routinized methods of government and financing that could function in a more or less satisfactory fashion even during a period of mediocre imperial leadership. Throughout the history of the Byzantine Empire, its emperors relied on a complex and changing system of bureaucratic checks and controls to preserve and expand their personal (and often familial) power. The emperors were able to succeed in this because the bureaucrats controlled access to the emperor, produced and authenticated documents and coins, as well as weights and measures, and of course they assessed, collected, recorded, and redistributed fiscal revenues and taxes, and disbursed and oversaw governmental expenditures for activities that ranged from public ceremonies to warfare. Byzantine bureaucracy was complex. Its complexity provided emperors with even more potential control for the prevention of the seizure of power by some rival, even though on relatively rare occasions such bureaucrats as Anastasius I and Nicephorus I became emperors themselves.

Byzantium was conscious of its Roman bureaucratic heritage, and to a lesser degree, of its important Hellenistic heritage, but it was not conscious of any debt to any Near Eastern or ancient Near Eastern heritage, even though a number of Byzantines admired the model of idealized Persian (Achaemenid) government order in the relatively popular *Cyropaideia* of Xenophon. Unlike some bureaucratic empires, Byzantium had no competitive examinations for its bureaucratic posts. Early in the empire's history, in the fourth and throughout much of the fifth centuries, a knowledge of Latin was a prerequisite for appointment to certain important positions. That requirement disappeared, but in subsequent centuries many higher positions in the bureaucracy were usually awarded to those who possessed, or who appeared to possess, a familiarity with at least some of the corpus of classical Greek literature, even though that literature provided no technical training for any given bureaucratic position. Education socialized many bureaucratic aspirants in Constantinople, although its socializing role in other areas of the empire is less clear. At Constantinople it was possible for a few teachers to earn a living from educating young men who sought varying governmental and ecclesiastical positions at Constantinople. The bureaucracy's archives do not survive, and therefore it is difficult to develop a detailed understanding of it comparable to that of some other bureaucratic empires. Its bureaucrats, like those of many other Near Eastern bureaucracies, were involved in sealing and authentication. Sealing was one of its most characteristic forms of bureaucratic control. Its lead seals constitute one of the most precious sources for the recovery of information about its offices, ranks, and personalities. There was a visual dimension to Byzantine bureaucracy: offices and their ranks had specific insignia, symbols, and in many cases, dress. Due respect for them contributed to *taxis* or order in the Byzantine world view and its society.

One of the most famous examples of bureaucratic control in Byzantium was the striking of coinage. The Comitiva Sacrarum Largitionum or office of the Count of the Sacred Largesses authenticated the purity of silver and gold sheet and objects between the fourth and seventh centuries, however, much more long-lived was another of its original responsibilities, the stability of the gold coin, the *nomisma* or *solidus*, which, stabilized normally at about four and a half grams of gold, remained the virtual symbol of imperial prestige between the fourth and eleventh centuries. The Comitiva Sacrarum Largitionum disappeared in the course of the seventh century, but the mint at Constantinople maintained effective control over the production and quality of gold coinage until the eleventh century.

Scholars are achieving, by means of the study of the lead seals, papyri, *praktika*, histories and literary works, an increasing amount of knowledge about Byzantine bureaucratic organization, and in particular, its slowly changing hierarchies. The sources are difficult to use for an understanding of many aspects of bureaucratic functioning. Such bureaucrats as John Lydos, Michael Attaleiates, Michael Psellos, Nicephorus Choumnos, and Theodore Metochites have left some written testimony about themselves, but not the kind of diaries from which a historian could reconstruct the detailed functioning, mentality, speed, and financial efficiency of Byzantine bureaus.

There are a substantial number of major aspects of bureaucracy that remain and perhaps will remain poorly understood. Without discussing the problems in understanding the evolution of every individual office, it is worth noting some major gaps in scholarly knowledge.

1. The precise evolution of municipal bureaucracy, from the fourth through the end of the seventh centuries, deserves more study.

2. Bureaucratic activities at Constantinople and elsewhere that were, by their nature, not recorded in official documents—signals, gestures, suppression and release of critical information at crucial moments, masking of intentions, deliberate misguidance and falsification of documents, and in general, concealed hatreds—should be the subject of a large inquiry.

3. Familial continuities and breaks within bureaucratic offices and ranks—there are too many breaks in historical knowledge about the relationships between bureaucrats, especially between the sixth and ninth centuries (this is especially true in Anatolia and what remained of the Byzantine Balkans)—are insufficiently understood.

4. Although there are some records of monastic landholdings, the absence of land registers, boundary markers, or other documentation on private landholding makes it impossible to know accurately the landholdings of bureaucrats, although a few, such as Michael Attaleiates, tell something about themselves and their properties.

5. The formation of a bureaucratic outlook, mentality, and group of customs at Constantinople is obscure. It took time for the various bureaucrats who were gathered from widely scattered parts of the Roman Empire in the fourth century to achieve an understanding of how to operate as bureaucrats at Constantinople. It took time to reach an appreciation of the range of alternative policies that might work when one controlled Constantinople and encountered internal rebellion or external invasion from either the Anatolian or Balkan areas of the empire. How did these mentalities develop and how long did it take for the essential features of these mentalities to form? It appears that a bureaucratic lore of how to operate at Constantinople had formed by early in the fifth century, but this is only an impression and it would be very difficult to provide solid documentation. The problem is an important one.

6. A substantial corpus of political and military advice existed at Constantinople concerning the use of cleverness, corruption, ruses, patience, and timing, instead of brute force, in order to achieve desirable ends in internal and foreign policy. Some of this advice had survived in aphoristic form from earlier Greek, Hellenistic, and Roman periods. Such advice, reinforced by the citation of specific historical precedents, aided some emperors and their bureaucrats in their efforts to avoid the risks of decisive warfare. Such compilations reinforced the confidence of Byzantine bureaucrats in their ability to overcome various challenges.

7. Bureaucratic rivalries require much more research, including the problems of rivalries between bureaus, techniques of bureaucratic rivalry, and the existence of esprit de corps and self-consciousness within bureaus.

8. Many aspects of time and timing deserve scholarly attention: the normal length of time necessary for the processing of certain types of documents, as well as bureaucrats' employment of time and exploitation of timing in handling problems of policy.

9. Fergus Millar has greatly contributed to scholarly understanding of Roman bureaucracy by the publication of his *Emperor in the Roman World, 31 B.C. – A.D. 337* (Ithaca, N.Y., 1977). A comparable book on the relationship between the Byzantine emperor and his bureaucrats would make an extremely valuable contribution to our understanding of the ways in which power flowed in Byzantium.

10. Some scholars, in particular, Alexander P. Kazhdan, have examined problems of the social origins, in particular, ethnic, religious, and familial, of Byzantine bureaucrats. This subject deserves much more work. Extant legal texts explain certain specific prohibitions of religious affiliation, i.e., heterodox affiliations, for officeholders, but the specific ways in which social origins and ties affected the selection, promotion, and retention of bureaucrats still deserve much more inquiry.

11. Many dimensions of venality and corruption deserve detailed study. Advances in scholarly understanding of these problems in the Late Roman period are contributing to a better knowledge of them in the Byzantine period.

12. Statistics are inadequate. Reports of travellers and Arab geographers require even more critical evaluation than they have thus far received.

13. No one has undertaken a serious investigation of the possibility of continuities in bureaucratic practices, organization, or outlook between the Byzantine Empire and ancient Near Eastern bureaucracies. Two decades ago Carl Kraeling suggested that it would be worthwhile to study various kinds of continuity between Byzantium and ancient Near Eastern entities that occupied what later became Byzantine territory. The project would require such formidable tools and range of knowledge that it would discourage most scholars from undertaking it. Kraeling's remarks, which he made in the course of a lengthy conversation, remain unpublished and unheeded.

14. A broad analytical study of categories and techniques of bureaucratic control and checks and balances in Byzantium could make a valuable contribution to the understanding of not only Byzantine bureaucracy, but also Byzantine imperial institutions and history in a wider perspective.

15. Informal groups existed within Byzantine bureaucracy. Sources occasionally use the term *hetaireia* for a particular bond or association of some persons. Thus far, only very scattered groupings have received scholarly notice. The references to the primary sources to this type of association are, however, likely to be parenthetical and brief.

16. An important issue is the existence or non-existence of bureaucratic solidarity. Did bureaucrats share a collective sense of identity which transcended family and bureau? The most frequently cited case for bureaucratic solidarity is one from the eleventh century. A number of scholars have argued that there was a "bureaucratic party" which was the rival of a "military party." Many scholars today believe, as I do, that it is inaccurate to assume such a clear dichotomy. The sources do not support such a sharp classification. It is inappropriate to use the modern concept of "party" in analyzing eleventh-century conditions. Even in the eleventh century the Byzantine bureaucracy was not homogeneous. It and the Byzantine armies were riddled with rivalries and complex personal ties. It is wrong to impute so much cohesion to Byzantine bureaucrats.

17. Another version of the hypothetical polarity between "bureaucratic" and "military" parties is the assumption of a polarity of Constantinople-centered bureaucrats and provincial, especially Anatolian, landholding military families. Once again, such a distinction is difficult to support in the late tenth and eleventh centuries because there was a tendency for bureaucrats who lived in Constantinople to purchase

land in areas that were very far away, and in addition, so-called bureaucratic and military families frequently had complex marital ties. It is an oversimplification to envisage some permanent and unvarying opposition on regional lines between a bureaucracy centered on the imperial capital and rural landholders. The real situation, in those periods when there are sufficient sources to make any worthwhile observations, was complex.

18. The traditional interpretation of Byzantine history has normally favored the argument that a strong central bureaucracy together with strict central controls was a constructive and indeed essential feature of Byzantine government and Byzantine history. A revisionist strain has developed in the past few years, however. Its adherents question whether one should necessarily assume that a very strong central government was good for the majority of Byzantine provincials. In short, the relative merits of centralization, embodied in a strong central bureaucracy, and decentralization are the subject of re-examination and doubt.

19. A neglected but very difficult to understand group of Byzantine bureaucrats were the eunuchs. The *notitiae* reveal which offices were reserved to eunuchs. No eunuch has left a memoir about his situation. References to eunuchs appear in scattered letters, histories, and literary works. It is extremely difficult to collect and analyze such disparate citations. Although some primary sources indicate that military commanders and soldiers felt hostility towards eunuchs—and sometimes openly expressed it—the pattern is not a uniform one. Comparative study of the use of eunuchs in other bureaucratic empires may illuminate Byzantine practices. It is significant that the Byzantines often employed eunuchs who were born within the borders of the empire and who maintained ties, sometimes ones that were very close, with other members of their families. The special problem of the imperial resort to the appointment of eunuchs to control armies met with very uneven success, although one of the greatest Byzantine generals, Narses, was a eunuch.

20. It is important to understand the views of non-bureaucrats in the Byzantine Empire on Byzantine bureaucrats. No one text provides an accurate picture. The eleventh-century *Strategikon* of Kekaumenos is an excellent source for one perspective on the Constantinopolitan bureaucracy, but there are other points of view. The Byzantine public was not uniformly hostile to bureaucrats, who appear to be accepted, if grudgingly, as part of government.

21. Few aspects of Byzantine bureaucracy have received more debate and less intelligent analysis than the possible interrelationship of Byzantine, Sassanian, Umayyad, and Ottoman bureaucratic institutions and practices. Many investigations have started with a *parti pris*. Very detailed and unbiased analyses are necessary, but at this time it is premature to draw broad conclusions. It is possible to conclude, however, that it is erroneous to attribute the origins of any of these bureaucratic systems to any one single external bureaucratic model. The unfortunate, although somewhat amusing, propensity of scholars to attribute any poorly understood Late Roman or Early Byzantine bureaucratic institution to some mysterious "Persian" origin has slackened, to the benefit of more rigorous research.

22. The most heatedly debated issue in the interpretation of the development of Byzantine bureaucracy is the explanation of the vast differences between the bureaucratic structures of the sixth century, which were essentially still Late Roman, and the distinctly "Middle Byzantine" ones of the ninth century. The dating and interpretation of those changes, including the disappearance of the Late Roman Praetorian Prefecture, the Count of the Sacred Largesses, and the related provincial structures of governors (*praesides*) and their *officia*, and the *provinciae* or provinces, as well as the military structure of *magistri militum* or Masters of the Soldiers, remain controversial. The tendency in most recent scholarship is to interpret these changes as gradual ones between the sixth and late eighth centuries, not

as the result of some sudden massive comprehensive social, economic, political, or military reforms of any one emperor.

The elucidation of these problems requires investigation of many kinds of primary sources, but among the most important of these are Muslim sources on the early Islamic conquests. Byzantinists thus far have not examined in detail the nature and character of institutions on the eve of the Muslim conquests in order to compare them with what followed in Syria, Palestine, Egypt, Byzantine Mesopotamia, and southeast Asia Minor. It is necessary to compare the institutions, but also to study the actual Muslim accounts of the conquests in order to understand, insofar as is possible, how Byzantine bureaucratic structures were still functioning during the course of that warfare. However imperfect, these sources provide some glimpses—at the last possible moment—of what was the character of Byzantine bureaucracy—terminology, offices, functions, practices, and deficiencies—during the strains of the invasions, before any new structures could replace them, in those areas. My present researches for a book, *Byzantium and the Early Islamic Conquests*, tentatively indicate that the very gradual change in Late Roman or Early Byzantine bureaucratic and military institutions persisted well into the 620s and even accompanied the restoration of Byzantine authority in the eastern provinces that the Sassanians evacuated after their crushing defeat by Emperor Heraclius in 628. However unsettling the lengthy and bloody war with the Sassanians had been, the decisive institutional changes in the Byzantine Empire happen not as a response to the Sassanian challenge, but in response to the Muslim one. Even these changes did not take place all at once, but appear to have started as *ad hoc* improvisations. A close analysis of Muslim reports about the activities of Heraclius in Syria and other provinces in the face of the Muslim invasions indicates that he appears to have appointed a number of military commanders with emergency powers to confront the urgent situation. These appointments, still very imperfectly understood, appear to be confirmed in several early Christian histories, and do represent a form of militarization of authority. It is incorrect to assume an absolute divergence between Muslim and early Christian traditions. Although the precise *stemma* of these Muslim and Christian traditions cannot yet, if ever, be determined, there are some remarkable convergences. The bureaucratic and institutional situation in Byzantine Anatolia, including its origins and development, cannot be understood in isolation from what was the bureaucratic and military institutional structure in Byzantine Mesopotamia and Syria as the Byzantine armies, with their command and logistical structures and the local bureaucratic apparatuses, improvised emergency governmental and logistical arrangements and then withdrew, under strong military pressure from the Muslims. There is a quickening of change in the 630s and early 640s, even though the total process of institutional change into a "Middle Byzantine" structure will be a very lengthy one. This does not solve the question of the dating of the regularization of the Greek word *thema* (plural, *themata*) for a new structure of provincial military districts. The study of the Byzantine fiscal bureaucracy's evolution reveals that the old Late Roman tax in kind called *annona militaris*, along with its complicated and controversial system of storehouses for rations for men and horses, survived in critical border provinces in the east until the Muslim conquests. This relatively unappreciated fact may be critical for understanding the nature of Byzantine bureaucracy in such provinces as Egypt, Syria, Palestine, Mesopotamia, and Armenia in the early seventh century, and may possibly have value in understanding the equally controversial fiscal situation in some of those areas immediately following the extension of Muslim authority there. It is important to understand that some Late Roman taxes in kind were still being assessed, paid, collected, and redistributed in kind, and not always commuted to gold or other monetary equivalent (*adaeratio*). This does not mean that the practice was universal throughout the empire, but in some areas where it was absolutely essential that soldiers and their mounts have adequate issues of food, some very old bureaucratic structures for the collection of such food supplies and their redistribution to soldiers and their mounts persisted until the disappearance of Byzantine authority. There is no evidence that any system of *stratiōtika ktēmata* or "soldiers' properties" (in the ninth-century sense) had yet come into existence. These very old bureaucratic structures were subject to extreme strain at the time of the Sassanian invasions in the early seventh century, but they nevertheless persisted and were part of the support structure for the Byzantine government and army in the 630s. The details of these structures may never be fully known, but it is essential for Byzantine historians and Islamicists to join in attempting to discern as much as possible of the nature of those bureaucratic institutions just as Byzantine authority was giving way to the Muslims. An understanding of the logistical problems of Byzantine armies can contribute to an understanding of the improvisations in the bureaucratic support system, in particular experimentation with the use of "prefects of the army" or extraordinary prefects, with the status of an ordinary praetorian prefect, to insure that soldiers received their appropriate pay and to observe and possibly serve as a potential check on any dangerous general. The solution of these formidable problems is not yet complete, but there has been substantial progress. This complex of problems involves some of the most significant topics of Byzantine and Islamic history.

23. Although bureaucracy is the subject of these remarks, it is important to remember that achievement of an understanding of the bureaucratic hierarchy of an institution such as the Byzantine army, however difficult, does not provide a full understanding of that institution and its functioning. It would be erroneous to neglect the importance of strategy, tactics, and combat performance, for example, in any discussion of the Byzantine army; the army was more than a bureaucracy. The study of bureaucracy is essential, but there are other perspectives of some institutions which deserve full analysis before there can be any possibility of a sophisticated comprehension.

24. Techniques of bureaucratic combat deserve study: the use of slander, falsified letters, inadvertent or deliberate release of incriminating information, perceptions within the bureaucracy of how to use one person or faction against another, and above all, how to fashion networks of alliances or factions.

25. There are pitfalls in any attempt to describe "the mentality" of the Byzantine bureaucrat or his bureaucracy, because any attempt to create a model or construct will probably have some gaps in its comprehensiveness. The exercise of attempting to create such a model might, however, uncover some valuable insights and at a minimum should form an awareness of the need for subtlety and qualification in the study of such problems.

26. Much more work is necessary on the experiences and perceptions of the empire's subjects who confronted or who feared to confront Byzantine bureaucracy. The sources are very scattered and complex.

27. The problem of bureaucratic change in Byzantium is complex. However difficult, the problem of understanding the changes in nomenclature of offices and titles and administrative restructuring is not as difficult as understanding how much change there was in the ways in which bureaucrats functioned and thought and perceived bureaucratic problems during the long history of the empire. How really different was a bureaucrat in the fourth century A.D. from one in the fourteenth? This is not an easy problem to analyze, but it is important to understand just how much continuity and change there was in broader bureaucratic processes.

28. A larger historical question remains: to what extent was the Byzantine bureaucracy responsible for the lengthy survival of the Byzantine Empire, and to what extent were its procedures and limitations responsible for its failure to exploit some major opportunities and for its eventual demise? The answers to these questions require efforts at interpretation that may never achieve any scholarly consensus. Yet the effort may be worthwhile.

29. This is not an exhaustive list of *desiderata*. It is a *tour d'horizon*, an attempt to point out some major opportunities, directions, and trends for future research and synthesis. Many of these topics are

very difficult to investigate and to interpret. Yet at the present time these problems challenge every historian who investigates Byzantine bureaucracy.

## SELECT BIBLIOGRAPHY

Ahrweiler, Hélène. "Recherches sur l'administration de l'empire byzantin des IX–XI$^e$ siècles," *Bulletin de correspondance hellénique* 84 (1960) 1–109.

Angold, Michael. *A Byzantine Government in Exile: Government and Society Under the Lascarids of Nicaea, 1204–1261.* Oxford: Clarendon Press, 1975.

Bury, John B. *The Imperial Administrative System in the Ninth Century.* British Academy Supplemental Papers, 1. London, 1911 and reprinted, New York, Burt Franklin, n.d.

*Catalogue of the Byzantine Coins in the Dumbarton Oaks Collection and in the Whittemore Collection.* Washington: Dumbarton Oaks, 1966– . 3 vols. published thus far.

Dodd, Erica C. *Byzantine Silver Stamps.* Dumbarton Oaks Studies, 8. Washington: Dumbarton Oaks, 1962.

Guilland, Rodolphe. *Recherches sur les institutions byzantines.* Amsterdam and Berlin: A. M. Hakkert and Akademie Verlag, 1967. 2 vols.

___. *Titres et fonctions de l'empire byzantin.* London: Variorum, 1976.

Hendy, Michael F. *Studies in the Byzantine Monetary Economy c. 300–1450.* Cambridge: Cambridge University Press, 1985.

Ioannes, Lydus. *On Powers or the Magistracies of the Roman State.* Ed. and trans. by Anastasius C. Bandy. Philadelphia: American Philosophical Society, 1983.

Jones, A. H. M. *The Later Roman Empire.* Oxford: Blackwell, 1964.

Kaegi, Walter Emil, Jr. *Army, Society and Religion in Byzantium.* London: Variorum, 1982.

___. *Byzantine Military Unrest 471–843: An Interpretation.* Amsterdam and Las Palmas: A. M. Hakkert, 1981.

___. "Heraklios and the Arabs," *Greek Orthodox Theological Review* 27 (1982) 109–33.

___. "Two Studies in the Continuity of Late Roman and Byzantine Military Institutions," *Byzantinische Forschungen* 8 (1982) 87–113.

Kazhdan, Alexander P. *Sotsial'nyi sostav gospostvuiushchego klassa Vizantii odinnadtsatogo–dvenadtsatogo vv.* Moscow: Nauka, 1974.

Kekaumenos. *Sovet'i i Rasskaz'i Kekavmena.* Ed., trans. and commentary by G. Litavrin. Moscow: Akademiia Nauk, 1972.

Maksimovic, Ljubomir. *The Byzantine Provincial Administration Under the Palaiologi* (in Serbo-Croatian with English summary). Belgrade, 1972.

Oikonomidès, Nicolas. *Les Listes de préséance byzantines des IX$^e$ et X$^e$ siècles.* Paris: Editions du Centre National de la Recherche Scientifique, 1972.

Pseudo-Codinos. Ed. and trans. by Jean Verpeaux. *Traité des offices.* Paris: Editions du Centre National de la Recherche Scientifique, 1966.

Stavrakas, Spyros. "The Byzantine Provincial Elite." Ph.D. diss., University of Chicago, 1977.

Stein, Ernest. *Histoire du Bas-Empire.* Ed. by J. Palanque. 2 vols. Paris: Desclée de Brouwer, 1949–59.

Weiss, Günter. *Oströmische Beamte im Spiegel der Schriften des Michael Psellos.* Miscellanea Byzantina Monacensia, 17. Munich, 1973.

Zacos, G. and A. Veglery. *Byzantine Lead Seals.* Vol. 1, Pts. 1–3. Basel: Distributed by J. J. Augustin, 1972; vol. 2. Bern: Benteli Publishers, 1985.

# CHAPTER 10

## THE ROLE OF BUREAUCRACY IN THE PROVISIONING OF CITIES: A FRAMEWORK FOR ANALYSIS OF THE ANCIENT NEAR EAST

ROBERT C. HUNT
*Brandeis University*

OUTLINE
Introduction
1.          Subsistence Model of Provisioning
2.          Simulation of an Urban Economy
2.1         Simulation of a Small Urban Economy
3.          Tasks and Bureaucrats
3.1.        Small Units of Production and Consumption
3.1.1.      Producing Food
3.1.2.      Extracting Food Surplus
3.1.3.      Processing Food
3.1.4.      Transporting Food
3.1.5.      Storing Food
3.1.6.      Distributing Food to Urbanites
3.1.6.1.    Market Exchange
3.1.6.2.    Redistributive Exchange
3.2.        Large Units of Production and Consumption
4.          Conclusions

INTRODUCTION[1]

In my oral comments at the conference on Middle Eastern bureaucracy held at The Oriental Institute in April, 1983, I posed questions about the work that bureaucrats do. The remarks I made at the end of that conference are here expanded in the direction of asking about the structure of the urban food

1.  The comparative work on irrigation has been supported by a grant from ACLS (1975–76), and by sabbaticals from Brandeis University (1975–76, 1983–84). The Egyptian field work in 1984 was supported by the Whiting Foundation. My students in the courses on agriculture and on the provisioning of cities have been a significant stimulus in working on this material. Piotr Steinkeller gave a guest lecture in the Provisioning of Cities course I gave at Brandeis during the spring term, 1985, and I learned much from that occasion. The manuscript has received careful readings from David Kaplan and Louis Levine. Irene Winter has read the manuscript with loving care and a creative eye. Any errors and infelicities which remain are my responsibility alone.

production and supply system. The framework of questions which I am posing is based in part on extensive field and comparative work on canal irrigation, in part on comparative research on agricultural systems, and in part on preliminary investigations of urban supply problems. As can be seen in the following essay, these three topics are systemically related to one another.

It is clear from a comparative study of the social organization of canal irrigation that there are a number of tasks which must be performed for the system to function.[2] These tasks are universally found, and are stable cross-culturally. Since they must be accomplished, there are task-driven performances required of the managers of irrigation systems. It has become clear that these tasks form a system, and that there is a close relationship between the tasks and the roles which manage those tasks.

Some of the tasks to be performed in the provisioning of cities have likewise been identified. There are systemic connections between some of these tasks, and between these tasks and the managerial structure of the economy. The analysis of all this for the provisioning of cities is clearly at an earlier stage than it is for irrigation. It is a hopeful sign however that the outlines of systems are becoming apparent.[3]

The present essay asks how bureaucrats can be, and might be, related to the tasks required for the provisioning of cities. These concerns seem particularly relevant for the present volume, as many of the empirical details in the substantive papers included here derive from the agricultural economy and its organization.

## 1. SUBSISTENCE MODEL OF PROVISIONING

Clearly cities have not always been a factor in human culture. The archaeological evidence is that agriculture preceded urban development, and therefore cities must have grown out of a situation of humans with agriculture, but with no cities. In order to provision a city, there are a series of problems that are created by the city, and which do not exist in the antecedent subsistence setting. I have found it useful to organize the discussion of the city against the background of a society which has agriculture, but which has no urban or town areas. Any economy which includes cities must solve a set of problems posed by the evolution out of a cityless subsistence economy.

In a hypothetical neolithic economy we can imagine that the largest settlements are villages with fewer than a few hundred people, and that most of the house-compounds in a particular village are occupied by fewer than thirty people. These people are probably related to one another by blood and marriage. For convenience I will call this unit a household. It is the primary unit of production, and will have access to farmland, to forest, and to fish stocks. It will provide most of the labor needed for agricultural and other kinds of production, most of the tools, most of the knowledge, and most of the genetic material. It will also provide itself with fuel, building materials, water, and fibers. Some of these

---

2. Robert C. Hunt, "The Comparative Method and the Study of Irrigation Social Organization," Cornell University, Department of Rural Sociology, *Bulletin Series*, No. 97 (Ithaca, 1979); idem, "Appropriate Social Organization? Water Users Associations in Bureaucratic Canal Irrigation Systems," *Human Organization* 48 (1989) 79–90; "Canal Irrigation in Egypt: Common Property Management," in *Proceedings of the Conference on Common Property Resource Management* (Washington, D.C., 1986) 199–214; "Size and the Structure of Authority in Canal Irrigation Systems," *Journal of Anthropological Research* 44 (1988) 335–55; "Hydraulic Management in Southern Mesopotamia in Sumerian Times: Some Observations," *Bulletin on Sumerian Agriculture* 4 (1988) 189–206; and "Bundles of Assets in Exchanges: Integrating the Formal and Informal in Canal Irrigation," in M. E. Smith, ed., *Perspectives on the Informal Economy*, Monographs in Economic Anthropology, No. 8 (Lanham, Maryland, 1990) 301–19.

3. See Robert McC. Adams, "Mesopotamian Social Evolution: Old Outlooks, New Goals," in T. Earle, ed., *On the Evolution of Complex Societies: Essays In Honor of Harry Hoijer, 1982*. (Malibu, 1984) 79–129, esp. 81.

materials will come in from other households, and some will come in from outside the village. So also this household will provide some materials for other households, and will be involved, however minutely, in export from the village. Every household in this village is involved in primary production.

The household is also the primary unit of consumption. A large fraction of the meals consumed by the full adults and the immature children will be prepared in the household. The clothing made by the household will be worn by members, as will tools used by members, etc. Distribution within the household will be managed by senior members, and will be based on seniority and on need. Much about these households conforms to the domestic mode of production, as discussed by Sahlins.[4]

The household provides the factors of production. It both produces what it consumes, and consumes what it produces. There is little surplus produced by the household, and few ways to invest such a surplus. There is little import-export trade, and most of that will be in small and high-value goods, such as feathers, shells, metal, etc. Some of this material will be highly desirable for production tools (obsidian, flint, and shells), perhaps, but most of it will be used in display items, or will be passed on in the trade. When there are shortfalls of food, people will travel to where there is food, and to where they have rights to that food, which usually involves going to where there are kin.

This household will, on the average, produce about what it consumes. Its production targets will be to provide for the household, which will include consumption and the degree of exchange that is required. For most households the total of goods and services exchanged outward will be roughly balanced by the goods and services which are exchanged inward, and will be a very small proportion of what is produced and consumed.

## 2. SIMULATION OF AN URBAN ECONOMY

In contrast to the subsistence picture drawn above, I now wish to consider a rather different situation, that of a city and its economic hinterland. The population of the urban area must be provisioned. It has to consume food, water, and fuel. It has to be provided with supplies for construction. It has to be provided with the raw materials for making clothing, and then the clothing has to be manufactured. All such populations have to have domestic tools, such as cooking pots, cutting implements, storage containers, etc.

The degree to which urban populations can provide these things for themselves, from their own productive activities, is unknown. Jacobs claims that early cities were entirely self-sufficient, a view which seems hardly credible.[5] Yet there is evidence that considerable production of food occurs within city boundaries,[6] and that some city dwellers produced substantial amounts of food.[7] The usual position in our tradition is to assume that we have a population in the central settlement which produces little of the basic materials needed, such as food, fuel, and fiber. I will accept that assumption for the purposes of this essay, and look forward to the day when there are sufficient data to confirm or amend that assumption.

I concentrate on food supplies because at this point far more is known about food than about fuel, building materials, etc. (although there is no reason to think that the food supply is inherently more important than, say, the water supply). And within the category of food, most attention will be paid to grain, again because it has received the lion's share of the attention of scholars.

---

4. M. Sahlins, "The Domestic Mode of Production" in idem, *Stone Age Economics* (Chicago, 1972) 41–148.
5. Jane Jacobs, *The Economy of Cities* (New York, 1969).
6. See H. D. Evers, "The Contribution of Urban Subsistence Production to Incomes in Jakarta," *Bulletin of Indonesian Economic Studies* 17 (1981) 89–96.
7. B. H. Slicher von Bath, *The Agrarian History of Western Europe A.D. 560–1850* (London, 1963).

This city is composed of units which we may again call households. These urban households will consist in most cases of a marital pair, with dependent children, and perhaps others as well. This will be a consumption unit, in the sense that some meals will be prepared and served here to all members.

In the countryside, even after extensive urbanization, people are living in a unit we can call a household, and at least some members of this household are involved in some form of production. This country household is also a unit of consumption. The members have to be housed, clothed, and fed. Reproduction is taking place, so the immature are being protected and trained. Assume also that this rural household is involved in agriculture on land to which it has some sort of right, and that it is operating as an independent production unit (I will relax this assumption below). A major fact follows from this: the rural households have to produce, and relinquish, sufficient surplus to keep the urban households functioning.[8]

## 2.1. SIMULATION OF A SMALL URBAN ECONOMY

For the purposes of this discussion I have modeled a small state in order to attach some numbers to the parameters. I have also concentrated on grain supply. I have assumed a total population of 100,000, and an urban population of 10,000. further assumptions: 1) mean size of household = 7;[9] 2) all rural households are farming; 3) the mean human energy consumption from grain is 1,000 kcal per day;[10] 4) there are 3,400 kcal of energy in a kg of grain;[11] 5) the seed/yield ratio is 1:10;[12] 6) the average yield of grain from a hectare (ha) of land is 1,000 kg (1 metric ton = mt);[13] 7) post-harvest losses average 15%.[14]

8. Another social arrangement is possible, whereby the urban households are provisioned in part by the productive efforts of their members in the countryside. The Mesoamerican vacant ceremonial centers are one example of this, whereby those who were serving in the center (for definite and limited periods of ritual duty) were supplied by their country households. See Alfonso Villa Rojas, *The Maya of East Central Quintana Roo*, Carnegie Institution of Washington, Publication No. 559 (Washington, D.C., 1945), for an example from Quintana Roo in the early part of this century. Yoruba cities were apparently supplied in part by the agricultural efforts of members of urban households. Some of these people would walk up to 120 km to their farms, work for a part of the year, and then walk back with the produce. See Peter Lloyd, "The Yoruba of Nigeria" in James Gibbs, ed., *Peoples of Africa* (New York, 1965) 549–82.

    Clearly many urban residents have relatives living in the country, and to a degree these urbanites will have a legitimate claim to some of the production of the rural part of the family estate (and vice versa). The proportion of the urban provisioning which can be provided in this way is a question worth pursuing.

    Urban society, or at least substantial portions of it, however, has often been provisioned largely outside of such personal and kinship connections, and it is the latter condition that I am exploring in this essay.

9. The size of this household does not affect the total production needed for the economy. Increasing or decreasing the size of the household will simply change the amount of surplus that each household must supply. Changing the size of the rural household, however, does significantly affect the labor pool available to that producing unit. See Morgan D. Maclachlan, *Why They Did Not Starve* (Philadelphia, 1983).

10. I am assuming that something on the order of 2,000 calories are needed per capita per day, and that about half of that is provided by grain (and grain products, such as beer). Fat of course is a more intensive source of calories, but it seems wise to assume that such products as butter, cheese, and meat are not very plentiful, and that most people will not get more than 1,000 calories per day from fat and protein. If the calories from grain are increased, then there will be an even greater demand on the grain production system, and vice versa. Of course, if the calories per day are increased to 2,500, or even to 3,000, then there are substantial consequences for the production system.

11. David and Marcia Pimentel in *Food, Energy and Society* (London, 1979) use 3,300 kcal/kg for wheat. Barley is given as 3,480 kcal/kg by Woot-Tsuen Wu Leung, *Food Composition Table for Use in Latin America* (Bethesda, 1961). I have assumed that the diet is a mixture of barley and wheat, and that therefore an energy figure of 3,400 kcal is reasonable. I have no idea whether modern caloric rates would apply to ancient grains.

12. This is certain to be a controversial figure. B. H. Slicher von Bath in *The Agrarian History of Western Europe, A.D. 500–1850* (London, 1963) reports seed-yield ratios for Europe in the Middle ages of 1:3. Bruce

The grain needs of such a population are as follows:

| | | |
|---|---|---|
| Rural nutrition: 90,000 × 365 × 1,000 / 3,400 | = | 9,661.8 mt |
| Urban nutrition: 10,000 × 365 × 1,000 / 3,400 | = | 1,073.5 mt |
| Storage losses: .15 × (9,661.8 + 1,073.5) | = | 1,610.3 mt |
| | | 12,345.6 mt |
| Seed: (1:10 ratio, + 15% for loss) | = | 1,419.7 mt |
| Total grain needed, average year | | 13,765.3 mt |
| Number rural households: 90,000/7 | = | 12,857 |
| Urban grain demands: (1,073.5 mt + 15%) | = | 1,234.5 mt |
| Grain demanded of average rural household | = | 1,070.6 kg |
| Surplus demanded of each rural household | = | 96.0 kg |
| Land needed for production / household | = | 1.1 ha |
| Percentage of surplus / rural household | = | 9 % |

Assume that half the crop land is fallow every year, and that there are 20,000 ha in woods, canals, swamps, pasture, roads, etc.

| | | |
|---|---|---|
| Area in grain in a given year | = | 14,000 ha |
| Area in fallow in a given year | = | 14,000 ha |
| Pasture, waste, woods, etc. | = | 20,000 ha |
| Total area of economy | = | 48,000 ha = 480 km$^2$ |
| Density of population | = | 208 / km$^2$ |

It seems reasonable to assume that such an economy might well be roughly circular (or hexagonal) in shape. The radius of the circle is the distance from the furthest-out farm to the center of the town. This is the maximum distance of any travel from center to periphery.

| | | |
|---|---|---|
| Radius of circle with city at center | = | 12.4 km |

---

Campbell has worked on the data from Norfolk and reports ratios in the range of 1:3 – 1:10 over several centuries; see "Agricultural Progress in Medieval England: Some Evidence from Eastern Norfolk," *The Economic History Review* 36 (1983) 26–46. The Iban in Borneo are getting results in the range of 1:20. It is hard to imagine how the medieval European farmer survived with such low ratios. I have chosen 1:10 for the purposes of this simulation. It is above the low medieval European rates, and well below most reports from modern times. If the ratio were lower, it would of course place greater pressure on the agricultural system. If the ratio were much higher then the surplus above nutrition would be much greater. Any society starting out at low seed-yield ratios that could raise them, either by genetic improvement or by seed storage technology, would have acquired a substantial advantage.

13. The figure of 1 mt/ha is derived from a sense of the central tendency in reports of contemporary paleotechnic agriculture. As reported by Pimentel and Pimentel, *Food, Energy and Society,* for example, the ranges seem to fall into 1 ⊺ 0.5 mt/ha. This is not a "strong" or solid mean because there are so few cases in the literature. If the average yields are in fact lower than this figure, it places even more stress on the agricultural system. Much higher yields would have the opposite effect.

14. Figure derived from National Academy of Sciences, *Postharvest Food Losses in Developing Countries* (Washington, D.C., 1978).

The sensitivity of the radius, the density, and the average amount of land cultivated per rural household to the assumptions of seed:yield ratio and of yield are of interest. If we simultaneously lower the seed yield ratio to 1:5, and the yield to 0.5 mt/ha, the effect is as follows:[15]

| | | |
|---|---|---|
| Total nutrition plus loss | = | 12,345.6 mt |
| Seed (1:5, + 15%) | = | 2,839.5 mt |
| Total grain needed, average year | = | 15,185.1 mt |
| Production per rural household | = | 1,181.1 kg |
| Surplus demanded of each rural household | = | 96.0 kg |
| Area needed/household (yield .5 mt / ha) | = | 2.4 ha |
|     Area in grain in a given year | = | 30,775 ha |
|     Area in fallow in a given year | = | 30,775 ha |
|     Pasture, waste, woods, etc. | = | 20,000 ha |
| Total area of economy | = | 81,550 ha = 815 km$^2$ |
| Population density | = | 123 km$^2$ |
| Radius of circle with city at center | = | 16.1 km |

As we can see, even with considerably lower yields the increase in the radius of the circle is only 3.7 km, which is 30%, and a small distance so far as human walking is concerned. If we assume a walking rate for oxen and humans of about 3 km/hour, then the extra distance is little more than one hour's travel.

The population density also was reduced, from 208/km$^2$ to 123/km$^2$. Although this is a large change, in percentage terms, it is not immediately apparent that there would be significant implications.

The two major changes, however, are in the amount of land which has to be cultivated by a household, and in that household's total production. The increase in area is 1.3 hectares, which is 118%. As we shall see in the next section, this is a massive increase, and poses some very interesting problems for the production process. The increase in total production is 111.9 kg (10%), which likewise poses a serious problem to the farmer. Nevertheless, our model in both cases produces an economy with a central urban settlement and a supporting hinterland, both adequately provisioned, well within the spatial range of Near Eastern settlement patterns.

## 3. TASKS AND BUREAUCRATS

In contrast to the hypothetical neolithic subsistence system presented in the previous section, we now have a very different set of circumstances. In the case of the city, there are a substantial number of households that are not producing their own food, fuel, water, building materials, etc.[16] In order for these non-producing households to be supplied, several major transformations of the subsistence production and exchange systems must take place. Those who do produce these materials must increase their production. That increase must then be transferred to the non-producing consumers. Produce must be moved some distance, probably stored, and then distributed to the urban consumers. All of these steps imply major differences in technology, social organization, and the organization of exchanges when

---

15. The lowering of productivity would be a concomitant of increasing salinity of the fields. There are other causes, such as drought, infestations of insects (locusts, for example), and floods.
16. We have assumed that no urban household is producing its own food. While it may be true of some, evidence of substantial urban subsistence production is beginning to appear. In Jakarta, it has been reported that the population sample with the lowest 20% of income is supplying up to 30% of household calories with urban farming and stock raising. See Evers, "Contribution of Urban Subsistence Production."

compared with the neolithic subsistence regime. The rest of this essay is an exploration of the system that evolves, and of the possible role of bureaucrats in managing that system.

## 3.1. SMALL UNITS OF PRODUCTION AND CONSUMPTION

### 3.1.1. PRODUCING FOOD

In order to support the aggregate of urban households, the rural household has to be persuaded to produce more than it needs to supply its own needs. The results of the simulation in the previous section are such that we may assume that if 11% of the households of the economy are not producing agricultural goods, the remaining 89% must increase total production by at least 9% in order to feed the urban households. The first problem we must face in this chain of consequences is that of raising the production of the rural sector by 9%. This can be done by raising productivity, or by increasing effort, or by some combination of the two.

Regardless of what some urbanites might imagine, an increase in agricultural production on the order of 9% is a major accomplishment, and an increase of this scale has grave implications for the production process. If 9% more land has to be brought into production, then 9% more labor hours have to be found. Since we are increasing the population to be fed *without* increasing the agricultural labor, we are faced with a potential constraint posed by labor.

One possibility is that the labor force is underutilized, and that the source of the extra 9% of labor hours could come out of leisure, sleep, etc.[17] There are widespread notions that peasants and other natives do not work as hard as they could. If they only wanted to, so the argument goes, there is much unutilized labor. Underemployment is a common term for this perception.

This position ignores a commonly found condition of the agricultural cycle. Agriculture is in large part constrained by the developmental cycles of the plants that are being grown, and that are in turn intercalated with the seasonal cycles. There are distinct phases of work in agriculture, starting with site selection, and proceeding through field preparation, planting, competitor control (particularly weeding), harvesting, threshing, and storing. Each of these phases must be performed at the appropriate time, and often there are natural limits on when a given phase can start, and when it must be finished. For example, in the cultivation of wet rice by the transplanting technique the seedlings must have been transplanted within forty days after germination. There are a large number of such time windows in agriculture, and they are determined by natural factors such as the genetics of the plant, climate, weather, and the "wild" flora and fauna.

The unit of agricultural production is never the rural sector as a whole, but some smaller unit. If it is the household, it is unlikely to contain more than four or five effective workers. The available labor which can perform any given task is limited, and must therefore be allocated to the phase of the cycle. Some tasks can be performed by anybody, but as Maclachlan has cogently argued, some tasks are best performed by laborers with particular characteristics.[18] Plowing with an animal, for example, is most

17. Those who believe that Sahlins' position on the affluent savage (see M. Sahlins, "The Original Affluent Society," *Stone Age Economics*, pp. 1–39) is correct will argue that production can be increased by simply increasing effort. The essence of this position is that the only constraint on increasing production is leisure. I think that it is as least as likely that other constraints are involved in most of the "simpler" agricultural regimes we know anything about. Field preparation time (see Morgan D. Maclachlan, *Why They Did Not Starve* [Philadelphia, 1983]), and weeding (see Derek Freeman, "Report on the Iban," *London School of Economics, Monographs on Social Anthropology*, No. 41 [London, 1970]) are two major bottlenecks in the agricultural cycle, and harvest can be as well. It is very attractive for us to think that levels of production are constrained. It is entirely possible that Sahlins' position is correct in some circumstances. I know of no demonstration of such a condition for agriculture in civilizations.

18. Maclachlan, *Why They Did Not Starve*.

often done by men, and there are gender-linked reasons of muscle mass which account for this. When time windows for completion of the agricultural phases are combined with a small number of laborers, it is immediately apparent that at some point in the agricultural cycle there may well be no excess labor. All the possible workers will be allotted to the crucial task, and it is this task that will limit or constrain any expansion of agricultural production. Investing labor in the other phases of production will be a waste, since the constraining phase will continue to be the limit. If the constraint is labor, it means that no further land can be brought into production without an increase in labor productivity for that constraining phase of the cycle. Land preparation can be the constraint. If the agricultural system includes weeding it is often the critical constraint on increasing the amount of land under production. With small households, harvesting labor can be the major constraint. (Of course there are many possible constraints other than labor, including tools, land, nitrogen, water, and competitors.)

In the ancient Near East, and over many parts of the globe prior to the mid-twentieth century, land shortage appears not to have been the constraint on increasing production. Rather, it appears to me to be the case that the major constraints would be the productivity of labor and water. In order then to raise permanently the production of these rural households by 9%, it would seem reasonable to look at problems associated with raising the productivity of the available labor.

There are several ways to raise the productivity of labor.[19] A major way is to add draft animals for the preparation of the land, and for threshing. From evidence by Pimentel and Pimentel, draft animals seem to save about half the labor needed in field preparation.[20] This would permit a doubling of land under cultivation, provided no other constraint were operating. Threshing is also made more labor-efficient. The animals provide other benefits, such as bulk transport, manure, milk, meat, and hides. On the other hand, there are costs. Animals absorb labor. They must be fed, watered, cared for, kept track of, and protected from thieves, the elements, and predators. Often high-quality forage must be grown for them, at least for periods of intensive work.

Another way to raise the productivity of labor is by means of irrigation, which will also relieve the constraint of insufficient water. If the minimum level of moisture can be raised then labor productivity and crop production will rise. The drier the area, the more the rise in such productivity. In this case, the productivity of the land will rise, but more important, the productivity of labor will rise as well.

However, as with animals so also with irrigation: there is no free lunch. There are both start-up and continuing costs associated with irrigation systems. Some tasks are universal to canal irrigation systems. All systems must be constructed, and this requires labor, tools, and some skilled judgment about placement. Once the system is built, the entropic pressures can be quite severe, and so maintenance has to be performed. Silt and weeds must be cleaned out of canals if flow rates are to be maintained. Leaks are another problem. The control structures, the dams, barrages, and gates have to be looked after. If a major point of such a system is to deliver water to the crop root zones, then allocation of the water in the system is a primary task. This means making, and carrying out, decisions about how much water is to flow where, and when. All canal irrigation systems generate conflict, and all such systems have institutionalized roles and processes for resolving the conflict. Finally, all such systems involve rights, duties, and performances, and there is an accounting system for keeping track of all this.

All of these tasks require labor and management, neither of which is free. Successfully completing a major construction project involves large amounts of labor, food, tools, planning, and managerial expertise. It is exciting to finish such a project, for one has made something new and substantial, at great

---

19. By productivity I do *not* mean the total production of the farm. It is possible to analyze the production process into factors of production, such as land, water, tools, labor, etc. In this case I am looking at the contribution that labor makes to agricultural output, separate from any contribution made by land, water, etc.
20. David and Marcia Pimentel, *Food, Energy and Society* (London, 1979).

cost and effort. Such construction projects are usually celebrated in myth and inscription. Maintenance, on the other hand, is drudgery, and is never celebrated; yet it is just as important as the construction phase. Without it the system will gradually run down, thereby reducing agricultural production. Allocation requires some staff who are skilled at the job, and who have authority to do their job, as do conflict resolution and accounting.[21] In short, these tasks do not get done without considerable human effort, taking time, calories, and scarce managerial talent. While the productivity of agriculture rises considerably with irrigation, so also does the demand for labor. (I know of no attempt to compare the managerial costs with the increased production. Such an effort would be very difficult, but very valuable if successful.)

A third way to raise productivity, and the one which has received the least attention, is changes in the genetics of the varieties grown. The biochemical revolution in agriculture in the past century has shown that yields of maize and rice can grow 5–10 fold, mainly through genetics. Such increases can be accomplished with no changes in the amount of land under production, and with little change in tools, or in the amount of labor (except at harvest time). What is involved is selection of new varieties, and a careful matching of the nutrient requirements of the new varieties with field management. This would seem to be a major strategy for raising the productivity of labor, especially in the early days of civilization. A careful study of yield figures from early sources, and of possible changes in the genetics of cereals from early sites, might well provide evidence of a subtle but crucial increase in agricultural productivity which made cities far more feasible and secure than they were earlier.

Assuming that by a combination of technical changes (animal traction, irrigation, crop genetics) the productivity of agriculture has been increased by the necessary percentage, how then is the farmer motivated to perform? This is no simple matter. There are comfortable myths, mostly based on a supposition of motivation, that the person working for himself outperforms a person working for others. The standard position is that modern state farms have low productivity, and that farmers who are working for themselves have high productivity. Then there is the question of the productivity of various kinds of labor contracts—slavery, share-croppers, permanent wage labor, migrant labor, etc. At this point we can say only that the question is important, and motivating factors, such as fear, added security, and access to non-agricultural goods need to be systematically sought.

The original conference and the written papers that have emerged from it pay little attention to the questions of what a bureaucracy is (with the notable exceptions of Michalowski and Morony), what a bureaucrat is, and, especially, what a bureaucrat does. For the purposes of this essay I assume a loosely-structured notion of bureaucracy and bureaucrat. All offices with titles which are chartered by either the state, or by a temple (in some circumstances these may be the same, but in others they may be different) will be treated as bureaucrats, and therefore as part of bureaucracy.

In the essays collected here we are provided with evidence for titles of officials, for offices, and for organizations such as the state and temples. The evidence is all derived from writing and other visual representations (non-verbal scenes on cylinder seals), so that literacy is automatically involved. There is also evidence that these officers/title holders are doing work—they are recording payments in and out, keeping track of stores, buying and selling slaves, sending taxes, signing contracts, making and paying loans, etc.

I am primarily interested in what these bureaucrats do, and with how their work is organized into larger systems of economic and political management. A full discussion of this would lead into a detailed classification of economic functions, which I do not wish to do here. For the present limited purposes I

---

21. R. Hunt, "The Comparative Method and the Study of Irrigation Social Organization," also idem, "Appropriate Social Organization? Water Users Associations in Bureaucratic Canal Irrigation Systems," and "Canal Irrigation in Egypt: Common Property Management."

will distinguish between 1) Production of goods, 2) Distribution of goods, 3) Cultic ritual activity, and 4) Governance. By production I mean mining, forestry, hunting, herding, fishing, agriculture, and manufacturing. This is the direct production of raw and intermediate materials, and of finished products. Distribution refers to the exchange or transfer of these materials and goods from one entity to another. These transfers can be multicentric (between one city-state and another, between one temple and another), or unicentric (between sub-units of a single entity). By cultic ritual activity I mean such acts as care and feeding of a temple statue, moving such a statue in a procession, etc. And by governance (which here is a residual category) I mean taking a census, collecting taxes, raising, arming, and directing an army, administering justice, etc.

In the long run it will probably be useful to define bureaucrats as those officers who are in the chain of command between the policy-makers and those who actually do the production work. They are the officers who have been delegated the authority to carry out policy decisions. In many cases each office will have a set of highly specific rules for the making of decisions. The further down the chain one proceeds, the less latitude the officer will have in making decisions. Given the lack of information on these intermediate offices in this collection of papers, I have assumed that any named office (other than the king) is a bureaucratic one.

It is very difficult for a member of any culture to "understand" the nuances of the institutions of another culture, as Civil (this volume) points out. Our modern image of a bureaucrat is that he or she is rarely involved in the direct production of anything, and when he or she is, it is a disaster. For most of us a bureaucrat is a captive of rigid rules and an inhibitor of production and distribution, rather than a facilitator or a doer. This set of expectations makes it very difficult for us to think clearly about the relationship of officials to production and distribution in systems other than our own. Such a view ignores essential public bureaucracies—air traffic controllers, health inspectors for restaurants, water supply boards, etc.—and the private bureaucracies functioning in large corporate firms. Further, bureaucracies are directly involved in managing production systems such as drinking water, in sewage disposal, coordinating traffic around ports and airports, and in producing cars, computers, or cabbages. In addition, the information collected by these agencies is oftentimes critical for health and prosperity. In fact most of us would not be able to manage for more than a few days without bureaucracy, and this is likely to have been the case throughout urban history.

In many of the papers in this volume there is evidence for offices and officers being involved in managing production, exchange, cultic activity, and governance. The evidence in the essays clearly supports the idea that a bureaucrat can be involved in directly managing production as well as distribution, ritual, and governing, and that furthermore bureaucrats were directly involved in provisioning cities in the ancient Near East.

To what extent are bureaucracies involved in agricultural production systems? We have assumed so far that the farms are small and independent units. The management of the farm therefore would almost certainly not be under bureaucratic control. Presumably the incentives to produce enough surplus will constitute sufficient motivation to ensure a reasonable amount of success. If we are assuming a large market function, then the "market" will determine what is planted. Alternatively, if there is a substantial tax or rent payment to be made in kind, the collector of these surpluses will have a strong hand in determining what is to be collected. If taxes must be paid in barley, then the farmer will either have to grow that barley, or count on somebody else growing enough so that he can acquire enough to pay taxes. In this context the tax and/or rent officials will influence agricultural management decisions by in effect setting targets for agricultural production. In other words a segment of the bureaucracy has indirect responsibility for agricultural production.

Comparable bureaucratic involvement may be seen in canal irrigation systems. If an irrigation system of any size (more than 50 ha),[22] is to be a part of agricultural production, then not only construction but also operation of that system must be explicitly managed.

The construction of an irrigation system on any substantial scale probably benefits from central and bureaucratic management. Central governments rarely fail to claim credit for such construction efforts, whatever the reality. Given the large-scale decisions to be made, including siting the headworks and the canals, assembling labor (plus their supplies, such as food and tools) and material, and coordinating the various jobs to be done, a central and specialized bureaucracy would seem to be advantageous.

In many cases it is not only possible but perhaps even desirable for farmers to manage the entirety of the irrigation system themselves. Comparative research has shown that there are a number of farmer-managed systems in the size range of 10,000 hectares, and with thousands of farmers.[23] In other words, it is not *necessary* that canal irrigation systems be run by specialized and centralized bureaucracies. Nevertheless, in fact systems on the order of 10,000 ha are often run by bureaucracies that receive their charter directly from the national polity. Since it is not necessary that they be so managed, the question becomes why the choice is made to manage certain irrigation systems centrally. Several possibilities may be suggested. First, control over the water system ensures some kind of control over the agricultural process, including timing. Second, such management might lead to more order, and greater peace, in the countryside. Third, control over the water system provides employment for would-be officers.

The problem with centralized management is that the operation of irrigation systems is difficult, time-consuming, and demands a thorough knowledge of local conditions on a day-to-day basis.[24] It is very difficult to find and keep staff who can and will do this job. The desirability of daily local information about the system is precisely what accounts for the ability of farmers to manage the systems. In other words, to work effectively, an irrigation system demands skilled administrative personnel, and to become skilled the people have to stay with, and know, the local system, local people, local land, and local crops.

For allocating water and maintaining the system, there is a great premium on this detailed and up-to-date local knowledge. Allocating the water also benefits from clear authority being vested in the people who do the work. Similarly with conflict, which is universal, and best solved when dealt with immediately, and as fairly as possible. This requires local knowledge by those with sufficient and appropriate authority. The same holds for accounting. For all these operational (as opposed to construction) tasks, then, there is a premium on having local knowledge, and therefore local people doing the work. This would seem to argue against the utility of having a centralized bureaucracy do the job. Any textual or archaeological evidence for management should then pay close attention to this issue. I would expect evidence for bureaucratic involvement in the construction of such systems. I would be surprised by evidence for substantial bureaucratic involvement in the operation of an irrigation system.

### 3.1.2. EXTRACTING FOOD SURPLUS

Let us assume that a farmer has been induced to increase his production. Now a portion of that production must be acquired from him. As long as we are assuming that the farmer owns the crop, there

---

22. See ibid.
23. Two good examples are Valencia in Spain, totaling about 16,000 ha (see Thomas F. Glick, *Irrigation and Society in Medieval Valencia* [Cambridge, Massachusetts, 1970] and Arthur Maass and Raymond Anderson, *... and the Desert Shall Rejoice* [Cambridge, Massachusetts, 1978]), and the 12-Go system in Japan, at about 5,000 ha (see Richard K. Beardsley, John Hall, and Robert Ward, *Village Japan* [Chicago, 1959]).
24. See D. Freeman, "Water, Water Everywhere."

are a very limited number of general forms of exchange for getting him to part with it: steal it, tax it, buy it, or take it in rent.[25] Theft is certainly not unknown, but most would concur that it is not a very effective way to achieve a sustained yield. Taxation is a common way to manage the situation. Taxes are collected by the superordinate and centralized authority, and may be collected in kind. The farmer as a member of the society is required to give up a certain amount of his harvest to a central authority. It is also possible to buy the produce from the farmer. Although it is conceivable that each farmer will sell small amounts of grain to individual urban consumers on a frequent basis, it seems very ineffective as a way to provision a city. It is far more likely that some agency will bulk the grain by acquiring small amounts of grain from large numbers of farmers. The agency may be the state or it may be a number of merchants. Several other institutional forms tend to go along with markets in grain. Credit is one such institution. The cash flow situation of farmers is different from that of most other producers. Farmers have to invest in the production process for months without having any output to market. Their cash needs during this period must be met from savings, or from credit which is advanced against the coming harvest. Classically the middlemen/grain merchants have also been primary conduits of credit to the farmers. The merchants also tend to be involved in handling, moving, storing, and processing the grain as it moves from the farmer towards the ultimate consumer, to which we shall return below.

Finally, the food may be acquired by means of rent. The situation here is that the "owner" of the land is not the operator of it, and charges a fee to the operator for the use of the land. Rent rates may follow laws of supply and demand (of labor and land). This kind of "ownership" of the land is deeply dependent upon the legal structure of the whole economy, and is likely to be constructed and enforced by the city, rather than by the countryside. If there are large landlords they will usually try (often successfully) to have considerable influence in the legal process.

"Ownership" is a critical matter. It implies a system of property relations. We assume that the produce of the field belongs to some owner, who may be the planter, or the owner of the land. Once the produce has been transferred via tax or sale, there is a new owner. It is my supposition that the produce is continuously owned until it enters the mouth of the consumer. Therefore the ownership, and the transfers of ownership, should be kept track of. Public goods, such as grain stored in a public warehouse, will be defined in this intermediate stage as owned by some public agency, which has the right (and duty) to guard it, and to distribute it in legitimate ways. Nevertheless, just because it is public property does not mean that any member of the public is permitted free access at any time. Prior to further distribution, "public" ownership is likely to be visible in terms of what agency has control over access to the goods, rather than by abstract notions such as "the citizens of the nation."

*Extracting Food Surplus and Bureaucracy.* When food surplus is being collected from more than a few dozen producers by a single enterprise, it seems virtually inevitable that the enterprise will have bureaucratic specialists for the job. One would expect written accounts as soon as writing came into existence, accounts that are likely to have a number of functions. Steinkeller provides evidence from writing that temple officials rented land from the temple; that the military officers in the peripheral provinces paid a kind of tax in animals sent to the regional redistribution center at Puzriš-Dagan; that a

25. It seems reasonable to assume that the goods are owned at every stage of their existence. It is clearly the case that the goods are often transferred from one person to another. Ultimately we will want to know enough about the property system, and about the exchanges, so that each stage of ownership, and each transaction, can be specified in great detail. When a sack of grain is exchanged, we would want to know the conditions of ownership of both parties, the process by which they arrived at the transfer, and the details of what was exchanged, *in both directions*. Rickman, for example, makes a heroic effort to understand the system of the grain supply of ancient Rome, but fails to keep track of the terms of each exchange (see Geoffrey Rickman, *The Corn Supply of Ancient Rome* [New York, 1980]). In consequence tax, rent, forced purchases, and market purchases are not kept distinct, and the resulting picture is confused.

similar place existed for the collection and redistribution of grain; that all major categories of temple personnel were required to pay various personal taxes; and that a significant portion of the intake of the "bala" system was used to provision various kinds of royal dependents.[26] The functions of writing here include evidence that producers have made their payment to the central enterprise, and documentation of asset holdings and management by and within the central enterprise itself. All of this argues for the strong presence of the bureaucracy in the acquisition (and later distribution) of provisions, in the Ur III period at least.

The degree of discretion allowed to bureaucratic personnel is a matter for empirical research. Who sets the rate of surplus to be extracted, and who is allowed to provide exceptions with respect to payment, needs to be established. Usually the highest authority sets the minimum target for collection. The target needs to be set in a timely fashion, and then needs to be communicated down the chain of command. The collection needs to be carried out, recorded, and communicated back up the line, and some of the surplus collected needs to be sent up the line as well. There is often some designed-in slippage down the line. And under a system of tax-farming the official target will be considerably below what is collected, with the difference going to support the intermediate hierarchy of collectors. This intermediate hierarchy can be a set of "private" operators, or it can be employees of the state or temple. It is important to note that all of the above-mentioned tasks will occupy a bureaucracy, but it is not clear that a specialized bureaucracy is necessary.

An interesting question is how expensive such bureaucrats might be. How many are needed to do the job? How many are needed to watch the ones who are needed to do the job? How much of the surplus is used to support those who are doing the collection and communicating? To what degree is this stream of wealth regarded as the "owner's," and to what degree can it be intercepted by the collectors for their own uses?

There is considerable evidence for ownership and contracts in the papers in this volume. In a complex society, where many participants are strangers to one another and where small-scale society sanctions are not operable, property transfers will need some basis for security. Johnson and Zettler both present cases of "lawsuits" over contracts. Part of the activity of the bureaucracy is to register ownership and contracts, to legitimize transfers of property, and then to be involved in the disputes which arise in the context of disagreements. This is another arena in which bureaucrats are implied in the provisioning of cities: that of recording and adjudicating contracts, in this case over ownership of land, as well as contracts for producing and transferring the fruits of that land.

### 3.1.3. PROCESSING FOOD

Once the "surplus" agricultural production has been acquired from the farmer, it then has to be transferred spatially and institutionally to the urban consumer. Some highly perishable items are distributed to the consumer without processing. Fresh vegetables, milk, meat, and fish are perhaps the major ones. For many food items some processing takes place, and this involves a technology, a facility, and usually some capital investment.

---

26. Steinkeller consistently refers to the "bala" as a system of taxation. I wonder if this is not a misleading translation. Taxation usually refers to the acquisition, by the central government, of resources from citizens and activities within the territory of the government. It usually does not include resources derived from means of production owned and operated by that government. The tax system does not usually include the expenditure side of government operations. The "bala" system as represented in Steinkeller's essay includes payments *to* royal dependents. In this respect "bala" reminds one of the Inka system of redistribution (see Terence N. D'altroy and T. K. Earle, "Staple Finance, Wealth Finance, and Storage in the Inka Political Economy," *Current Anthropology* 26 [1985] 187–206). In any case, until the entire extent of "bala" rights and duties are described, it would seem preferable to refer to it simply by name.

For the grain staples, preservation is improved as the moisture composition of the grain decreases. After harvest, then, it is common, and desirable, to dry the grain. The usual way to do this is to spread the grain to dry in the sun for several days. The objective is to reduce the moisture content to about ten percent, which will inhibit germination and the growth of fungi and bacteria. Perhaps not so incidentally, it also reduces the weight of the grain. Fresh milk is also processed for storage in the form of cheese and yogurt.

For some agricultural products there can be a small steady stream reaching a city over a period of many months. Fresh fish are caught on a daily basis; sheep, goats, and fowl are small units when slaughtered; cheese, milk, and eggs arrive in small daily batches, etc. For the major staple grains, however, much of the yearly supply becomes available within a short time period, and the bulk of it has to be stored for use during the rest of the year. Requirements are therefore successful processing to ensure sufficiently clean and dry grain, and then successful storage facilities to ensure preservation.

*Processing Food and Bureaucrats.* Most of the processing will be done to small batches of raw material (milk, meat, fish). I judge it likely that these are under the control of producing households, not of bureaucracies. Grain, on the other hand, is accumulated in large amounts at central storage places. Maximum storability requires high quality processing. Grain that is too wet, or that is already contaminated with mold or bacteria, will wreak havoc in the storehouse, for the results will not be confined to that batch alone but will spread to every other batch with which it is in contact. I think it likely that once the relationship between quality of grain and storability was realized, the managers would want to exercise a great deal of control over the whole of the processing. These quality-control problems appear to constitute a strong case for a team of specialists to manage the storehouse for grain. They would have a great deal to say about the quality and condition of what enters the storage facility. They might have responsibility for drying and grading the grain, but they might not. The advantage of doing so is quality control, but the disadvantage is the need for massive processing facilities, labor, and security. This would also shift the risk to the warehouse from the farmer or collector.

If the farmer is responsible for processing the agricultural produce, then the bureaucrat would be responsible only for keeping track of quality. If this were a factor in the ancient Near East then there should be textual comment on it at some point in time (the farmers from a certain region might be notorious for trying to pay taxes in inferior grain, etc.).

If, on the other hand, the bureaucrats are responsible for some of the processing, and actually organize the work, then it implies a labor force, facilities, and capital assets. Some sort of textual reference (construction costs, inventory of facilities, etc.) and/or archaeological remains could well exist.

### 3.1.4. TRANSPORTING FOOD

Insofar as the urban food supply is coming in from the rural areas, transport is involved. For the smaller quantities of fresh supplies, such as milk, presumably the producer/processor can move them. Mammals destined for meat can be walked to the slaughter place, which is usually adjacent to an urban area. Fowl and fish will be carried in small amounts, also posing no particular transport problem. Grain, however, is bulky, heavy, and comes in very small pieces. The technology and organization of grain transport is always a factor. The grain first has to be moved from the field to the threshing floor, which the harvest crew usually does. In modern times, the distribution of the various shares of the crop usually takes place on that threshing floor, where the size of the whole crop is plain for everybody to see.[27] The various people with interests in the crop (merchants, share-croppers, owners, laborers) are all present to collect their share and to see that their own interests are protected.

---

27. See R. R. Leach, *Pul Eliya: A Village in Ceylon* (Cambridge, 1961) for an example.

That part of the harvest which is to be sent off as tax, rent payment, or for sale will have to be moved to a central storage facility. Somebody will have to take the responsibility for this move, and it may be either the farmer or the entity which has taken ownership of the appropriated portion of the crop. In addition to the question of responsibility, there is also the physical fact of a large amount of loose grain, heavy in the aggregate, which now has to be moved a considerable distance. It will have to be collected in movable containers, such as sacks or barrels, loaded onto humans or animals, or into carts or boats, and then physically transported.[28] If the grain is being moved by humans, then it requires a certain number of person-trips to accomplish the job, and this becomes a labor demand of considerable size.

Returning to our hypothetical rural population of 90,000 producing grain, each household would need to send about 96 kg of grain (9% of the household production of 1070 kg) to the warehouse. If we assume that a standard load is 20–25 kg, it would constitute 4 or 5 loads for a human. Given a radius of 12.4 km, it seems evident that each trip could be completed in one day. This means that each household must provide 5 person-days of labor to move the grain to the warehouse. I would suspect that the economics of this situation would tend to encourage the authorities to force the farmer to deliver the grain to the warehouse, and that the cost (time, energy) of transportation therefore becomes a part of the payment. The areal extent of an economy with 100,000 people and a density of 200/km$^2$ is small enough so that every farmer could move grain to the urban warehouse with ease. With much larger states it would probably be the case that regional towns would have warehouses.

The labor force and technology for moving the grain from the countryside to the city should be apparent in documentary evidence. If there are canals or rivers, then boat transport is the obvious solution. Animal and human transport, however, are equally effective (if not as efficient). When an authority as opposed to individual farmers is responsible for transporting the grain from the countryside to the urban location, then that authority must control the technology (animals, boats, carts, sacks) and a labor force to operate that technology. If this labor force is needed only for this operation, and if the job is accomplished in a short time period, then the contracts for that labor become very interesting. Does it imply that this is a corvée, a duty of the citizen? Or can it be organized as wage labor? And if the latter, what work do these people do at other times of the year? Is there a floating pool of wage laborers, who work in transportation, construction, agriculture, etc., and always for a wage? Are they then buying their sustenance and housing in a market? Does this not imply that the market is deep and wide, such that most of the necessities and luxuries of life can be acquired in the market? And does this not imply a money-substance which is in small denominations, hard to counterfeit, durable, and widespread?

If instead this labor force is being fed and housed by the current employer, then it implies that employers have large-scale housing facilities and food supplies for gangs, which must in turn be administered.

*Transporting Food and Bureaucrats.* In small states the transport will be the responsibility of the farmers who will need to provide the necessary supplies. Bureaucrats will be there to do the accounting, and to keep track of fulfillment of obligations.

In larger entities there may well be another stage of this transport process, which is moving the grain from rural assembly points to urban warehouses. Bureaucrats may well be in charge of this process. They

---

28. We moderns tend to think that there is an efficiency limit to how far such grain can be moved, and it is supposed to be a function of the total amount of calories moved, relative to how many calories it takes to move the load. Some personal experience with the landscape, and ethnohistory, of Mesoamerica, leads one to be skeptical of such generalizations. While doing fieldwork in rural Mexico in the 1960s, I found it was common for my informants to ignore such factors as mountains and rivers in transportation by foot. And in pre-hispanic times large loads were moved many kilometers on human backs. There must be some sort of limit where the energy expended to move something approaches the value of what is being moved. I suspect that we know very little about where such limits are located.

will organize it, find labor and containers, manage the timing, etc. If such is the case, then these bureaucrats cum managers will have to have the resources necessary for the tasks. They have to have slaves, or money to hire laborers, or the right to call people out on corvée. If boats or animals are to be used, then they must be assembled, must be in working order and have to be owned, paid for, or called out on corvée.

It is presumed that efficient use of capital goods (such as donkeys, oxen, and boats) would be of some interest to these people. No such capital good is exempt form entropy. They must be maintained if they are to be in working order. A barge that is used only one month a year, for grain transport, is not a very efficiently used barge. For the rest of the year it must be tied up, kept secure, patched, repaired, etc. Likewise with a donkey. A donkey has to eat twelve months a year, not just while it is working. There is probably an optimal amount of use for such capital goods. If one can at least presume that all managers want to achieve some minimal degree of efficiency, then the scheduling of work of such assets would indicate that the barges, etc., would either be used full time for a single purpose, or that the organization would find other uses for the assets. If a barge could be used for grain transport for part of the year, could it be used for firewood for other parts? If a donkey is needed for grain transport for two months, could it not be used for onions for another month? The implication of this kind of thinking is either that the "owner" of the asset has sufficient work of varied kinds so that the asset is optimally used, or that there is some mechanism for exchanging the use of the asset. A market is one such mechanism, but taxation (i.e., corvée) is another. If either of these two modes of exchange for the use of capital goods existed in any substantial quantity, there should be textual evidence for it. There are likely to be contracts and lawsuits over the former, and duty-rosters and administrative complaints for the latter.

### 3.1.5. STORING FOOD

Substantial amounts of food must be stored in both rural and urban areas. The farmers will try to store a supply of grain sufficient to feed the household until the next harvest. In addition, farmers have to have seed, and it must be stored safely until the next planting season. Perishable food moved to the town will be consumed within a day or two of acquisition. Some things, like salt and spices, occur in small amounts, and the storage problems can be handled easily. Grain, however, presents problems. It is heavy, vulnerable to human theft, and to competition from other life forms large and small (from errant donkeys to microorganisms that fly, walk, drop, crawl, and burrow). There are no reliable measures of the loss to competitors from grain storage,[29] but most estimates of annual losses are in the 10–25% range. Without efforts to control such waste, presumably the figures could go as high as 75–100%.

Because grain is heavy, storage facilities must be strong. Chambers should be watertight and dark. To support the weight they will be built on ground level, or perhaps recessed. Many small storage containers in rural areas are built on posts, or the containers are kept up high inside the house, which provides protection against several kinds of competitors. I have seen no engineering study of the support system. I would expect that massive storage areas would not be suspended well above ground. Since moisture is a prime enemy, there should be protection against groundwater, floods, or heavy rain. The interior walls and floors will almost certainly be covered with a thin hard substance, such as plaster, to inhibit the passage of moisture and insects, and to facilitate thorough cleaning. The storage chambers should be dark, for light promotes germination. There would presumably be few entrances, probably just one. That entrance should be such that it can be kept under observation by guards, with access thereby controlled. The chambers should also be relatively handy to a road or dock. Zettler suggests that two gates or doors of the Inanna Temple in the Ur III period probably fronted on a major canal. I would

---

29. See National Academy of Sciences, *Postharvest Food Losses in Developing Countries.*

expect that grain storage areas would be relatively close to one of those two gates or doors. Safety of storage (against theft and pest) is a primary consideration, as is the integrity of the structure.[30]

Storage facilities are probably under the control of the entity owning the grain. If the acquisition has been by tax or rent, and it is taken into possession at the time of the harvest, then the collection entity will presumably have the storage facility. These warehouses are likely to have permanent staffs. There will be one person who is in charge, and, depending upon size and complexity, other managers and workers. The construction and maintenance of the structure have to be accomplished, the intake has to be kept track of, the security and integrity of what is stored monitored and managed, and then withdrawals managed as well.

Accounting would seem to be an integral part of the operation of any storehouse. Once recording systems are available, physical accounts of the contents, and movements in and out of any storehouse can be sent to higher authorities, to other parts of the territory, etc.

I have so far assumed that only urban warehouses are necessary. All such warehouses are likely to be located in a town or other densely settled place. Isolated country storehouses full of grain would be an irresistible attraction to any heterotroph. There would thus be great incentive to moving the grain quickly from the countryside to the towns and cities as security against theft and war.

*Storing Food and Bureaucrats.* While all farmers do some storage of their produce, even if only the seed, the kinds of large-scale storage I am referring to here are probably under the control of a bureaucratic authority. Some coordinating agency seems highly desirable, if not necessary, to manage the bulking of relatively small amounts of produce from relatively large numbers of producers. This coordinating agency is going to employ bureaucrats, who will actually manage the work.

First there is a major capital investment, the facility itself. Not only must it be built, but it must be maintained as well. Second, the facility must be operated. It must be ready for the grain when the grain arrives. It must get the new grain into proper storage in a timely fashion. Third, there will be constant withdrawal from the storage facility, and this will require decision-making, labor, supervision, and record-keeping. If, as seems likely, the supervisory work is closely associated with record-keeping, then such bureaucrats will be literate, and there will be accounts for that facility.

Accounts might well include information on deposits, withdrawals, and costs of operation. There are a large number of producers who are "paying" into the warehouse. There is clearly some interest in keeping track of who has paid in, how much they have paid in, and how much is in the warehouse. The modern rational man wants inventory control so that unmet obligations can be differentiated from those already met, and so that future planning for use can be based on a realistic notion of how much grain is yet in storage.[31]

Part of the accounting process is for management of large volumes, surely. But part of it is also no doubt to help deal with the "free-rider" problem. A "free-rider" is a person who will underperform some obligation, in the calculation that if he or she does so, others will not.[32] If this happens, the "free-rider" will continue to enjoy the benefits derived from the participation of most of the other members, but will have relieved himself of some of the costs. A classic case of this is in those canal irrigation systems where every farmer is supposed to participate in maintenance. If one person does less, the irrigator's benefit stream will not be reduced significantly, but the irrigator's costs of operation will be. A major

---

30. See Geoffrey Rickman, *Roman Granaries and Store Buildings* (Cambridge, 1971) on Rome.
31. It is not clear to me how much of this accounting is natural or necessary; the anthropologist in me becomes deeply suspicious of arguments about necessity and rationality that are so closely allied with our own deeply rooted practice.
32. See Mancur Olson, *The Logic of Collective Action* (Cambridge, Massachusetts, 1965).

problem in all irrigation systems, therefore, is how to ensure compliance in the most cost-effective way.[33] Accounting in these warehouses will be in part to inhibit or prevent free-riding. The accounts will be a record of who has paid, and how much, making non-payment easier to detect.

### 3.1.6. DISTRIBUTING FOOD TO URBANITES

So far we have assumed that the agricultural producers are large in number, and are not organized together in production groups. On this basis the urban food supply has been tracked from the producer to an urban warehouse. The next set of problems to be discussed is the method of transferring that portion of the food designated for urban consumption to the urban households.[34]

As far as I can see, there are only two widely-found systematic general ways to transfer this food from the organization running the warehouse(s) to consumers: by market, and by redistribution.[35] Many contemporary nations use a combination of these two practices. For example, both market and redistribution systems are in use in the USA, Egypt, India, the Soviet Union, and in many other nations. Each has its own problems, costs, and benefits.

#### 3.1.6.1. MARKET EXCHANGE

The market form of distribution is complex and far-reaching. We will start with an assumption of many sellers, none of whom has a market share so large as to affect prices and supplies.[36] We will also assume that there are a large number of purchasing units.

The urban consumer both establishes eligibility, and has access to particular quantities or particular products, through one single identification device, money.[37] Each consuming unit, in our case still

---

33. See R. Hunt, "Canal Irrigation in Egypt: Common Property Management."
34. If the storage facilities are under central control it should be noted that a portion of the materials will be available for uses other than urban consumption, trade being a major example. With the simulation in section 2.1. there is little surplus for trade. However, with some changes in the assumptions the situation is very different. Current paleotechnic dry grain farmers often realize a seed-yield ratio of 1:30 (see examples in Pimentel and Pimentel, *Food, Energy and Society*). Because Mesopotamia was irrigated, assume a grain yield of 2 mt/ha and that each rural household has only one hectare of grain under cultivation in any given year (alternatively, a yield of 1 mt/ha, but cultivating 2 ha gives the same results). The resulting surplus (beyond seed, loss, and nutrition) amounts to 8,980 mt in one year. This is a substantial amount, nearly equal to the nutritional demands of the entire rural population, and would provide a very comfortable surplus for emergency stores (against a crop failure), with considerable left over for trade, feeding animals, etc. It should also be noted that yields of this size would pose serious problems for collecting and using harvest labor.
35. By market I mean that the exchange takes place in terms of a price which varies with supply and demand. It may or may not involve a marketplace. It will involve some idea of a money-substance, although that substance may not actually change hands. Fixed and customary prices are not part of this market exchange. By redistribution I mean those exchanges which are determined and managed by a central authority. The items are collected on the basis of the domination of that authority, and may subsequently be allocated down the hierarchy by that authority (see Timothy K. Earle, "A Reappraisal of Redistribution: Complex Hawaiian Chiefdoms," in T. Earle and J. Ericson, eds., *Exchange Systems in Prehistory* [New York, 1977] for a clear discussion). If the society has a money, some of the payments into, and payments from, the central authority may be phrased in terms of that money. It is crucial to note that such exchanges are not market exchanges in the sense used here.
36. It is unclear whether this was the original situation or not. In the context of many agrarian states, there are both a large number of small producers, and a small number of large producers. The large-scale producers (ancient agribusiness?) must have outlets for their produce; urban markets and export trade are the two obvious ones.
37. Some might object that barter could do the job, and that therefore money is not necessary. The problem with barter as the source of exchangeable goods is that the urban household is unlikely to produce very much that

assuming urban households, will enter the market with the means of exchange, make decisions about what and how much is to be acquired, and often through a bargaining process establish the price. Once the price is established, the exchange can take place: goods for money.

The apparent simplicity of this transaction is very misleading. Each individual exchange may be fairly simple, but the complexity derives from the long string of antecedent and subsequent conditions which are necessary for this "simple" purchase and sale to take place. Let us begin with the consumer side of the matter. The implication that food provisioning is a series of market transactions implies that there is an extensive market economy. One problem that each household must solve is to acquire the money needed to buy the food. This implies a whole series of institutions.

First, there must be some sort of widely accepted money-stuff. This often implies a government or bank, some central institution which produces, or at least guarantees, the value and stability of the money. Such money-stuff will often be fairly inert (although cloth and cacao beans have been used), will be clearly marked if it is officially sanctioned, and the purity of the substance will be a serious concern.

Second, each household that provides its food from market transactions must be able to generate demand by earning money. The implication of this condition is that these households are themselves producing and selling things. Using the market to provision urban households implies, in other words, that there is a rather complex and widespread market economy for the city households. There might well be archaeological and textual evidence for this kind of division of labor, and for this mode of exchange. Steinkeller refers to private merchants, craftsmen, shepherds, and fishermen, which supports the idea that a market for foodstuffs existed, at least during the Ur III period.

Turning now to the implications of this market for the producers, we find that they are no less pervasive. We will continue to assume a large number of consuming units, and a large number of producing/selling units. Assuming as well a 1:9 ratio of urban to rural households, we have determined that on the average each agricultural unit has to sell an average of 9% of its production. There has to be some way in which buyer and seller can communicate with one another, inspect the goods, establish the price, and arrange for a transfer to take place. The usual location for much of this activity is a marketplace.[38] Often located near the center of towns and cities, they are also connected to major traffic routes, and are usually surrounded by permanent shops, restaurants, inexpensive lodgings, etc. These markets may be daily in frequency, but in the lesser towns they will be periodic, and in many parts of the world these periodic markets form an interlocking rotation.

Each seller will bring what is for sale to the marketplace, and each buyer also goes. The sellers display, the buyers inspect, both haggle, and if eventually a price is agreed upon, the transfer takes place. All that each participant needs is some knowledge of the cultural process of the market, and either something to sell, or the means to buy it. Thus communication and exchange can take place with a minimum of common language. This would greatly facilitate exchanges in economies which contain multiple cultures and languages. These conditions become increasingly common as the state develops, and may well be a widely distributed characteristic of the nation-state.

One of the problems of the agricultural seller is transport. The seller, and his or her goods, must be transported to the marketplace, and then the seller must return home. As we have seen in the simulation, an urban economy of 100,000 people, with a density of 200/km$^2$, has a radius of less than 13 km. It is therefore possible in this circumstance for even the most remotely located farmer to get to market and

---

is desired by the rural, food-producing household. Some sort of money is far more flexible and therefore effective for managing a large number of exchanges, each of which is relatively small in scale.

38. It should be emphasized that market transactions do not imply marketplaces, nor do marketplaces imply market transactions. Neither can be inferred from the other. See Paul J. Bohannan and George Dalton, *Markets in Africa* (Garden City, 1965).

back in a single day. Even much more populous economies will have a very large proportion of their rural members located less than half a day's walk away. Food for the journey is required and may be carried from home or purchased. If the transport requires or uses an animal, then the animal has to be parked somewhere, fed, watered, and kept safe from theft. If a cart is used to bring these goods to market, then the cart itself has to be parked and protected for the time the seller is engaged. If an overnight stay is necessary, then some safe place to sleep is needed. One solution, of course, is to sell from and sleep with the cart itself. This will be attractive to the farmer for it will save him money, a highly desirable goal for households with minimal cash flows, but this implies a very large (and messy) market place. All of these problems are soluble. My point is that the problems cannot be ignored if there is to be a marketplace. The solutions might be visible archaeologically, and perhaps textually as well.

The next set of problems is concerned with the terms of trade between urban and rural zones. Once the seller receives his money in exchange for the produce, the question is what is done with that money? If we assume that the costs of the agricultural operation are largely borne by the farm itself (that is, no inputs, such as seed, are purchased, but are all generated on the farm), then what will the farmer spend his money on? We are back to the problem of the motivation of the farmer. In this market context, the farmer is not forced to provide food to city dwellers. He is motivated to grow by the market. In order for this motivation to work, he has to have something he finds desirable to do with the money he receives. If the farming operation cannot absorb this money, then it has to be something else. It could be land, and Steinkeller mentions that land was involved in the private sector. It could be taxes, and this strategy was used by European colonial powers to draw farmers into cash-crop production. It could be the consumption of urban manufactured goods. It could be education for the children (and social mobility out of farming for them).

One question to ask of farmers who produce for an urban market then is what they are spending their money on. This is the issue of the terms of trade between the city and these agricultural producers. No market will be viable unless the terms of trade are sufficiently attractive to the producers.

*Market Exchange and Bureaucrats.* While most market transactions seem simple, and hence would not require bureaucrats, there are many peripheral aspects which do encourage, if they do not actually require, bureaucratic management (Kaegi, this volume). As noted above, a money-substance has to exist. It is often manufactured and regulated. To the extent that this is a function of the state, or of some other large organization, then the manufacture and certification of this substance has to be organized and very carefully supervised. Any such substance invites counterfeiting, so some staff that searches for, and tries to identify and punish the perpetrators of counterfeiting is also a possibility.[39]

Almost all marketplaces operate with standardized measures of weight and volume. These also may well be certified by the authorities (as Kaegi points out, this volume). As a case in point, Steinkeller reports that one of Šulgi's changes was the reorganization of the system of weights and measures. It would be interesting to know whether there was continuing management and surveillance over these weights and measures.

The marketplace itself is a good candidate for managerial activity. First, it must be cleaned up. Food marketplaces, especially if live animals are involved, are very messy. There is much organic debris that must be dealt with in some way or another: the vast accumulations of food and refuse attract pests, such as rats and mice. Second, a marketplace invites conflict. Weights and measures may be altered from true, and people may cheat and steal. Furthermore, the marketplace is often connected with entertainment, including gambling, intoxicants, and prostitutes. These activities often breed conflict.

---

39. While money and market exchange are often associated with each other, there are exceptions. The existence of something that we call money (especially minted coins) does not necessarily imply the presence of market exchange.

Peace in the market is usually desired by most, and is under the control of some sort of authority. Finally, the marketplace is an attractive resource for generating income for the state. Taxes on sellers, on buyers, or on transactions are hard to resist for most modern states, and may well have been in operation in ancient times as well. This means surveillance, which therefore means staff.

All in all, then, a marketplace may simplify some aspects of exchange, but there are transaction costs, as well as managerial duties, and these often fall to, or are captured by, bureaucracies. There may well be textual evidence for such activities, at least for titles of officers, and perhaps for the income generated from the posts.

### 3.1.6.2. REDISTRIBUTIVE EXCHANGE

Rationing is the redistributive mode which is most familiar to Western readers. In a ration system, a superordinate authority (today usually the state) determines that a given amount of a material (sugar, meat, bread, natural gas, water) exists, and is to be distributed in proportional ways to predetermined units (persons, households, hospitals, factories). Each of the receiving units is to get no more than some fixed proportion of the supply.

The first job for the consumer is to establish eligibility. In the case of food supplies and households, each household must establish that it is eligible for the food distribution. This eligibility can be a kinship connection, or an ethnic connection, with a distributor, but is more usually a matter of citizenship in a polity. The problem from the point of view of the distributor is often to establish the legitimacy of each unit of eligibility, and then to confine that unit to its share of the distribution. In other words, the problem first is to confine disbursals to those eligible, and then to confine the amount disbursed to the appropriate share. Unless the disburser and the receiver are known to each other personally, the first condition must be met in some other way. A common way to identify eligibles is by some token, which is to be acquired through the official apparatus. Such tokens can be identity cards, or ration books.[40] Acquiring such tokens is usually done in an official place, and from an official in that place. A major problem is counterfeiting; if there is any serious attempt to limit the distribution to those eligible, and if this is accompanied by a substantial demand for the goods, counterfeiting and black or gray markets are almost certain to exist.

Once the token is acquired, then the recipient usually has to present the token at the distribution center as proof of eligibility. At this point the distributory system has another problem to solve, which is how to organize the supply of the goods spatially. If there is only one warehouse, then all recipients must come to that one warehouse. In a territory of any substantial size and population, however, this means that a large number of people have to travel a rather large distance to get to that warehouse, and then have to move the goods back to the household. It also means problems of scheduling and congestion around the central warehouse. If the warehouses are split into several smaller ones, then the congestion is less, the distance traveled is less, but the cost is one of matching the supply with the recipients, or allocating the goods to the warehouses nearest to where the recipients are to be found. Easing the logistical problem for the recipients intensifies the logistical problem for the distributors.

The solution to this problem in contemporary Egypt is to have every eligible family register at one and only one shop. All rationed goods are to be acquired at that shop, and only at that shop. Since the number of eligible recipients at each shop is known quite precisely, the distribution of the goods can be allocated to the shops with equal precision. The problem that this creates is that the recipients are not

---

40. On the other side, Winter (this volume) has argued that cylinder seals, used to confirm commodity transactions, functioned as tokens of the bureaucratic system to designate the legitimate authority of certain sets of officials. The point is also made by Morony.

eligible for rations at any other place. This means that citizens cannot travel to another city, on business, or for religious purposes, etc., and receive their rations while away from their neighborhood store.[41]

The solution in the USA, with food stamps, is quite different. The US food stamps are a special purpose money, and can be spent any place in the country. One has to establish eligibility for the stamps locally, which involves identity papers and statements about income and assets. And one has to buy the stamps with general purpose money. But once one has the stamps, they can be spent at any of the many stores which accept them. One of the multiple purposes of the food stamp program in the US is to increase the income of farmers and merchants. Since the food stamps can be used for almost any domestic food item, there is no special distribution problem to be solved.

To sum up, most redistribution systems specify how much of which commodities the recipient is eligible for. Goods are usually located in specific places, and the recipient has to go to that place, often at particular times, to receive them. Problems with this system are the travel time and waiting time for the recipient (transaction costs can be very high), and the problems of distributing the goods among the various warehouses. Proof of eligibility is fundamental to the system, and has to be based either upon being personally known, or upon some form of identity document. Counterfeiting, peculation, and black markets are challenges to the integrity of such a system.

*Redistributive Exchange and Bureaucrats*. Redistribution has far more scope for direct involvement of bureaucracy than does a market form mode of exchange. Criteria for eligibility, certification of eligibility, creation of portable proof of eligibility all imply (if they do not require) officials, official places, and official substances (tokens). The places where the transfer of the rationed goods takes place must be managed. It is hard to see how such places of any size could work over the long term without bureaucrats. The "bala" system was clearly operated (at least in part) as a bureaucratically managed redistribution system. Provinces and military personnel paid into it, and various kinds of entities (including royal shepherds) withdrew from it. Steinkeller notes that a substantial portion of the "bala" contributions were withdrawn as provisions for royal dependents. It was monitored, if not run, by bureaucrats using writing.

A major problem requiring management is the determination of how to allocate the available goods, assuming there is more than a single warehouse. There must be a policy about allocation. Therefore, there must be a system to monitor the total amount available at any given time, and an awareness of the costs and benefits of distributing the total amount to the various distribution points. If proportional distribution is desired, then it also implies a knowledge of the relative number of recipients per distribution point. This in turn implies information about number and location of recipients, plus amount and location of the supplies, and therefore some practice of decentralized measuring, as well as centralized coordination of the resultant numbers. It is difficult to imagine how this could be done without some overall authority and managerial capacity. This task is well suited to a state bureaucracy (authority, and spatial coverage), although it probably need not be confined to one.

A very general problem in economies is how signals to the producers are constituted and conveyed. In a true market system, with prices being determined by supply and demand, the prices of goods constitute signals to producers. These prices help the producer to set targets for production. It may well be the case that all production systems operate with a set of targets. The information needed to set these targets will constitute a set of signals, which will include household needs (how household production

---

41. Harold Alderman, J. von Braun and S. A. Sakr, *Egypt's Food Subsidy and Rationing System: A Description*, International Food Policy Research Institute, Research Report No. 34 (Washington, D.C., 1982).

varies with household composition was a major contribution of Chayanov),[42] market prices, tax and rent demands, etc.

One aspect of this problem, which is rarely given much attention, is that of bureaucratic control or influence on the amount and kind of foodstuffs that enter the system. The modern Egyptian case is particularly clear in this regard. The Ministry of Supply determines how much wheat and rice are needed for the coming crop-year. The Ministries of Agriculture and Irrigation then organize to produce at least that amount. Individual farmers are given figures for the area to be planted in particular crops at particular seasons, and the necessary inputs (fertilizer, pesticides, etc.) are also made available.[43] The point here is that there is a large bureaucratic apparatus, involving at least three ministries, which sets targets for (i.e., gives the signals for) agricultural production. Not only is the distribution managed (in part) by bureaucracy, but so also is at least part of agricultural production.

It seems to me that no large redistribution system can work for long without establishing clear and legitimate targets for production. As Steinkeller points out, the military who had to pay livestock as a tax had a fixed amount to pay every year, and it was graduated by military rank. Some sort of official must have set these tax rates, and the collection must have been carried out by, or at least monitored by, a bureaucrat. This implies that bureaucracy is managing not only distribution, but also setting the minimal goal for production. And this in turn leads back to the problem of motivation of the farmer. It is apparently a problem in command economies to keep agricultural production at sufficiently high levels. Somehow the terms of trade between the bureaucracy and the farmers must be managed so that production levels reasonably close to target levels are maintained. The main point here is that in order to meet distribution requirements, the bureaucracy is led to become involved in production.

In sum, the city economy must collect agricultural surplus. It may further try to determine directly how much of what goods will be delivered. If the agricultural producer is delivering food as the payment of the surplus, then the recipient has to be able to consume and/or distribute it. If there are substantial amounts (1200 metric tons of grain) then some sort of exchange mechanism must exist. Markets, and redistribution, seem to be the major choices. Bureaucracies are almost certainly required in the latter, are probably implied by the former, and both mechanisms seem to be supported by Steinkeller's materials from the Ur III period.

3.2. LARGE UNITS OF PRODUCTION AND CONSUMPTION

Thus far we have been assuming an economy made up of many independent producing units, and many independent consuming units. Certainly these assumptions have been met many times in the the history of civilization; but so also has history seen the existence of large scale production and consumption units.

Many of these large enterprises have upwards of several hundred members, plus an additional number of temporary hired laborers. These operations own land, beasts of burden, tools, buildings, and other capital goods. They produce raw materials on their land with their tools and labor, process those materials to some degree, and export some amount of raw material and/or processed goods. Often a large portion of what is consumed in the enterprise is produced by that enterprise. If the enterprise has several locations, including some in the country and at least one in the city, then the city consumption is likely to be supplied at least in part by the country efforts.

42. A. V. Chayanov, *The Theory of Peasant Economy* (Homewood, Ill., 1966).
43. See R. Hunt, "Canal Irrigation in Egypt: Common Property Management"; Alderman, et al., *Egypt's Food Subsidy and Rationing System*; and Alderman and J. von Braun, *The Effects of the Egyptian Food Ration and Subsidy System on Income Distribution and Consumption*, International Food Policy Research Institute, Research Report No. 45 (Washington, D.C., 1984).

Much of the provisioning of the urban seats of such large enterprises comes directly from the rural estates. Members of these estates could number in the hundreds. Some individuals were permanently in the countryside, others permanently in the city, while a third set frequently went back and forth. The "owner" could spend particular seasons, according to taste, in the various places; managers (bailiffs, majordomos) would probably go back and forth continuously as part of their duties.

Given the size, complexity, and division of labor of such an enterprise, production and internal distribution have to be centrally managed. Production targets and schedules have to exist, tools, animals, seed, and labor have to be acquired, scheduled, deployed, and supervised, and entropy has to be continually fought through maintenance. Production will be of sufficient size that storage and processing will be non-trivial problems. If the enterprise is disposing of some of its production outside of its own membership, usually through a market or a central taxing agency, then this, too, has to be managed and supervised. If supplies are to be moved from one site to another (say from a rural estate to a temple, or city house), then the amounts and timing have to be managed, as does the transport.

One of the consequences of a spatially and temporally diverse organization is absentee authority. A problem for all absent authorities is how to extend their authority into times and places where they are not present. This is generally accomplished in our tradition by a concretized signal. It is visual, it is materially present, and it is tangible. It also has a tendency towards permanence (carved in stone would be the ultimate metaphor). It has often consisted of (or included) the impression of some sort of object, such as a signet ring, or a seal. In the ancient world the cylinder seal was a prime means for extending authority into the distance. As Winter has implied, cylinder seals operate as effective mechanisms for signaling authority, particularly in the tightly centralized environment of the Ur III period. Morony discusses the problem more generally, for cases in the ancient Near East, and the Byzantine era. Certainly the Ur III state is large and complex enough to need such extensions. The question arises then of how a temple household would extend such authority.

While it is by no means necessary that writing be employed in all this, it is clear why it is attractive. Information can be collected over seasons and years, and transferred from one place or time to another, with some degree of insulation against memory loss, distortion, and falsification. An official in one place can send information to another place without going there in person. If parts of the enterprise are widely scattered, this can be an advantage. Tokens of authority become very useful, and they will almost certainly be visual. The problem of how to send an authoritative message is solved with the institution of the seal of that authority, as Winter has shown with respect to the seals of officials and as Morony has argued in general. Cylinder and other forms of seals can therefore be understood as conveying the authority of an office from one place to another, and thus are essential artifacts of the bureaucratic system.

Most large enterprises own land. This land is often willed to the enterprise, but it may also be a royal gift, some other kind of gift, or it may be purchased. How the land is acquired cannot be understood separately from the land tenure rules of the particular society. The land held by the enterprise may be worked directly by the enterprise, or it may be lent or rented out to other parties. Zettler reports, for example, that the Inanna Temple rented land to some of its officials.

Labor must also be acquired for production. Some of that labor will be provided by "members," however they are recruited. Recruitment by birth is clearly one means, and voluntary recruitment another. Slavery would seem to be a less than totally voluntary form, but this would depend upon the transaction rules of slavery in the society. Some systems of slavery permit or encourage the slave to initiate the status of slavery, and to initiate terminating the status. The owner usually has these rights as well. How it works in any given society has to be determined empirically. Zettler and Steinkeller refer to "slaves" in the context of the Ur III period, Zettler in the context of a temple. Another means of recruiting labor is to buy it in a market.

That the temple may be involved in agricultural production is very clear from Zettler's account. The Ur III Inanna Temple at Nippur stored, and distributed, seeds and fodder, owned land, and managed agricultural labor.

Rations, of which there is little mention in these essays, could be a form of remuneration of labor, as well as a form of provisioning of the labor force, some of which is clearly urban (Inanna Temple). It would be of interest to know if the rations are regarded as a means to solve nutritional problems, or are a wage paid in special-purpose money. If the latter is the case, then the rate of pay would vary with the evaluation (time, quality) of the labor provided. If that is the case, then a secondary market (or some other mode of exchange) is probably implied, for the recipient would have to find some way of using the rations which are in excess of domestic nutritional requirements.

Whatever else they are doing, the temples are clearly operating storehouses. Storehouse records are being kept. If rations are being distributed to large numbers of members, then the connection between the storehouse and the members becomes clear. There are royal industrial complexes, reported here by Steinkeller for Ur III, and in these cases as well there must be wages, or food rations, and perhaps both, made available to the labor force. The "bala" payments to royal dependents should also be looked at in terms of the question of provisioning vs. food as a special purpose money.

Almost all of the evidence we have for these phenomena come from written records. In interpreting them it is important to be careful not to presume too much. First, we cannot know, from the written records, how much of the economy took place outside the realm of these written records. For Steinkeller to conclude that the private economy was not important, as he does, seems premature. Second, it is by no means the case that these written records have been analyzed to the fullest. For example, as Winter points out, there has been no analysis of the relationship of seals, sealings, and the contents of the documents sealed. An analysis of this relationship would reveal much more about the workings of at least part of the economy.

We have been using the term "household" to refer to a residential unit comprising something on the order of seven persons, recruited by birth and marriage, and with a division of labor (and of ranking) based on age and gender alone. In Ur III times the temples were called the "households" of the gods, and metaphorically perhaps the whole of the city-state is called a "household." These are clearly two very different notions of household, and a brief exploration of these differences is revealing.

A small familial household handles recruitment by birth and marriage, and the division of labor uses only principles of age and gender. As discussed above, it is the locus of the domestic mode of distribution. Such households can expand solely by means of birth and marriage, and they can become extended. They can become fairly large (30+) in size, but still operate with the same principles.

Households can also add members by other principles of recruitment. Apprentices, servants, slaves, and employees can be members of the household in the sense that they sleep and eat there, and are widely known to "belong" there. In these cases, the division of labor (and the distribution of resources) is based on principles other than age and gender. There will be a ranking of personnel into two or more tiers, members of each recruited by different principles, having different jobs, and perhaps most important, having different kinds of rights to the resources of the household. Such households can be very small, with perhaps a marital pair, a child or two, and a slave. Alternatively, they can be very large, with hundreds of members, a high degree of economic differentiation, and several locations. Some examples of the latter might include the medieval European manor house, the Spanish colonial hacienda, and perhaps the monastery. The Ur III temple is perhaps another example. What is interesting in the latter case is the ideology behind the household metaphor. In some economic terms, these enterprises might be called vertically integrated industries which are largely self-sufficient (they produce raw materials, tools and capital goods, and reproduce their own labor). Yet they are called households. This would seem to imply either that there is an attempt to construct a familial ideology for them, or that "household" is a bad translation. In any case, there is a puzzle here which would probably reward some detailed investigation.

*Large Enterprises and Bureaucrats.* The large enterprises were involved in production, processing, transport, storage, and distribution of food, and were also involved in a great deal of processing and manufacturing. For units of any size to maintain this kind of complexity, there had to be managers. It is probably the case that we know more about the management officials of such enterprises than we know of any other role (e.g., weaver, cook), for it is they who have left documents, collected in archives, attesting to their existence. These documents were very specific in reference and use, have been the subject of fruitful analysis from which most of our evidence derives (Civil and Zettler, this volume). Clearly, these managers used written records as tools of their management activities, and they often, if not always, had titles derived from temple or state authorities. By the definition used in this paper, then, they were bureaucrats.

Production clearly has to be organized by the central authority of the enterprise. What is to be produced, how much, by whom, and when, has to be centrally determined. While much decision making will be guided by tradition, it will also be guided by the managers.

The amount of the goods that are to be shipped to the central place (often a temple) is also determined by some sort of authority. Timing and the mode of transportation are likewise the responsibility of the managers, as is processing, storage, accounting, and the disbursals from storage.

In sum, the management of any large enterprise is likely to be under the control of bureaucrats. This is certainly true for a large part of the economy of the temple during the Ur III period, as is shown by Zettler. Another clear case of this is presented by Roth in her discussion of the organization of the royal mortuary temples in Old Kingdom Egypt. These large enterprises could each contain, and support, large numbers of people. It would be interesting to know, and perhaps impossible to determine, the proportion of any state economy that was under the control of such large enterprises at any given time.

A major issue lurking behind our discussion of bureaucracies is the degree to which there existed a concurrent private economy. Evidence from the papers presented here suggests that there was a well-developed private economic sector. Johnson presents a protracted inheritance case, argued before bureaucrats, which shows a substantial private economy functioning in Ptolemaic Egypt. Winter, referring to the seals of merchants in the Ur III period, argues that the merchants stood outside the official state bureaucracy. Steinkeller, as well, refers to merchants existing in the private economic sector. In Zettler's essay there is a reference to the Chief Administrator of the Inanna Temple leasing land from the temple in return for a share of produce. At one point a Chief Administrator was charged by his principal heir with intercepting and diverting sheep, butter, and flour intended for the royal offering, for intercepting the butter for regular offerings, and for diluting the butter of the regular offering. On another occasion the brother of the Chief Administrator received a loan of 1,440 silas of grain from the cupbearer of the king, could not repay, and so the Chief Administrator paid off the loan.

All this would seem to indicate that the Chief Administrator of the temple, along with members of his family, was involved in "private" economic deals. Surely his produce from the rented temple lands was not simply contributed to the temple accounts, but was disposed of outside of the temple economy. Assuming that there is some truth in the allegations of peculation with respect to temple offering materials, one interpretation is that these materials were being diverted into a "private" economic stream. This in turn suggests that there is a fairly vigorous economy outside the official temple and royal economies. There must be destinations for the goods that are being produced on rented land or diverted from temple receipts, and there has to be some motivation to produce or divert. The only destination which makes immediate sense is a private sector of the economy, and probably it is market dominated.

One interesting consideration to be pursued, therefore, is the degree to which the private sector co-existed with, and competed with, the official sectors in a given political economy.

4. CONCLUSIONS

The title of this essay highlights the provisioning of cities; the focus has been on the tasks which must be involved in such provisioning, and especially on how those tasks might or must involve bureaucrats in the ancient Near East.

Simulation of a hypothetical urban economy revealed two very interesting conditions. The first condition is that at reasonable rates of productivity a city-state with 100,000 people has a radius of only about 12–17 km. A major implication of this is that any resident can easily get from the periphery to the center and back in one day. This means that all city services are within reach of all members of the state, at least in terms of transportation. The second condition is the effect of yields per hectare. Simply reducing yields and seed: yield ratios by 1/2 results in increasing cultivated area by over 100%. This has enormous significance for the generation of surplus. One suggestion that results from this simulation is for analysts of textual and archaeological sources to try to pin down levels of agricultural productivity and changes in them, particularly the genetic changes which I believe were certain to have occurred.

Within such a hypothetical urban economy, *production* was the first task considered. It is clear that agricultural production when managed by large-scale enterprises (such as temple estates or royal farms) necessitates intensive involvement by bureaucrats in the management of that production. Production targets have to be set, the factors of production (tools, labor, land, seed, animals) acquired and kept in working order, and the phases of the agricultural cycle have to be organized. This is not surprising. What is surprising is the implied presence of bureaucrats for the production of many small household farms. Taxes and rent are probably major means for the extraction of surplus, and these imply that a production target is being set by somebody other than the farmer. Bureaucracies seem the most likely locus for this task.

The next task considered was the *extraction of surplus production* from the farmer. The amounts to be extracted need to be targeted and communicated, and the amounts actually extracted need to be collected and recorded. Targets, deliveries, and record keeping imply the involvement of bureaucrats.

Once acquired, the surplus has to be *processed, transported,* and *stored.* For many agricultural products, such as melons, milk, and mullet, there is little large-scale organization required. As we have argued, grain is another story. Due to the nature of grain agriculture, the harvest becomes available in very large amounts during very short time periods. It must therefore be dealt with quickly, or losses will occur. As noted above, the processing of the harvested grain is all-important in guaranteeing storability. Almost certainly there will be a bureaucracy involved, at least in quality control about what actually enters the storage bins. Due to the small radius of the economy (in the simulation), it is clearly the case that every farming household can easily deliver its surplus grain to a central warehouse, so that transportation is not a major obstacle. However, the recording of such deliveries would certainly be in the interest of the receiving authorities, and therefore a bureaucracy is implied for this task as well. Finally, a grain warehouse has to be actively managed, and it is difficult to imagine an urban grain storehouse without bureaucratic management.

*Distribution* of the food from any collecting agency to the consumer was the final task considered, and turns out to be a very complex operation. Two ways of achieving it on a substantial scale seem reasonable—market transactions and redistribution. The market mode of distribution is attractive for its simplicity, and yet it implies many other social institutions. It implies that the (urban) purchasers of the food are deeply involved in a market economy—that they have something to sell on a regular basis. Since they are probably not producing food, they must be doing something else in the market, such as manufacturing or providing services, that in turn require substantial numbers of people involved in market transactions. This in itself probably does not require a bureaucracy. Nevertheless markets typically pose problems of standardization of the money-stuff and of weights and measures, while the marketplaces must be managed in terms of spatial allocation, cleanliness, and freedom from conflict. This all implies, if it does not require, bureaucratic management.

Distribution of goods to consumers by means of redistribution for a population of any size certainly requires a bureaucracy. First, there is the matter of proving eligibility, which means a token if people are not known to one another personally. Such tokens are usually issued by, and authenticated by, bureaucratic authorities. Second, disbursements need to be managed, and are often written down, again requiring bureaucrats. Finally, the flow of goods in such a system must be planned and managed, and this too requires some central direction and active management, bringing us around to bureaucracy once again. In short, the redistribution mode apparently requires bureaucracy at every step.

It is thus apparent, at least as concerns the provisioning of cities, that the tasks of production, extraction, transport, storage, processing, and distribution turn out to be interconnected, and there are a large number of times where a bureaucracy might, or does, become involved. Evidence for many of these phenomena can be found in the papers included in this volume.

Students of the ancient Near East have paid a great deal of attention to the titles and perquisites of bureaucrats. The analysis contained in this essay suggests that an investigation of the evidence of what bureaucrats do and how they are organized would pay off handsomely in terms of systematic knowledge of the workings of ancient society.